W9-BCB-968

Recent years have witnessed a considerable flowering of efforts to decentralise decision-making and planning in the developing countries of Asia. The range and diversity of these initiatives reflect the different historical, cultural and political conditions of the countries concerned. At the same time, there are many common threads and features running through them. This volume examines the theoretical underpinnings of decentralisation, the origins of the various systems, their common and distinctive features, and their efficacy in terms of ensuring the meaningful participation of citizens.

Six Asian countries have been studied in depth by the contributors: India, China, Bangladesh, Nepal, the Philippines and Sri Lanka. Two papers are presented for each country—the first is an overview paper and the other a field level account. The volume, thus, provides a unique combination of theory and practice—of how the system of decentralised governance in each country should function and how it is actually working. In the process, the contributors assess the extent to which the positive values of democracy and development have been promoted in each of the six countries. Since the systems of self-governance pertaining to these countries have been examined at different stages of implementation, this volume also provides a bird's eye view of what obtains at a particular point in time in the evolution of decentralised governance.

By documenting the factors that have encouraged and facilitated decentralisation and by presenting first-hand accounts, this volume will go a long way towards furthering the process of civic participation and making decentralised governance more effective and meaningful. It will be of immense use to planners, policy-makers, administrators, political scientists, economists and sociologists.

# Decentralised Governance in Asian Countries

# Decentralised Governance in Asian Countries

## EDITED BY

## ABDUL AZIZ
## DAVID D. ARNOLD

**Sage Publications**
*New Delhi/Thousand Oaks/London*

WINGATE UNIVERSITY LIBRARY

*Copyright © Institute for Social and Economic Change, 1996*

All rights reserved. No part of this book may be reproduced or utilised in any form or by any means, electronic or mechanical, including photocopying, recording or by any information storage or retrieval system, without permission in writing from the publisher.

*First published in 1996 by*

**Sage Publications India Pvt Ltd**
M-32, Greater Kailash Market I
New Delhi 110 048

**Sage Publications Inc**
2455 Teller Road
Thousand Oaks, California 91320

**Sage Publications Ltd**
6, Bonhill Street
London EC2A 4PU

Published by Tejeshwar Singh for Sage Publications India Pvt Ltd, Phototypeset by Pagewell Photosetters, Pondicherry and printed at Chaman Enterprises, Delhi.

**Library of Congress Cataloging-in-Publication Data**

Decentralised governance in Asian countries / edited by Abdul Aziz, David D. Arnold.
      p.    cm.
    Includes bibliographical references and index.
    1. Decentralisation in government—Asia. 2. Local government—Asia. I. Aziz, Abdul, 1937–    II. Arnold, David D., 1952–
JS6950.3.A3D43    1996    352.05—dc20    95–26755

**ISBN**: 0–8039–9292–0 (US-hb)
       81–7036–527–9 (India-hb)

*Sage Production Editors*: Sarita Vellani and Sona Sabharwal

**Dedicated
to
Dr. G.V.K. Rao**

# Contents

# List of Tables and Figures

# Acknowledgements

The present volume is the product of an experience-sharing international seminar held in the Institute for Social and Economic
Change (ISEC), Bangalore during March 1993. The seminar was
sponsored by the Ford Foundation, New Delhi, in conjunction
with the Ford Foundation offices located in Dhaka, Manila and
Beijing. We are grateful to them for making this seminar possible.
We are also obliged to Professor Rajni Kothari for his stimulating
keynote address. Since his address raised many important issues
on decentralised governance, we felt that it would be appropriate
to include it in the present volume. The concluding remarks by
T.R. Satish Chandran, Professors D.M. Nanjundappa and
Raymond D. Horton in the wrap-up sessions, and the remarks
made by Jonathan Hecht, David Chiel, Kamal Siddiqui, David D.
Arnold, V.S. Angadi and Revathi Narayanan, who presided over
the technical sessions of the seminar, were helpful in capturing the
main contours of the discussion and in drawing up the last chapter
of this volume. To them all we owe a great measure of indebted-
ness. In addition, we are grateful to those participants who, apart
from preparing the papers within the short time limit prescribed,
found time to come down to Bangalore to make presentations and
to participate in the discussion.

No less important was the administrative support provided by
Dr. M. Nageswara Rao, Registrar, ISEC and his colleagues, the
secretarial assistance given by M.S. Nagavalli, and the technical
assistance extended by M. Mahadeva, C. Charles Nelson and
Devendra Babu. It is our privilege to record our deep sense of
gratitude to all of them. Last but not the least, we are grateful to
Sage Publications (India) Private Limited, New Delhi, and particularly to Harsh Sethi for his help in bringing together this volume.
We have dedicated the volume to Dr. G.V.K. Rao, former member

of the Planning Commission, who was largely responsible for inviting Professor V.K.R.V. Rao to found the Institute for Social and Economic Change, Bangalore.

ABDUL AZIZ
DAVID D. ARNOLD

# 1

# Introduction

ABDUL AZIZ
DAVID D. ARNOLD

In recent years there has been a dramatic flowering of decentralisation initiatives among the developing countries of Asia. The range and diversity of these initiatives is quite impressive, reflecting the different historical, cultural and political conditions of the various countries. At the same time, there are many common threads and features running through the different systems that are beginning to emerge. Given the likelihood that pressures for political devolution will increase in the future, it is worthwhile examining the theoretical underpinnings of decentralisation, the origins of the various systems, their common and distinctive features, their effectiveness in providing for meaningful citizen involvement in the local governance process and the future directions in which decentralised governance systems should move. Drawing mainly from the papers presented in this volume, an attempt is made here to comment on these dimensions of decentralised governance systems.

## A Theoretical Perspective

The fact that decentralised decision-making ensures the well-being of all of those who are likely to be affected by such decisions is now well known. The rationale of this premise is derived from the political (democratic) imperative that all those whose interests are affected by decisions ought to take part in the decision-making process. When everybody takes part in the decision-making process, self-interest is supposed to guide them to arrive at decisions that are consistent with everybody's good. This logic provides the theoretical basis for the evolution of decentralised political institutions which are looked upon as institutions that promote decentralised decision-making.

The rationale of decentralised governance is also derived from the known drawbacks of centralised decision-making at the macro governmental levels. Being away from the basic spatial units such as hamlets and villages and with power concentrated at the top of the space in a pyramidic power base, the state and the union government power structures draw representatives from well-endowed sub-regions and sections of the community, leaving the backward regions and weaker sections unrepresented. This gives rise to the emergence of enclave-type power bases and unequal distribution of power among people. The interests, felt needs and aspirations of some sections and of people living in backward and interior regions are thus likely to be overlooked under the centralised decision-making system. Secondly, in the centralised system, where there is not much scope for people's participation, the implementation of decisions taken at top government levels becomes weak as it does not inspire or motivate people to extend their cooperation. On the other hand, under the decentralised governance system, since the representatives are drawn from all sub-regions, including villages and hamlets, and from all sections of the community (through a system of positive discrimination, if necessary), two important results can be expected: (*a*) the emerging power structure would not be all that unequal or of the enclave type; and (*b*) the articulation in the decision-making process of local needs and aspirations of people belonging to different sections would be more probable. Also, as people's participation is ensured by inspiring them and by creating some special institutional mechanisms, implementation of decisions is more likely to be effective under decentralised governance. The association of non-government organisations (NGOs) and people's organisations with decentralised government units, which is most likely to happen at the grassroots level, would help mobilise resources, especially voluntary labour, for development and would facilitate monitoring of the implementation process.

The tasks involved in local governance are to:

1. identify local problems and ascertain the felt needs and aspirations of the people;
2. take an inventory of locally available manpower and natural resources and assess the development potential of the sub-regions in the light of the availability of these resources;
3. estimate the financial resources required to promote regional development in view of the local problems identified and carry out the inventory of the available resources;
4. set out a strategy of resource mobilisation, both financial and physical, and implement projects and programs that promote the development of the sub-region;
5. decide on the location of projects in different villages and hamlets, and accordingly allocate financial resources for their development;
6. determine the implementation and monitoring procedure such that there is no let-up in the implementation of the projects and programs taken up by them; and
7. evolve appropriate rules and regulations regarding the use of community resources such as common property resources, community assets like irrigation tanks, community buildings, schools and hospitals, and take appropriate action in the case of misuse of these resources.

The effective implementation of these tasks under the decentralised governance system calls for appropriate logistics in terms of institutional structures and conducive environment. The institutional structures required are:

(a) a decentralised political institution to identify and to articulate people's felt needs and aspirations and to formulate rules and regulations relating to the use of the community's resources and assets;
(b) a decentralised administrative structure to formulate and implement the plans and programs of the local governments keeping in view the felt needs of the people; and

(c) a decentralised data collecting machinery to provide the required grassroots level statistical data to the planning agencies of these bodies.

For the decentralised governance system to operate more effectively, there should also obtain a conducive environment for carrying out decentralised decision-making in the appropriate manner. To effect such an environment it is first necessary that the decentralised political structures provide all citizens access to the decision-making process. But if these structures are such that access to decision-making is restricted only to some individuals or to some sections of the community, then political decentralisation would be incapable of ensuring the well-being of all citizens. In other words, the decentralised political institutions should have a representative character in the true sense of the term, giving every section or interest group of the community the opportunity to participate in the decision-making process. This can be accomplished by using the instrument of positive discrimination i.e., reservation of seats for the weaker sections and backward regions. The autonomy of the decision-making authority is the second component of a conducive environment: the decision-making authority should be capable of taking decisions independently and not be amenable to pressures either from the state or from the central government. This requires that local institutions enjoy both political and financial autonomy. The existence of decentralised governments should not be at the mercy of the higher level governments, nor should they be over-dependent on higher level governments for their financial needs. They should be able to generate their own resources and to carry out developmental activities on their own. Also, there should be an arrangement for the devolution of funds to them from higher level governments on the basis of recommendations made and the principles evolved by a periodically constituted state finance commission.

It is, however, necessary to say at this point that autonomy does not amount to freedom from the state level political institutions. In order to prevent different tiers of government from working at cross-purposes, local level political institutions need to be integrated into a system of state and central government institutions, at least to some degree. In other words, while political and financial autonomy is a desirable goal, there must also be some degree of meshing between the decentralised and state level governments so that their efforts complement rather than compete with each other. In view of this, it is necessary that decentralised governments function within the framework laid down by the national Constitution. At the same time, it is equally important that national and state level governments allow local governments some constitutional rights so that the latter enjoy legal recognition and rights with minimum or no interference from unscrupulous politicians at the state and the national levels.

An important logistic is the need on the part of the local governments to promote positive democratic values. These values include peaceful electoral processes, accountability of elected representatives, and regular consultation with the people on issues that affect them. It is also desirable that local governments work closely with people's organisations and NGOs, since such organisations can not only provide them with feedback, they may also assist in the implementation of schemes and projects. The promotion of positive development values is another important logistic. For instance, local governments should identify the needs and aspirations of the people and match these needs with available local resources by formulating development projects and implement these projects in a cost-effective manner so as to promote community and economic development.

In the following pages we propose to present the experiences of Asian countries in relation to decentralisation, keeping in mind the following parameters: the representative character of the decentralised bodies, the political and financial autonomy of these bodies, the integration of decentralised institutions into the state governance system, and the extent to which these bodies have promoted positive democratic and development values.

## Emergence of Decentralisation: Causes

What accounts for the sudden emergence of decentralisation as a major theme in countries as diverse as Bangladesh, India, the Philippines, Nepal, China and Sri Lanka? Part of the explanation lies in the political demands for democratic self-rule in countries previously governed by authoritarian regimes. This is the case in the Philippines, Nepal and Bangladesh, each of which has undergone the transition from autocratic to democratic rule in the recent past. The installation of a representative form of democracy at the national level is often seen as only the first step toward returning power back to the people. Political devolution from the centre to state, provincial or local governments often comes fast on the heels of national redemocratisation. In the Philippines, for example, the recent enactment of the sweeping Local Government Code represented a major plank in the Aquino government's 'people power' platform. Nepal enacted a decentralisation program within a year of its first national elections being held, and one of the first acts of the newly installed government in Bangladesh was to establish a presidential commission to recommend local government reforms to replace the upazilla system of the Ershad regime. In these countries, decentralisation can be seen as the 'second wave' of democratic reform, depending and building on the democratisation process taking place at the national level.

A second factor in the movement toward political devolution is the ethnic diversity of some of the countries in the region, and the growing demand of different groups within Asian societies for greater political autonomy. In India, for example, over-concentration of power at the centre is frequently cited as a factor contributing to the unrest in regions such as Punjab, Kashmir and Assam. Similarly, the growing strength of the Jharkand movement in southern Bihar can be traced in part to the refusal of the state government to share power with local authorities, evidenced by its failure to hold local elections for more than 15 years. The gradual emergence in India of an all-party consensus that states should be mandated to establish functioning panchayati raj systems represents a widespread recognition of the essential need for political decentralisation to manage the stresses and strains of India's ethnic, regional and religious diversity. A similar set of factors clearly underlays Sri Lanka's establishment in 1987 of elected provincial councils, in a move designed to defuse Tamil demands for political autonomy in the island's strife-torn north-eastern region.

China's move in the direction of granting villages greater autonomy through a system of 'basic level democracy' deserves special mention, coming as it does amidst China's rapid economic liberalisation and its continuing resistance to the democratisation of its single party political system. Architects of the 1987 Village Committee Organization Law and subsequent experiments with democratically elected village councils perceive these reforms as responding to grassroots demands for greater control over village affairs. While much of the rationale and justification for the reforms is cast in terms of contributing to social and economic development objectives, there is little doubt about the fundamental political character of the village councils. There are numerous questions about how far the Chinese experiment in village level democracy will be permitted to go, particularly when inevitable conflicts arise with formal state structures, but the fact remains that villages now enjoy a degree of 'democratic space' that did not previously exist within the Chinese political system.

Political forces and factors provide some, but not all of the answers to the question of why decentralisation has arisen recently as such a widespread phenomenon. An equally compelling explanation can be found in the failure of large, centralised development schemes to reach intended beneficiaries and deliver tangible benefits to rural communities. As just noted, China's foray into village level democracy is justified largely on the grounds of promoting rural development. India's new constitutional amendment mandating all states to establish panchayati raj systems also drew its strength from the failure of various centrally sponsored development schemes to achieve the desired impacts 'on the ground'. Indeed, some analysts have argued that such schemes have created an attitude of government dependence on the part of villagers, which can only be overcome by revitalising village level institutions. The fact that responsibility for overseeing the implementation of the new panchayati raj is vested with the Rural Development Ministry is indicative of the close linkage that exists between rural development and village democracy in India.

It is not just the 'mega-states' of India and China that have seized on the social and economic development benefits of decentralisation. Nepal's new network of district development councils and village development committees arose out of a clear recognition that it is impossible for Kathmandu's helping hand to reach remote mountain hamlets, which are often several days' walk from the nearest road. Similarly, the new Local Government Code in the Philippines places major emphasis on provinces and municipalities assuming greater responsibility for local development, and carves out a special role in the development planning and implementation process for local non-government organisations.

It cannot escape notice that in several Asian countries, the process of government decentralisation is taking place simultaneously with the introduction of structural adjustment and economic liberalisation policies. Conceptually, there is a logical connection between privatisation and decentralisation, if the primary objective is to reduce the control of central state structures over economic decision-making. Some international lenders and multi-lateral donor agencies have strongly encouraged decentralisation as part of an overall structural adjustment package, although this has not risen to the level of 'conditionality'. While it would be a mistake to attribute too much weight to economic liberalisation as a factor in the decentralisation process, it has definitely helped to create a favourable policy climate for the advancement of local governance reforms.

## The Papers

Recent decentralisation initiatives in most countries of the Asian region have thus moved forward under the dual banner of 'democracy *and* development'. The extent to which they succeed in delivering the positive values of *either* democracy *or* development is a question for research and policy debate, and it is this question which the papers presented in this volume seek to address. Essentially, the papers attempt to provide early feedback on how well recently adopted decentralisation reforms seem to be performing with regard to both political and socio-economic objectives. Since most of the reforms are quite recent in origin, the findings and conclusions must necessarily be regarded as tentative. Longer-term and more systematic monitoring studies are clearly necessary to yield definitive results and answers. However, since policy-makers rarely wait for definitive studies before embarking on ambitious policy changes (including reversals in previously adopted policies), it is important to marshall whatever evidence we can even at this early stage of the process.

The papers included in this book were originally commissioned for an Asia regional seminar on decentralised governance. The purpose of the seminar was to provide an opportunity for sharing results of research and for a comparative assessment of several Asian countries' experience with decentralised governance initiatives. Scholars and policy-makers were invited from six countries— Bangladesh, China, India, Nepal, the Philippines and Sri Lanka— each of which has had recent experience with local elected government bodies of various forms.

For each of the countries represented at the seminar, two papers were commissioned. The first was intended to provide an overview of the system of decentralised governance, including its historical background, legal status, fiscal arrangements, current political context and future outlook. The overview papers were primarily descriptive, but in many instances also provided analytical insights into structural strengths and weaknesses of the various systems. The second paper for each country was designed to provide a micro level assessment of how local governance actually functions at the grassroots level. In contrast to the overview papers, which provide the 'theory' of how different systems should work, the field level papers give a first-hand account of local governance 'practice'. As the reader will quickly discern, there is often a considerable gap between the two.

The local governance systems examined by the authors of the papers are all at different stages of implementation and are in a continuous state of flux, reflecting the unique political, economic and social dynamics of the societies in which they are embedded. In this sense, the current volume must be considered a 'snapshot' of the arrangements that exist at a particular point in time. Moreover, the micro level papers have a place-specific quality that makes broader generalisation somewhat risky. Nevertheless, taken as a collection, the papers provide a finely textured picture of an understudied but potentially significant movement throughout Asia toward the devolution of basic governance and development responsibilities to lower levels of government. It is hoped that the issues and questions they raise will be the focus of future scholarly research, as well as informed debate and discussion among concerned policy-makers, community activists and the public. It is only through such a process of sustained inquiry and policy dialogue over time that the positive benefits of local self-governance can be realised and widely acknowledged, and weaknesses and drawbacks reduced.

## The Contours of Decentralised Governance

It may be of some interest now to present the contours of decentralised governance systems in the Asian countries under reference
as they have emerged in the papers included in this volume. The
paper by Rajni Kothari provides a perspective for understanding
decentralised governance practices in Asia in general and India in
particular. He looks upon the system of decentralised governance
not only as a means of effective democratic functioning of the
governing system but also as an instrument of social and economic
transformation of the rural society. Rajni Kothari notes that there
is an absence of consensus across countries on the issue of decentralisation. There are some who are afraid that decentralisation of
power may lead to the emergence of centrifugal forces endangering
national unity and there are others who hold that it may, by
removing economic disparities, provide stability to the union
government. Notwithstanding such dissensions, he holds that
decentralisation should be seen as extremely desirable. However,
he is of the view that decentralised governance can succeed only
when (a) the process of decentralisation is seen as a continuum of
the governing structure of the nation, (b) a dynamic 'bottom up'
structure of the local government set-up is evolved on a voluntaristic
basis, (c) the power of decision-making at this level is equitably
shared by all the social and economic classes, and (d) people are
mobilised to continue their struggles for democratic rights through
their own organisations.

The papers that follow present the main features of the decentralised governance system in each of the six Asian countries that
are experimenting with this system. The Bangladesh system, being
a part of what was evolved in the Indian subcontinent from ancient
times, shows new strains after independence in 1971. As Mohammad Mohabbat Khan argues, the system has gone through three
phases since independence—each time subjecting itself to modifications based on the self-interest and perceptions of the leaders
holding power at the centre. After experimenting with different
systems (tier-wise), the previous government has finally settled for
a three-tier decentralised system consisting of a union parishad, an
upazilla parishad and a zilla parishad respectively at the village

cluster, sub-division and district levels. The working of these institutions, particularly the upazilla parishad, as gathered by Khan
from several field studies, is somewhat perturbing, considering
that elections have been marred by disturbances and violence,
local level planning has been devoid of people's participation,
corruption has been endemic, the relationship between elected
representatives and bureaucrats has not been all that cordial and
accountability has been given a go by. Because of this, the present
democratic government has taken steps to strengthen grassroots
level governance and established a two-tier local government with
a union parishad and a zilla parishad. It is hoped that in due
course, some meaningful decentralised governance will emerge in
the new setting.

The experience with the new set-up—especially the impact of
Bangladesh's experiment with decentralised governance on its
rural society—has been vividly captured by Zarina Rahman Khan.
Decentralisation implies the devolution of political and administrative functions to the local bodies, political and financial autonomy and full scope for people's participation in decision-making.
This calls for such logistics as clear demarcation of functions between
different layers of government, access of all people, especially the
weaker sections, to the governing bodies through the electoral
process, a mechanism for the devolution of financial power and an
efficient administrative and project implementing machinery. The
efficient functioning of these bodies is judged not only in terms of
their style of functioning but also in terms of how effectively they
identify and articulate the needs of the people, formulate and
implement local resource-specific projects through a well-thought-
out planning process.

Viewed in the light of the above criteria, the functioning of the
Dighi Union Parishad studied by Zarina R. Khan leaves much to be
desired. Its composition is such that it is dominated by the rich and
powerful sections of the rural society with no representation to
women despite a provision for two women nominees. Regular
meetings are not held and no real attempt is made to collect taxes.
Corruption and favouritism in the dispensation of justice, absence
of popular participation in the planning process and lack of
accountability on the part of elected representatives are some of
the charges levied against the parishad. With such a system of

decentralised governance, the kind of impact it can have on the rural society is anybody's guess.

Surprisingly, China presents a contrasting picture. The abolition of the commune system in 1983 represents the real beginning of the establishment of an enduring grassroots level governance system, although in China the system existed in some form or the other, through the years of dynastic rule and even after the founding of the People's Republic. But as Wang Zhenyao points out, while the rural social, economic and political structures of the dynastic rule allowed peasants to manage production for their own subsistence, hardly anything was done to promote the greater public good. Up until 1958, China was dominated by township governments. It was only with the replacement of these governments by people's communes that village governments became important. The latter not only succeeded in creating a strong economic cohesiveness within Chinese rural society, they also generated a significant amount of non-agricultural capital required for rural industrialisation and mobilised masses to live and work together for a common goal. Laudable though this was, it was nevertheless inadequate for creating a modern system of democratic self-government. A conducive environment for such a system emerged only after the advent of the household responsibility system in 1979 and the phasing out of people's communes, subsequently replacing them with elected village committees.

The Chinese village committee is a grassroots level autonomous body run by people who are responsible for local administration, public projects, mediation of disputes and public security. There were, of course, initial teething troubles like soured relations between peasants and cadres, an unorthodox election process and general resistance to the new system. But gradually, with experience and by painstakingly dispelling people's misgivings about grassroots democracy, the situation improved. Elections became formal and standardised competitive election campaigns became the norm. Election to the village committee is direct and any peasant irrespective of age, sex, wealth and education can get elected if supported by the people. The possibility of corrupt practices at the time of elections does exist but, if discovered, the legal system takes action against them. The village committee which generally meets once a month, is greatly influenced by the villager council conference comprising not only members of the village committees but also citizens of the village and representatives of people's congresses at various levels.

The village autonomy ensured in the new system provided instruments to (*a*) resolve rural contradictions propelled by the new direction given to Chinese politics; (*b*) train peasants in the art of democracy; and (*c*) accelerate the pace of rural development while maintaining political stability. The extent to which these gains were secured and the basic constraints imposed on the functioning of the villagers' group are illustrated in a case study of the Lishu county by Cao Guoying and Zhang Houan. This paper also illustrates in detail the electoral process—the nomination of the candidates for election, the election speeches, voting procedures and the declaration of election results—all of which seem akin to the presidential election system in USA! The other good features of the system, as illustrated by the case study, are group networking for developing common facilities and making village financial accounts available for public scrutiny. The upsurge of democratic feelings among the rural Chinese peasants has been very well channelised by the new system which has, in turn, laid the foundation for the sustainable economic and social development of rural China.

In India, too, this democratic upsurge was exploited by the political leadership. But initially this was done only to entrust responsibility for implementing community development projects to the people. However, as George Mathew very rightly says, it was only following the recommendations of the Ashok Mehta Committee that these bodies were transformed from being mere development organisations into political institutions. The high level of political perception among the rural masses, the emergence of a new and young rural leadership, the devolution of powers and resources to local governments, the participation of political parties at this level of governance and the recent amendment to the Constitution giving these bodies a statutory status and permanency have created the necessary conditions for the emergence of a sustainable governance system at the grassroots level.

The interest groups that the panchayati raj institutions in India have had to take into account are more numerous than elsewhere because of the complicated social stratification in terms of caste.

Therefore, in addition to gender bias, the membership composition needs to be in favour of depressed castes. This also explains the reservation of seats for the weaker sections.

The Indian model of decentralised governance is generally three-tiered and functions at the district, block and village cluster levels. The most important responsibility of these bodies is to plan for their respective regions. But they have been ineffective in this task mainly because of unwillingness on the part of the government at higher levels to share power and resources, the dominance of these bodies by the rural elites and the lack of political will. The latter is reflected in the failure of these bodies to regularly hold elections and the propensity of the political elite to dance to the tune of the bureaucracy which does not seem to have taken very kindly to the notion of decentralising decision-making power.

It is this important issue of the devolution of power and resources that is discussed in the field-based paper by Abdul Aziz, Charles Nelson and Devendra Babu. The Karnataka experiment with decentralised governance, which has attracted a good deal of attention, provides an indication of the extent to which people can share power and resources. The authors point out that though members of the weaker sections of society could be elected to the mandal panchayats through seat reservation, positions of power were not available to them. The political autonomy supposed to be enjoyed by these bodies has been eroded by their recent supersession by the state. Forced to operate with limited resources, they could not possibly give much attention to production-oriented development projects, although their track record with regard to provision of amenities has been fairly good. It seems that these amenities are now more equitably located than they were earlier—an achievement of which decentralised governments can be legitimately proud. Nevertheless, they still have to go a long way in inspiring the citizens to develop an interest in and awareness about decentralised governance, and to make voluntary contributions in cash and kind to support community development projects.

The case of Nepal is unique in that in recent years there has been a transition from centralised autocracy to decentralised democracy. What is important is that this transition has been peaceful and has been made with the concurrence of the ruling monarchy. Though initially, decentralisation was modelled after

India's community development approach seeking to mobilise people's support for self-help projects, in due course, with a series of legislative measures, politico–administrative decentralisation has emerged which has since been engaged in carrying out decentralised planning exercises. The paper by Soorya L..Amatya presents a detailed account of the institutional structure of decentralised governments: the village and the district development committees and the process of decentralised planning followed by them. An interesting feature of decentralisation in Nepal is that the NGOs and user groups are brought into its ambit and NGO projects are also integrated into the local planning frame. Also, both the NGOs and user groups are involved in the implementation of local development projects. Both the village and the district development committees formulate development plans for areas under their jurisdiction that involve the people and give priority to programs that increase income, employment and agricultural production, utilise local resources and skills and protect the environment. The planning process operates within a time schedule, and includes such tasks as identifying projects, prioritising them and getting them approved. The planning agency employs a committee approach, involving people's representatives, bureaucrats, NGOs and representatives of users' groups, and provides for quarterly and annual progress reviews. In practice, however, the decentralised governments, especially the village committees, are found to be working with a low financial base; there is much to be desired with regard to accountability on the part of elected representatives; and there is also a need to reduce interventions from the central government and higher level bureaucracies.

These drawbacks of decentralised governance in Nepal have been brought out more sharply by Sant B. Gurung in his field-based paper. While presenting a case study of the K-BIRD project, which is formulated and implemented in the decentralised plan framework, Gurung lists out a series of constraints the planner faces. These are: lack of data base at the village and district level; delay in receiving a budget ceiling and guidelines from the central government, and even delay in budget disbursement; lack of awareness about the decentralised planning process among politicians, and lack of planning skills within the lower level bureaucracy; frequent transfer of project staff; poor standards of coordination among sectoral agencies; and lack of people's participation. Obviously, there is a need for change in these parameters if a meaningful decentralised planning process is to be ensured.

In his paper, Alex B. Brillantes, Jr., identifies the various phases in the development of a decentralised governance system in the Philippines and also points out a few loopholes in the latest legislation introduced by the government. The Philippines also had a history of local governance till the arrival of Americans who effected centralisation of the politico–administrative system to ensure the consolidation of their power. However, after 1935, and more particularly since 1946, local governments began to enjoy some degree of autonomy in fiscal, planning and regulatory areas. Though this autonomy was restricted between 1972 and 1986, during Marcos' authoritarian regime, the passing of the Local Government Code of 1991 provided the much needed constitutionally guaranteed autonomy for local governments in respect to fiscal, planning and regulatory functions.

The outstanding features of this code are: sharing of proceeds of natural resources in their jurisdiction, rise in the proportion of the internal revenue allotment, direct participation of NGOs and people's organisations in the local governmental special bodies and allotment of seats in the local legislative bodies to marginalised interest groups like women, labour, the disabled and tribals. However, the cost of devolved services is borne by the local governments, and this has proved to be a point of contention. As has the possibility of the provision facilitating people's organisations and NGO participation being misused. Another contentious issue has been the delay in implementing the provision relating to empowerment of weaker sections on the grounds of heavy costs incurred on this account. While presenting her case study of a municipality, Jessica K. Carino goes deeper into the problems of implementing this code. She sketches in detail the functioning of decentralised governmental bodies, especially with regard to their planning tasks. The municipal government, it is to be noted, is expected to prepare both the long-term six-year plan and the annual plan. But owing to delays in constituting the municipal development council, which includes NGOs and people's organisations, the plans were prepared without the latter's participation. And what is worse, instead of preparing comprehensive socio–economic development plans, the council just restricted itself to reviewing proposed development projects. Thirdly, the devolution of powers with regard to delivery of services by the municipality such as agricultural extension, health services and the construction of a school building was also delayed. Fourth, on the question of sectoral representation (to women etc.) it is argued, particularly by the officials, that they need not be represented at all as in any case men represent women's interests as well. The formation of local bodies has also been delayed on various grounds, the foremost among them being financial constraints and failure to accredit NGOs and public organisations. One reason for all these delays is procedural problems. Also, it is too early to expect the government machinery to move so fast as to complete all the required formalities, considering the fact that the code was passed only recently and that its provisions have to be understood by all concerned before action can be initiated.

The case of Sri Lanka is more akin to India. It, too, has had a long tradition of political devolution which came to an abrupt end with the advent of colonial rule. However, a new phase of devolution, albeit in a small measure, began from the last quarter of the 19th century. But this only took definite shape with the beginning of the Bandaranaike era. The latest decentralised governing units are the provincial councils, the pradeshiya sabhas (PS) and the gramodaya mandalayas (GM).

In his paper C. Suriyakumaran discusses the experience with the various aspects of devolutionary system in Sri Lanka during the last four decades—an experience which is seen in the context of the growth of an ethnic dimension in the country. There has been a universal commitment to the values of local governance and people's participation, and this is reflected in the 13th Amendment to the Constitution which relates to the creation of local government structures. Although there is still room for improvement with regard to administrative and fiscal devolution and people's participation, there have been some notable achievements. For instance, NGO participation and the disappearance of latent dyarchy with the phasing out of the government agent system.

A detailed account of the functioning of the pradeshiya sabha is presented by H.A.P. Abeyawardana in his field-based paper. The pradeshiya sabha is assigned the responsibility of providing amenities. Funds for these activities are collected from the users as rates and grants from provincial councils. The pradeshiya sabhas and the Grama Mandalayas function in a coordinated manner and provide amenities to citizens from their funds, occasionally drafting communal labour and involving people's organisations and NGOs. However, as in other countries, participation by women was found to be very poor, mainly because of ignorance, lack of awareness and inability to take time off from routine household responsibilities.

One of the main functions of these bodies is local level planning but Abeyawardana's study does not give them full marks in this task. For them, planning continues to be a routine exercise, as illustrated by their use of project compilation for the purpose of requesting funds. The 'basket projects' concept was proposed to overcome overlapping duplication and wastage of resources, but according to the study this has not met with much success.

## Future Directions

Before we close this chapter, a point that needs examining is: what does all this add up to? Is the effort to promote decentralised decision-making been justified in the light of experience gained? It should, at the very outset, be admitted that justification or no justification, political decentralisation has become inevitable in the Asian region. There have been compelling reasons, as mentioned in earlier pages, for centralised decision-making authorities to devolve power and resources to local government bodies. But a crucial point to be raised at this stage is: have these bodies played their roles to the expected levels and have they thereby justified their existence as separate political units of decision-making? As decentralised decision-making units, they should be seen as units which deliver positive values of democracy and promote local development. Therefore, the question is whether they have delivered these goods in a measure such that they command all-round acceptance. On this issue, the findings of the papers in this volume are not unanimous. Thus, while positive democratic values such as a peaceful electoral process, a representative political structure, devolution of power and finances, accountability of the elected representatives and people's participation are evident in the Chinese system in a large measure, they are somewhat satisfactory in the Indian, the Philippines and Sri Lankan systems, and not so satisfactory in Bangladesh and Nepal. Positive development values such as the identification of needs and aspirations of people and local resources, matching of these two by formulating development projects and implementing them in a cost-effective manner so as to promote community and economic development show a more or less similar spread across countries. That is, the Chinese system has in a large measure promoted community and economic development; the Indian and Sri Lankan systems have produced moderate results; but Bangladesh, Nepal and the Philippines are yet to produce results even in a moderate measure.

It is difficult to categorically state why this has happened. Nevertheless, it should be possible to make an educated guess. As stated earlier, a basic pre-requisite for the delivery of positive democratic values is the presence of strong and democratic governments at the higher layers of governance and a leadership that is readily prepared to devolve adequate powers and resources to the lower echelons of the governing system. Minimum interference from above and the permanency of local governments are added advantages. Deliberate attempts by state governments to delay elections to local bodies or to supersede them by taking over administration can hardly provide the conducive environment needed for delivering positive democratic values. Similarly, adequate resource-raising powers, devolution of funds in appropriate measure, the presence of skilled man-power which formulates and implements local plans, people's and NGO participation in the planning process are pre-requisites for the delivery of positive development values. Appropriate logistics for supporting and facilitating decentralised governance and decentralised planning are the other pre-requisites. These comprise: (*a*) fully decentralised political institutional structures which are strongly linked to the higher level governance bodies; (*b*) a decentralised administrative system which is again linked to the higher level government administrative system; and (*c*) a decentralised data gathering machinery which collects and disseminates data about the micro regions for the benefit of the decentralised governing and planning bodies. Variations in the creation and availability of these prerequisites may be at the base of the differential performance of decentralised governments in different countries and this issue could well become a potential area of study for future research workers.

Having made some general comments about the factors that might have contributed to the differential performance of decentralised governments with regard to the delivery of positive democratic and development values, we shall now move on to the future directions that the decentralised governance system should and will take. Although, in the countries under reference, these systems exhibit divergent characteristics, some commonalities can also be discerned. In all these countries, the system and its structure has been evolving over time partly in response to the will of the political bosses but more importantly, in answer to the changing needs of the overall political imperatives. We can therefore, expect, with a reasonable degree of confidence, that as the philosophy of decentralisation catches on in the Asian countries and that as it spreads spatially, the system will have much more in common across countries. Second, there have been initial teething troubles such as opposition from vested political and economic interests, dominance by social and economic classes, corruption and election violence. But with the spread of awareness and more accurate perceptions about and higher levels of participation in decentralised governance by citizens, officials and people's organisations, and with the system acquiring permanency and acceptance, it is expected that these teething troubles will subside. Third, these decentralised governing bodies are being slowly but steadily transformed from mere development organisations into political institutions. Though the extent to which this has happened varies across countries, the direction, however, remains intact. And in some countries, such as India, these bodies have acquired statutory status, permanency and some degree of political and financial autonomy. There has also been an attempt to make them more representative by introducing seat reservation or allotment for economically and socially weaker sections of the society. This trend, if it continues, is likely to transform the decentralised governance bodies into a truly representative body of the people, particularly of the weaker sections. There are, however, some gaps in the working of these bodies. First, planning for promoting development among backward regions and weaker sections is undoubtedly an important common thread that passes through decentralised governance systems in Asia. However, the impact of planning on the community and economic development has not been significant mainly because of lack of planning skills and financial bottlenecks. Second, there is some degree of participation by NGOs and people's organisations in decentralised governance, but not enough. Third, there is still much left to be desired with regard to financial and power devolution from the upper to lower level governments. Future efforts will therefore have to concentrate on removing these disabilities so that decentralised governance becomes more effective and meaningful.

# 2

# Issues in Decentralised Governance

## RAJNI KOTHARI*

Decentralisation should be viewed in the context of an emerging need to reconcile two contrary tendencies: globalisation on the one hand and local self-governance on the other. The entire world is undergoing wide-ranging change. A renewed North–South dialogue, democratic upsurges, the decline of authoritarian regimes, experimentation with new institutions, problems of ethnicity, religiosity and basic social identities—some of these now need redefinition and a political orientation. This need is being felt everywhere but more particularly by Asian countries. There is a remarkable shift of interest and concern today in favour of giving a concrete shape to the democratic upsurge and to local self-government institutions. There is a special reason for this. An immediate effect of globalisation has been the impact of the world capital market on centralised and decentralised governance, especially in respect of the making of vital decisions that affect the lives of the people. It is in this changed context of economic and technological development that there has emerged a need to understand the imperatives of decentralised governance and to develop commitment to the philosophy of decentralisation.

Indeed, some degree of commitment to decentralised governance can already be seen all over the world. The emerging commitment should, however, be seen as an end product of a given historical

* Excerpts prepared by Dr. N. Sivanna and Dr. Abdul Aziz from the keynote address delivered by Professor Rajni Kothari at the inaugural session.

process. One has to perceive this commitment among the political parties and in their ideologies, in the upsurges among the people and their recognition of persisting disparities, underdevelopment, poverty, rural and urban disparities, centre–periphery problems and in their growing awareness of environmental concerns. It should also be seen in the context of political mobilisation in rural areas, the appalling conditions of women and the poor, in respect of poor literacy and growing urbanisation, and of growing incapacity, even unwillingness, on the part of the state to solve problems. By and large, emphasis has always been on macro economic development. Because of this, the gap between macro and micro economic development continues to be accentuated.

A related problem in this regard is the lack of fit between institutional backwardness and popular awareness. During 1960s, the benefits of economic development did not percolate down to the grassroots level, and even the radical measures adopted by regimes in 1970s could not handle and control the upsurges. The institutions that were created for promoting the necessary social and economic development have become almost moribund due to their dependent nature and inadequate ideologies. The alternative framework of policies formulated and implemented during the 1980s also failed and were unable to check the growing unemployment, economic disparities and other related problems. The purchasing power of rural incomes had dwindled. Coupled with all these, the authority structures and institutions and policies always depended on the national bureaucracy. The national planning system addressed only 'national' issues and not the constellation of interests that had emerged at other levels, including the most local. Hence the need arose to distribute power to grassroots level institutions and committees and, with this in view, for restructuring the nature of the state by evolving a structure where people themselves came to the centre of power and participated in decision-making on issues that affected them.

Decentralisation soon began to be seen as an alternative system of governance where a 'people-centred' approach to resolving local problems is followed to ensure economic and social justice. The entire process would be for locating people at the centre of power so that they become the basic engine of the development process and not, as hitherto, merely its beneficiaries.

There does not, however, appear to be consensus on the issue of decentralisation across countries and political ideologies. In some countries, leaders are afraid of decentralising power, that is, to share power with different levels of the governance system. The question is often posed: what will happen if power is decentralised? Will it not create space for the emergence of 'centrifugal' forces which endanger national unity and strength? And as a result, would not forces of disintegration emerge and work to destabilise the system? A related fear is that if power is decentralised it may land up in the hands of dominant caste groups who may try to advance their own interests. If this were to happen, local elites would rule and in the course of time might both challenge state authority and jeopardise public policy designed to benefit the people at large.

In contrast, those who favour decentralisation argue that not only is centralised power incapable of providing stability to the government but, being colonial and bureaucratic, it may well give rise to religious, ethnic and minority upsurges. It is admitted that monolithic states and progressive socialist states, where power is vested in a central government, are more enlightened than local governments as far as protecting the larger interests of the poor and minorities is concerned. Also, centralised government structures are successful to a larger extent in removing disparities. But at the same time, it has also been observed that under centralised governance, it is not possible to have a stable political system. Further, centralised power is inimical to democratic values and approaches to solving problems. This is mainly due to the nature of the state which is a gift of colonisation. In such an environment, what is the position of the poor who are largely located in rural areas? Since real power is concentrated in urban and metropolitan cities, there is hardly any chance for the rural poor to share the benefits of development. As a result, migration has taken place and the trend is towards degeneration of rural assets and ecological imbalances. To put the rural economy back on the rails, local governments and decentralised development planning have become a political necessity.

Present-day society is a mixture of both traditional and modern values, this is particularly true of developing countries. On the one side, we can see the impact of urbanisation, the mass media and a high level of education—each trying to provide a framework for modernisation. On the other, most countries have their own cultures and values which are deeply ingrained in traditional relationships, especially in the countryside. State-sponsored development of the modern kind has often led to regional disparities, social disparities, backwardness among some sections of the society, and rural–urban conflicts. A larger issue to be debated in this context is: if a backward region is given 'statehood', would it not be in a position to enjoy political autonomy, make better use of local resources and lessen disparities with regard to rural and urban areas? This question has come up in various countries and needs to be thoroughly examined in the light of available experience.

As far as the rationale of decentralisation is concerned, there is need to see the evolution of decentralised processes in terms of a continuum. Merely setting up governing structures would in no way promise effective decentralisation. The commitment here needs to extend beyond it, to ensuring the devolution of real powers and resources. Only then would it be possible to pursue a real democratic path. There is also the question of whether we can have local self-government directly, without the backing of a federal structure and process? And, at the same time, in the absence of well-equipped state level governments, is it necessary to intervene directly and instal local institutions? Decentralised governance is required in the sense that the people have the ultimate authority to take decisions since there is no direct sharing of power along the federal dimensions. But this is by no means assured. What happened in Germany during the reign of Bismark, who was the first exponent of 'adult franchise'? In the so-called Bismarkian model, which espoused decentralisation, there was no effective devolution of power as there were no intermediate structures through which such power could be devolved. While efforts are being made to create local self-government institutions in most centralised regimes such as the colonial regime of British India, as well as in highly authoritarian regimes like Nepal and in various military regimes, the national leadership always seems reluctant when it comes to sharing power. Unfortunately, no inherent correlation is found between local government set-ups and democracy. Countries like Indonesia, Egypt, Pakistan or, until recently, Nepal, each of which tried one or another model of 'local democracy' and each of which tried to establish local government institutions that were supposedly endowed with special powers, have not really shown much interest in the advancement of the democratic process.

There is another question: What type of set-up will promote effective decentralised governance? In this context, there is need to distinguish between a local government set-up established by a central authority and a dynamic 'bottom-up' local government structure of a voluntaristic kind. The latter is the result of the processes of civil society, wherein the local community wields power. Local self-government perceived in this way will be a measure for containing discontent and channellising available local energy and skills for promoting grassroots level development. Of course, to achieve such governance, the central government too should be interested and, to the extent interested, channellise funds to the local committees. In China, the central government finds it easier to channellise funds than redistribute power. As I see it, however, what is required is a local government set-up established by the central authority which perceives the need for and the advantage of channelling local energies and skills for development.

Merely setting up local self-government committees does not necessarily amount to the advancement of democratic politics. On the contrary, such an attempt may prove to be quite counter-productive. The basic issue is: how should decentralised systems enhance the powers originally given to them and, in turn, contain the power of dominant groups and the muscle power used for manipulating the election process? Failure to understand such imperatives has often led to the growth of the 'mafia' phenomenon in local governance which keeps the weak away from the political process. If this happens, the very purpose and philosophy of decentralisation is defeated.

There are certain important socio–economic correlates of decentralisation. By itself, decentralised governance is an inadequate tool to empower people socially, economically, educationally and in respect to access to decent standards of livelihood—health, housing, etc.—unless the economic policies of the central government are employment-oriented. It may be noted that employment generation is constantly ignored in the Indian planning process and this, in turn, has affected the social development of the weaker sections. There is now an increasing demand for the 'right to work'—a right which is also emphasised by the ILO and the Commission on Human Rights. It is now realised that people should be empowered politically, economically and socially by ensuring them various rights so that they can participate in decentralised governance more effectively. The most important is the right to work—in the sense that every citizen should be able to get work commensurate with his skills and abilities. Decentralised governments can ensure work to all those who need it by appropriately planning for the development of the local economy.

But above all, what is the point of having decentralisation when local power structures and the distribution of economic power are extremely skewed? The skewed power structure has emerged due to ineffective implementation of land reforms. In this context, the discussion should focus on the relationship between what decentralisation represents and the kind of structural changes that are required in the prevailing rural power structure. The related issues are: what are the rights of women and youth, and of weaker sections and minorities in a decentralised system of governance?

A larger issue to be discussed is the kind of policies that need to be framed for empowering people who are prevented from participating in decentralized governance. Unless people are equipped in the way they want, any talk of decentralised governance would be mere sloganising. Reservation of seats for the weaker sections is one way of giving them access to decentralised governments. But having done that, if these persons are not trained in the art of governance through the creation of social awareness among them and not provided with the requisite information, then they would be no better off than they were earlier. This again raises the issue of the kind of training modules that need to be prepared, the training methodology to be employed and the follow-up measures that must be adopted.

There is a strong need to remove poverty. To do this the poor have to be empowered with income-yielding assets and increasing access to natural resources. Also, it calls for higher allocation of budgetary resources for providing the social basis of poverty alleviation. If people are better educated, have better clothing, health and access to living space, they could take care of themselves. It must be remembered that poverty cannot be removed bureaucratically and by central planning. People have to be empowered with education, health, housing and should have access to common property resources. It is therefore essential that they participate in the planning process, identify their needs and aspirations and provide inputs for planning and implementing projects at the local level. It is generally complained that there is a great deal of 'leakage' from the poverty alleviation programmes on account of misidentification of beneficiaries and misutilisation of funds. People's participation in the process of beneficiary identification and in monitoring the programme may, perhaps, minimise leakages.

I would like to go a little further and say that I see decentralisation as a clear counter to the processes of homogenisation, globalisation, modernisation, liberalisation and privatisation. We should build a system such that people become the sources of decentralised governance, which should also mean a differentiated and pluralist structure of governance. Of course, in the context of the globalising process, there is need to view the world as a 'global village', a concept that has been gaining ground in recent times. But we need to be clear about what exactly this concept means in our time and about how we can make that global village truly decentralised. In effect, decentralisation should be seen as an important correlate of development policies to equip local groups and bodies to become qualified members of the global village.

Another correlate of decentralisation is the grassroots political process. People's initiative is necessary for grassroots struggle, for justice and for self-determination by ethnic groups. Regional groups are more basic to decentralisation of power. Local committees should be responsive to the urges of the people. People should fight for justice and against the structure of domination. In this kind of struggle, traditional values and practices should be given due consideration since traditional society had its own way of dealing with local problems. Hence, the grassroots political process should be treated as part of decentralisation. The entire process should not merely be for the delegation of power but also allow people to create their own new and dynamic structures of power. Only then will they even get close to real decentralisation of power.

The importance of people's struggle in the process of development lies in mobilising them from the bottom based on their own assertions and upsurge. Failure to recognise such upsurge by any decentralised structure would make the latter a manipulative one. Installation of local government committees must be in response to the need for giving power to the people. For the development of local self-government to become real, there is need for (*a*) effective participation by the people, and (*b*) voluntarism of the civil society. But in India, the voluntaristic ethos, which at one time was very much alive, has been suppressed as a result of colonialism, transfer of power to centralised regimes, bureaucratisation and homogenisation. In such a situation how does one regenerate voluntarism and keep it alive? That is, perhaps, the key question which needs to engage our minds.

To sum up, the entire process of decentralisation should thus be seen as a means of effective democratic functioning. In such a process social problems should be given due consideration both in respect of building the necessary social pre-requisites of nation-building and the removal of poverty and unemployment and in the context of resolving fundamental social and economic problems faced by diverse communities and across constellations of class and ethnicity. Decentralised governments should, therefore, be seen as instruments of social and economic transformation. Any model of decentralised governance should keep this larger historical imperative in view.

# 3

# Local Self-government System in Rural Bangladesh

## MOHAMMAD MOHABBAT KHAN

In recent years there has been an increasing interest in Asian countries to analyse the role of local governments from the perspectives of autonomy and economic self-sustenance. To be effective, local governments need to be premised on certain bases since efficient and effective management of local affairs is neither possible nor desirable when the central government is located far away from the local units of governance. Secondly, political and economic development at the local level requires participation of the local people on a regular basis. Thirdly, locally elected leaders, in order to maintain their autonomy, must try to increasingly lessen their dependence on central government grants and instead generate resources from within. Lastly, for local level democracy to take shape, local people need to be aware of and trained to manage their own affairs so that their reliance on central bureaucracy is reduced to the minimum.

One way by which local self-governments can be strengthened is through devolution of authority from the central government to local level elected bodies. Devolution as a form of decentralisation has certain characteristics.[1] First, it requires that local governments be given autonomy and independence and be clearly perceived as a separate level over which central authorities exercise little or no direct control. Second, the local units must have clear and legally recognised geographical boundaries over which they exercise their power and authority and within which they perform public functions. Third, local governments must be given corporate status and power to raise sufficient resources to perform specified functions. Fourth, devolution also implies a need to develop local governments as institutions perceived by local citizens as organisations providing services for satisfying their needs, and as governmental units over which they have some influence. Finally, devolution is an arrangement in which there are reciprocal, mutually benefiting and co-ordinated relationships between central and local governments. Local self-government and devolution of authority from the central to local governments go hand-in-hand. One cannot survive without the other. Both for conceptual and practical purposes the inter-relatedness of the two needs to be understood and accepted. In the present context, local government means local self-government and decentralisation implies devolution.

This paper describes and analyses Bangladesh's experience with local governance and devolution in rural areas from a historical perspective.

## Historical Development

To trace the lineage of local self-government in today's Bangladesh, one has to look at its development in the Indian subcontinent for a number of centuries. Even then, there are controversies as to which accounts of local governments can be accepted as authoritative. This is specially the case pertaining to the ancient period.

### The Ancient Period

It is usually accepted that in the Indian subcontinent, the institution of village self-government (VSG) is as old as villages themselves. These VSGs were supposedly autonomous units responsible for their internal administration and socio-economic development.[2] But VSGs took different forms and functions in different times and places.[3] Nevertheless, two institutions—of the headman and the panchayat—seem to have been in existence since ancient times, with considerable variation in their powers and functions. The headman usually belonged to the most powerful family of the dominant caste in the village. He was not elected by the people; his importance rested on the fact that all political and administrative contacts between the village and higher authorities were exclusively routed through him. The village panchayat was an elected body with executive and judicial functions.[4] It has been suggested that these panchayats were controlled by the leaders of upper castes and often by the headman.[5]

## The Mughal Period

The panchayati system disappeared in medieval times during the Mughal rule of the Indian subcontinent. This happened due to the curtailment of the law and order functions of panchayats, the growing importance of the headman, and a taxation system which led to the creation of an intermediary class of people between the tax administration and tax payers.[6]

## The British Period

The main objectives of British rule in India were to maximise land revenue collection and maintain law and order. As an imperial power, the British had little interest and inclination to understand and appreciate the indigenous local self-government system. As a result, the ancient system of local governments became inoperative and ineffectual, and then disappeared altogether. Instead, the British sought to introduce a system of local government which would suit their imperial interests.

The developments in the area of local government during British rule can be divided into two broad phases. The first phase loosely corresponds to the rule by the British East India Company. The second phase roughly coincides with the formal taking over of India by the Crown and the consequent consolidation of its power.

During the first phase there had been little progress in local rural government. In 1870 the Village Chowkidari Act in Bengal established union panchayats to collect taxes to maintain Chowkidars (village police). However, these panchayats were not representative bodies.

The foundations of local self-government in rural British India were laid by Lord Ripon's famous Resolution of Local Self-Government.[7] This Resolution of 18 May 1882 is important for two reasons. First, it set out general principles for the development of local institutions in the future; and second, it provided the rationale behind the functions of local bodies. Ripon believed that local government was to function (*a*) as a means of devolution of authority in administration and in the decentralisation of financial resources; and (*b*) as a means of providing political education that would mobilise popular participation in finding solutions to the problems of government.

However, the Ripon Resolution was never implemented in its true sense. It proposed a two-tier—union committees and local boards—system of local self-government. Union committees were to be elected bodies with a number of specified functions to perform. Above them, the local boards were to consist of members, the majority of whom would be elected. Local officials would have considerable say in the functioning of the Boards. But when the Ripon Resolution became a law, i.e. as Act III of 1885, another layer, the district board, was added. The lower bodies were bereft of all functions and made dependent on the district board. The Royal Commission of Decentralisation, 1907–1909, though it favoured democratising local bodies, still recommended control of such bodies by government officials. The Report of the Bengal Administrative Committee, 1913–1914, which advocated the institution of union boards, was critical of the state of the local government system in general and deemed it a failure. The Bengal Village Self-Government Act, 1919, abolished union committees and substituted them with union boards. The union boards would consist of members two-thirds of whom would be elected and the rest nominated. The chairman of the board would be elected from among the members. The union boards were given certain specific functions including the authority to levy taxes. By the end of 1920, in Bengal, all the district boards came under non-official chairmen.[8] Also, the revival of panchayats in Bengal led to the establishment of one panchayat for a number of villages.

Efforts during the Mughal period, Company rule and Crown administration until the 1880s in the area of local self-government can only be described as piecemeal, narrow and restrictive.[9] Though there had been considerable progress in democratising the local government system by the British after 1882, 'the Indian local self-government was . . . in many ways a democratic facade to an autocratic structure'.[10]

## The Pakistan Period

After independence in 1947, Pakistan continued the local government system it inherited from the British. The union boards and the district boards kept on functioning as in the past but the local boards disappeared.

In 1959 a new system of local government was introduced. The system, known as Basic Democracies (BD) had a twofold objective. It was designed to prepare the base on which an upward pyramid of a sound political system would be developed. It was also intended to achieve true democracy suited to the genius of the Pakistani people in place of Western democracy.

The four-tier BD system comprised of the union council, the thana council, the district council and the divisional council. Except for the union council, which stood at the base of the system, none of the other three bodies was fully elective. The thana council, considered an innovation at the time, had very little to do except coordinate the activities of union councils and liaise between the union council and the district council. The district council, like the thana council, was dominated by officials. Both bodies were headed by civil servants. The district council was responsible for coordinating the activities of the union council and municipalities within its jurisdiction. It also performed a variety of other functions. The sources of the council's revenue were land taxes and direct grants received from the government. The divisional council, yet another innovation, was designed to complete the coordination chain at the divisional level, and was headed by the divisional commissioner, a senior civil servant.

A keen observer of rural local government in Pakistan summarised what actually went on in the name of achieving true democracy at the local level. According to him, 'a powerful district council remains the primary agent of administration, and an even more powerful government at higher levels can easily view the union councils as convenient administrative adjuncts'.[11]

## Institutional Structure of Decentralised Government in Bangladesh

The local self-government system in Bangladesh has passed through three distinct periods which symbolise the political priorities of the regimes in power and the changed circumstances.

### Mujib Period (1972–1975)

The first period covers the initial years after independence. This period witnessed the rule of the Awami League under the leadership of Sheikh Mujibur Rahman (Mujib). Having been an opposition leader Mujib found it difficult to adjust to his newly-found role of supreme leader. Moreover, social unrest, mounting economic problems and lack of accommodation of various political forces in the governance system made nation-building activities and the institutionalisation of the democratic system of governance Herculean tasks for Mujib and his party to undertake. Added to these, Mujib lacked a vision for the future and failed to project himself as a leader who was above partisan politics. He continued to remain the leader of his political party, the Awami League. His only concern was to concentrate all powers in his hands and to suppress opposition to his regime. This led to the creation of the monolith, Bangladesh Krishak Sramik Awami League (BKSAL). All these factors shaped Mujib's and the Awami League's policy towards local self-government.

The government dissolved all local government bodies inherited from the days immediately after Pakistan's independence. This radical decision was followed by two other decisions to fill the void created by the dissolution. Public officials were authorised to form committees at different tiers as an interim arrangement for the temporary performance of local functions. Also, the names of different bodies were changed and the union council became the union panchayat; the union committee became the *nagar* panchayat and the town committee was known as *shahar* committee. The thana council and the district council were respectively designated as the thana development committee and the zilla board. The interim arrangements included nomination of persons by the national government to these local bodies, except for the thana development committee whose affairs were looked after by the circle officer in charge of development activities in the thana. Though there was a system of nomination to involve local influential persons in various local bodies, the actual control on them was exercised by the deputy commissioners, sub-divisional officers and circle officers.

The President's Order No. 22 of 1973 defined the composition, functions and sources of income of union parishads on a more or less similar line as the Basic Democracy Order of 1959. The name of the union panchayat was again changed to union parishad. A system of election was introduced to elect a chairman and a vice-chairman and nine members for each union parishad. Each union consisted of three wards and each ward returned three members.

## Zia Period (1975–1981)

The second period covers Lt. Gen. Ziaur Rahman's (Zia) accession to state power, its consolidation and his assassination. Zia's assumption of power came at a critical time of the nation's history. He succeeded the interim President Khondokar Mushtaq Ahmad (Mushtaq). Mushtaq was a beneficiary of the coup which toppled the Mujib government and culminated in his brutal killing. Zia was installed by those army officers and jawans who opposed Maj. Gen. Khalid Mosharraf's stay in power. Zia moved systematically to consolidate his hold over state power. He began the process of providing alternate strategies and policies pertaining to politics, the economy and society. All these contrasted sharply with Mujib's strategies. Zia wanted to achieve his goals through widening and consolidating his political base in the rural areas. This was in line with the policies he pursued at the national level.

Through the Local Government Ordinance of 1976, Zia's government clearly spelled out the structure and functions of local bodies in rural areas. The Ordinance has been considered by some scholars as the constitution of local government in rural Bangladesh.[12] It led to the creation of three tiers of local government—the union parishad for a union, the thana parishad for a thana and a zilla parishad for a zilla. All three were declared to be corporate bodies with typical features. Of the three, only the union parishad had a representative character with the chairman and nine other members being directly elected on the basis of universal adult franchise. The thana parishad was a quasi-representative body. The positions of chairman and vice-chairman were manned by the sub-divisional officer and the circle officer (development). Only the chairmen of the union parishads within the thana were representative members of the thana parishad. The other members were officials of different nation-building departments working at that level. Though the zilla parishad was to consist of elected members, official members and women members, no elections were held. Consequently, the deputy commissioner functioned as the chairman of the zilla parishad and another junior official assisted him as the secretary of the parishad.

All three bodies were assigned a number of similar functions and responsibilities. The union parishad was to undertake civic, police, defence, revenue, and general administrative and development functions. The chairman of the union parishad was to assist in the collection of rent and land taxes and help in the preparation of records and assessment. The thana parishad had the responsibility to prepare development plans, to oversee their implementation and to provide assistance to the union parishad. The major functions of the zilla parishad were of a maintenance nature. The zilla parishad was also empowered to coordinate the activities of all other local parishads.

The swanirvar gram sarkar (SGS) was introduced at the village level in April 1980 by amending the Local Government Ordinance of 1976. The micro governmental system was actually an amalgamation of two experiments—the swanirvar andolan (movement for self-reliance) and the gram sarkar (village government), which were attempted at non-governmental levels, initially without government support.[13] The swanirvar andolan aimed at achieving a breakthrough in agricultural production together with reducing population growth.[14] Emanating from this movement for self-reliance, gram sarkar, on the other hand, was an administrative arrangement to ensure better mobilisation of development efforts and fuller utilisation of existing indigenous resources.[15]

The SGS consisted of one gram pradhan (village chief) and eleven members including two women. The members of the SGS were to be chosen through consensus of the gram sabha (village assembly) composed of all adult members of the village. It was responsible for doubling food production, eradicating illiteracy, reducing population growth, invigorating rural cooperatives and maintaining law and order within the village.

These SGS bodies did not function for any considerable period of time and were abolished by a Martial Law Order in July 1982. But even during their existence, they were perceived as being used for partisan political purposes: to widen the base of Zia's newly-formed political party, the Bangladesh Nationalist Party (BNP).[16]

### Ershad Period (1982–1990)

Lt. Gen. H.M. Ershad (Ershad), who seized power in a bloodless coup on 24 March 1982, moved swiftly to consolidate his hold over state power. Ershad's usurpation of power was possible mainly due to extreme factionalism within the ruling party, i.e. the BNP, the failure of the president to effectively assert his authority over key party members including ministers, Ershad's over-ambition.

By any measure, the Ershad regime introduced significant changes in the area of local government. These changes were supposed to 'bolster' rural local bodies, to take administration 'nearer to the people' through local government bodies and to 'facilitate people's participation' in administration and development.[17]

The government appointed a high-powered Committee for Administrative Reorganisation/Reform (CARR) with the Deputy Chief Martial Law Administrator (DCMLA) and Chief of Navy as its chairman in April 1982. The members of CARR included individuals from various professions: the army, civil services, teaching and journalism. The intention was obviously to give it the appearance of a 'representative' body consisting of members from different segments of the society.

The recommendations of CARR included a directly elected chief executive (Chairman) and a representative parishad (council) at each successive sub-national and local level: zilla (district), upa-zilla (sub-district) and union; popularly elected chairmen to be chief coordinators at all levels and provided with adequate staff support; elected councils at each level to possess full functional control over officials working there, and adequate devolution of administrative, judicial and financial powers at the zilla and upazilla levels; elimination of sub-division and division as tiers of administration; elected chairmen of lower councils to be ex-officio members of immediately higher councils; and the development of infrastructure at the upazilla level.[18]

An implementation body was created entitled the National Implementation Committee for Administrative Reorganisation/ Reform (NICARR) to direct, oversee and coordinate the implementation of reform measures recommended by CARR. In fact, CARR specifically called for the establishment of a powerful National Implementation Committee (NIC). Unfortunately, the government did not adhere to the recommendations of CARR with regard to the composition and functions of the NICARR.[19] Its role was restricted to identifying thanas for their phase-wise upgrading into upazillas, fixing the number of officers and staff of the national government to be deputed to the upazillas, approving upazilla parishad business and taxation rates, calling for fixed financial allocation of resources on a yearly basis by the national government for upazillas and recommending the conversion of 64 urban thanas into upazillas.[20]

The legal coverage of the decentralisation effort was provided by the promulgation of the Local Government (Upazila Parishad and Upazila Administration Reorganisation) Ordinance, 1982. The Ordinance had been revised a number of times. It laid down, among other things, the composition and functions of the representative council (upazilla parishad), the nature and transfer of functions from the council to the national government and *vice versa*.[21] It also identified the manner in which the council could undertake developmental activities, levy taxes on specified items for the generation of revenue, prepare and maintain accounts and ensure their proper audit.[22]

An upazilla parishad, the centerpiece of Ershad's reform, consisted of (*a*) an elected chairman; (*b*) representative members, i.e. all chairmen of the union parishads within the jurisdiction of the upazilla; (*c*) three women members nominated by the national government from among the residents of the upazilla; (*d*) official members, i.e. national government officers working in the upazilla; (*e*) chairman of the Upazila Central Cooperative Association; and (*f*) one nominated male member.[23] All members, except the official ones, had the right to vote in upazilla parishad meetings. But like other members, official members could participate in the parishad meetings. The tenure of the parishad, which was initially for three years, was subsequently raised to five years. The chairman of the parishad was directly elected by all adult inhabitants of the upazilla.

With the assistance of a number of civil servants, the chairman of the parishad performed a variety of functions. He supervised and exercised control over the personnel deputed to the upazilla, coordinated development activities, initiated the formulation of plans and programmes pertaining to local development and ensured the proper implementation of projects and their monitoring and evaluation, promoted and organised employment-generation activities and maintained liaison with other levels of administration and public agencies.[24] He also initiated the annual confidential reports (ACRs) of the upazilla nirbahi officer (UNO).

Among the national government officials at the upazilla level, the upazilla nirbahi officer was the principal functionary of the parishad. He was responsible to the chairman and assisted the latter in the execution of the parishad's decisions. He supervised and controlled revenue and budget administration, coordinated all training activities at the upazilla level and initiated the annual confidential reports of all upazilla officials except the magistrate.[25]

Besides the UNO, the other key person was the planning and finance officer who played the role of financial advisor to the upazilla chairman and assisted him in the administration of the parishad fund. His responsibilities included the preparation of the upazilla budget, advising on authorisation of development and non-development expenditures from the fund, assistance in the preparation of upazilla development plans (UDP), and monitoring the progress of development projects, undertaking socio-economic surveys in the upazilla, and providing assistance in the evaluation and appraisal of projects.[26]

Many other national government officials posted at the upazilla level worked under the guidance of the parishad in general and the UNO in particular, dealing with subjects such as agriculture, primary education, health and family planning, cooperatives, fisheries, livestock and rural water supply.

The upazilla parishad performed five sets of functions: financial, developmental, operational, coordinative and miscellaneous. The financial functions included the management of the parishad fund, preparation of annual budget, annual statement of accounts and audit reports. The developmental functions were concerned with preparation of the upazilla plan book, formulation of annual development and five-year plans, and approval and implementation of development projects. The personnel administration of the parishad, formation of committees and sub-committees and setting down procedures to regulate the execution of contracts by the parishad were some of the operational functions. The parishad periodically reviewed developmental and regulatory activities of public agencies not directly associated with the upazilla administration, i.e. those agencies which were controlled at the national level, in performing its coordinative functions. The parishad also reviewed its own activities, which fell outside the purview of the four sets of functions just mentioned.

The upazilla parishad (UZP) could levy taxes, rates, tolls and fees with the general or special sanction of the national government on the following sources of income: (*a*) lease money on jalmahals (inland natural fisheries) situated within upazilla boundaries; (*b*) tax on professions, trades and callings; (*c*) tax on dramatic and theatrical shows and other entertainment and amusements; (*d*) street lighting tax; (*e*) fees for fairs, agricultural and industrial shows, exhibitions and tournaments; (*f*) fees for licences and permits granted by the UZP; (*g*) tolls on services and facilities maintained by the UZP; and (*h*) lease money from specific bazars and ferries to be determined by the government.[28]

As has been indicated, the UZPs had been given some authority to raise revenue. Additionally, a UZP might manage, maintain, inspect, develop or improve any property which it either owned, or which was placed under its charge, or which it acquired or transferred by grant, gift, sale, mortgage, lease exchange or otherwise.[29]

Notwithstanding the power to impose such a wide range of taxes, the national government's grants were the most important sources of revenue for local government institutions during the Ershad period. The UZP finances were met almost entirely from government grants, as the national government provided all the manpower and undertook to provide necessary monies to meet the cost of establishing the upazilla parishad and to pay the salaries of its personnel.[30] But this dependence of local councils on national government grants had two negative consequences. First, mobilisation of local resources was callously neglected. Second, it seriously undermined the autonomy of local councils and adversely affected their authority to set priorities for local level development. The personnel mobilisation

Apart from upazilla parishads there were two other rural local government bodies. These were union parishads (UPs) and zilla parishads (ZPs). The Local Government (Union Parishad) Ordinance, 1983, provided for a directly elected chairman and nine members for a UP on the basis of universal adult franchise. The functions of the UPs were primarily confined to assessment and collection of taxes, maintenance of law and order, construction of village roads, bridges, culverts, ponds and maintenance of cottage industries.[31] The term of office of the UP chairman and members was three years.

A zilla parishad was constituted in each district as per the Local Government (Zilla Parishad) Act, 1988. Its members, who enjoyed a three-year tenure, consisted of public representatives, nominated male and female members and some officials. The national government retained the right to appoint the chairman. Like the union parishads and upazilla parishads the zilla parishads had many powers on paper. Until their dissolution in December 1990, their most important function was planning and the promotion and execution of development and welfare programmes within the district.[32]

Both the union and zilla parishads depended heavily on government grants to maintain personnel, meet establishment costs and perform mandated functions.

## Nature of Local Level Planning

Planning, budgeting and resource allocation were closely related. Three directives[33] prepared and circulated by the national government indicated the nature and extent of control exercised by it over upazillas. Of the three, two directives on the utilisation of development assistance by the UZP attempted to control each and every aspect of the planning and resource allocation process in the upazilla. The directive stated in unambiguous terms the intention of the national government towards local level planning at the upazilla level:

1. Criteria were established for the local government division to follow in allocating funds to different upazillas. Four criteria with different weights were used for the allocation: population (40 per cent), area (20 per cent), extent of backwardness (20 per cent) and performance (20 per cent).
2. Upazillas were asked to prepare an Annual Upazilla Development Programme (AUDP) and an Upazilla Development Plan (UDP) and to maintain a plan book. Upazillas were then told that since they had little experience and expertise, their developmental activities were to be restricted to nine broad areas. Then a strict sectoral allocation pattern in AUDP was shown for all nine areas, with the minimum and maximum shares for each one of them.
3. The upazilla parishads had to be aware of the objectives and priorities of the national plan before undertaking any developmental activities.
4. They were advised to take up only those projects which could be completed within two years.
5. They were advised to constitute a project selection committee, a project evaluation committee and a tender committee. The composition and functions of the three committees were also specified. In all the committees, the predominance of centrally-recruited, directed and controlled officials deputed at the upazilla level was noticeable.
6. Upazilla parishads had been barred from using development funds for 20 different types of work.
7. Central civil servants at district, division and the secretariat levels were allowed to inspect project activities in upazillas and were required to send their findings in the form of advice, comments and suggestions to respective upazilla chairmen with copies of the same to the Cabinet Division, Local Government Division or any other concerned ministry/ division.
8. Every upazilla parishad was required to send copies of the annual report detailing the cost of all development activities

and physical progress of work at the end of each financial
year to the Cabinet Division, the Local Government Division,
the Planning Commission and the concerned Deputy.
9. A project proforma was supplied by the national government to be followed by the upazilla parishads for preparing
project proposals.

## Nature of Elections and Electoral Process

Local level elections have been held periodically under the overall
supervision of the Election Commission (EC) which is a constitutional body. So far, five union parishad elections and two upazilla
parishad elections have been held under different regimes in Bangladesh. The process of organising and holding local level elections
has been beset with a number of problems.[34] First, the small size of
the EC compels it to depend rather heavily on public servants who
are deputed by the government to work under the supervision of
the EC's senior officials in the various facets of the election process.
Second, though corrupt practices have always been part of the
election process, under the Ershad government they crossed all
limits. The alarming increase in practices like vote-buying, bogus
voting, and ballot box snatching during the 1985 and 1990 upazilla
parishad elections and the 1988 union parishad elections cast a
shadow of doubt over elections as a mechanism for selection of
local leaders. The caretaker government of Justice Shahabuddin
Ahmed took a number of steps like reconstituting the EC and
giving it wider powers with regard to the conduct of civil servants
involved in the election process. The present government, too, has
shown its willingness to enable the EC to function in an independent
manner. Third, violence in one form or another has always characterised elections, specially the local ones. In this regard, the
1988 UP elections broke all records. Over a thousand people were
killed and several thousands were injured in election-related inci-
dents. Finally, the selection process of local leaders is dominated
by a few individuals. Field-level data clearly point to the elite
domination of the electoral system and local institutions.[35]

## Assessment of the Working of Decentralised Governments

Assessing the performance of any institution is a difficult task because an institution performs its functions within an environment over which it has little control. This is especially true of local government institutions in Bangladesh. In this section, attention will be focused only on the upazilla system—for two reasons. First, during both the Mujib and Zia regimes, very little power was transferred to local bodies. Secondly, administrative, financial and judicial powers were transferred by legal instruments during Ershad's rule to local bodies composed of elected, nominated and official members.

A number of scholars and researchers have examined different aspects of the upazilla system and have produced some serious field based studies. For instance, Khan and Zafarullah[36] focused on the decentralised planning process at the upazilla level. Pilot studies were conducted in 15 upazillas of 11 districts covering 3,300 villages in 197 unions in different parts of Bangladesh. Then detailed investigation was undertaken on the nature and dynamics of local level planning in two more upazillas: Savar and Comilla Kotwali. The findings of the study were both revealing and shocking. First, the vast majority of the rural population was kept completely in the dark about the planning process at the level nearest to them. The planning function at that level remained the responsibility of either politicians or civil servants. Second, planning relied rather heavily on the influence of the elite in the selection of project sites and the manner of project implementation. Local level planning did not benefit the majority of the local population. At no stage of the planning process were the common people even consulted. The participation of the rural poor in local projects occurred at the implementation stage—as hired labourers. Third, the relation between the elected representatives and the officials at the upazilla level was based on suspicion and uncertainty. Fourth, technical expertise available at the local level was inadequate. Elected representatives had no knowledge about even the basics of local level planning and this situation was exploited by civil servants. Fifth, corruption became endemic at the upazilla level with upazilla chairmen and upazilla engineers being the principal beneficiaries of the situation. Practices like graft, tender manipulation, misuse of funds and nepotism became common. Sixth, there was lack of coordination in development planning between the upazilla parishads and other public agencies in relation to projects at the local level.

Blair[37] and his associates studied a single but complex issue of local resource mobilisation (LRM) in the rural areas of the country. They conducted field research in the Bhanga and Nagarkanda upazillas of Faridpur district and Lakshmipur and Ramgoti upazillas of Lakshmipur district. The findings of the study make for disturbing reading. First, rural elites were taking advantage of whatever local governmental autonomy existed to further their own interests, often at the expense of the community's welfare. Second, there was very little interest in local tax collection at either local or central level. Third, there was a powerful bias towards infrastructure which pervaded the representative government at the local level. Fourth, the central government determined, by what it did, the bias towards infrastructure in allocating resources for rural development. Fifth, there was no accountability to anyone for LRM. Sixth, LRM was quite uneven between one locality and another.

Murshed and Quddus conducted field studies in two upazillas—Mirsarai in Chittagong district and Saharasti in Chandpur district—to determine among other things, whether noticeable socio–economic changes had taken place among the rural poor after the adoption of decentralised governance. The study, heavily criticised for its methodological and other flaws, found that villagers did benefit from the implementation of projects by these two upazilla parishads.

### Current Policy Issues and Future Outlook

The present democratic government has shown considerable interest in the local governance system. This is reflected in a number of steps the government has taken since assuming power in March 1991. First, the union parishads were allowed to function. In fact, elections to the union parishads were held rather peacefully. Second, the elective component of the upazilla system was abolished. All the functions of the upazilla parishad and the upazilla chairmen are now performed by officials. Third, a Local Government Structural Review Commission (LGSRC) was formed to establish a local government system based on democratic principles. The commission was composed of 17 members of which six, including the chairman, were members of parliament, four belonged to the teaching profession and the rest were civil servants. The commission recommended[39] a two-tiered structure of local government: gram sabha (village council) and union parishad (UP) at the village level and a zilla parishad (district council) in every district. The chairmen and members of all the bodies would be elected. The other recommendations[40] of the LGSRC included an indirectly elected Thana Development Coordination Committee and an independent and permanent Local Government Commission. Finally, the government accepted the major recommendations of the LGSRC regarding the institution of a union parishad at the union level and zilla parishad at the district level. As a follow-up, an ordinance was promulgated to give effect to the government's decision. Later, a Bill was passed by the parliament to regularise the government decision. The government did not accept the LGSRC proposal to constitute a gram sabha at the village level.

It would appear that the government's policy considerations include, among other things, institutionalisation and democratisation of the local government system. But some problems and confusions can be seen in the government's actions. The present government has followed its predecessors in scrapping the local government structure it found in place and substituting it with a new and different scheme, which it regards as the centerpiece of its rural development policy.[41] Also, it did not take into confidence the members of parliament after the LGSRC submitted its report. Rather, through an executive action, i.e., the promulgation of an ordinance, it gave effect to the accepted recommendations of the LGSRC. The local government reform proposals were then presented to the parliament as a *fait accompli*.

It is hazardous to try to predict what will happen in the area of local government in the future that will depend upon a number of factors. First, the credibility and popularity of the present government will determine how quickly and systematically actions can be initiated to institutionalise a viable local governance system. The second factor concerns the manner in which the policy planners within the ruling party (BNP) view the relationship between the national government and representative local institutions in terms of autonomy and control. And third, it would depend on how seriously the government has considered the recommendations of the LGSRC and their long-term political, economic and administrative implications.

## Conclusions

The account of decentralised governance presented in the preceding sections shows that there are serious problems which have undermined the development of local self-governing institutions. The national governments have dominated local self-governments leaving the latter with little scope to do anything meaningful. The domination of successive national governments has been motivated by political considerations. Both General Zia and General Ershad utilised local government bodies to mobilise public support for their regimes. This enabled General Ershad particularly to civilianise his military rule in the face of mounting political opposition in the urban areas. An almost total dependence of local bodies on national government grants and their unwillingness to mobilise resources from within have further emboldened the national government to interfere in the affairs of the former. Further, the existing rural power structure has not been conducive to foster people's active participation in local councils affairs. Local councils, like upazilla parishads, have been dominated by the triumvirate of the centrally-deputed civil servants, locally elected politicians and local influential persons, leaving no room for the rural poor to voice their needs. Also, political commitment to devolution of power to sub-national and local levels, measured in terms of the nature and support provided by the national political leadership in power, has been at best marginal. The actual degree of decentralisation has been rather limited.

## Notes

1. Rondinelli, D.A. 1981. 'Government Decentralisation in Comparative Perspective: Theory and Practice in Developing Countries'. *International Review of Administrative Sciences*, Vol. XIVII, No. 2: 138.

2. Alderfor, H.F. 1969. *Local Government in Developing Countries*. New York: McGraw Hill, p. 69.
3. Siddiqui, K. (ed.) 1992. *Local Government in South Asia: A Comparative Study*. Dhaka: University Press Limited, p. 13.
4. Malaviya, H.P. 1956. *Village Panchayats in India*. New Delhi: All India Congress Committee, p. 66 and 68.
5. Siddiqui, K. *op. cit*. p. 15.
6. *Ibid*, p. 17.
7. Banerjee, A.C. (ed.) 1946. *Indian Constitutional Documents, 1758–1945*, Volume 1, Calcutta: p. 644.
8. Siddiqui, K. *op. cit*. p. 21.
9. Khan, M.M. and H.M. Zafarullah. 1979. 'Rural Government in Bangladesh: Past and Present'. *Journal of the Institute of Local Government Administrators*, Vol. XX, No. 2: 9.
10. Tinker, H. 1954. *The Foundations of Local Self-Government in India, Pakistan and Burma*. London: The Athlone Press, p. 70.
11. Tepper, P. 1966. *Changing Patterns of Administration in Rural East Pakistan*. New York: Maxwell School, Syracuse University, p. 107.
12. Khan and Zafarullah, *op. cit*. p. 10.
13. Khan, M.M. and H.M. Zafarullah. 1980. 'Rural Development in Bangladesh: Policies, Plans and Programmes' *Indian Journal of Public Administration*, Vol. XXVI, No. 3: 3.
14. Tepper, P. *op. cit*. p. 3.
15. Khan, M.M. and H.M. Zafarullah. 1981. 'Innovations in Village Government in Bangladesh'. *Asian Profile*, Vol. IX, No. 5: 119.
16. Zafarullah, H.M. and M.M. Khan. 1989, 'The Politics of Rural Development in Bangladesh' . *Asian Journal of Public Administration*, Vol. XI, No. 1: 16.
17. Siddiqui, K. *op. cit*. p. 152.
18. Khan, M.M. 1988. 'Major Administrative Reform and Reorganisation in Bangladesh, 1971–1985' in C. Campbell and B.G. Peters (eds) *Organizing Governance: Governing Organizations*. Pittsburgh: University of Pittsburgh Press, p. 369.
19. Khan, M.M. 1987. 'Politics of Administrative Reform and Reorganization in Bangladesh'. *Public Administration and Development*, Vol. VII, No. 1: 353.
20. Khan, M.M. 1990. 'The Policy Significance of Decentralization in Bangladesh'. *South Asia Journal*, Vol. 111, No. 3: 281.
21. *Ibid*, p. 281.
22. Khan, M.M. 1986. 'The Process of Decentralization in Bangladesh'. *Community Development Journal*, Vol. XXI, No. 2: 121.
23. Siddiqui, K. *op. cit*. p. 153.
24. Khan, M.M. and H.M. Zafarullah. 1988. *The Decentralized Planning Process in Bangladesh*. Bangkok: Division of Human Settlements Development, Asian Institute of Technology, p. 14.
25. *Ibid*, p. 13.
26. *Ibid*, p. 15.
27. *Ibid*, p. 16.
28. Government of Bangladesh (GOB). 1983. *Manual on Thana Administration*, Dhaka: Bangladesh Government Press (BGP). Vol. 1, p. 20.

29. *Ibid*, p. 12.
30. Siddiqui, K. *op. cit.* p. 170.
31. *Ibid*, p. 158.
32. *Ibid*, p. 161.
33. Government of Bangladesh. *op. cit.* Vol. 2, pp. 7–12; 'Guidelines for Upazila Parishad for Utilization of the Development provided by the National Government through the ADP'. Vol. 2, pp. 13–15; 'Instruction for Utilization of Development Assistance Fund by Upazila Parishads'. 1985. Vol. 3, pp. 100–112.
34. Khan, M.M. 1989. 'The Electoral Process in Bangladesh'. *Regional Studies*, Vol. VII, No. 3: 95–111; Khan, M.M. 'Critical Issues in the Selection Process of Local Leaders in Rural Bangladesh'. *The Journal of Local Government*, Vol. XX, No. 1.
35. Suqui, Q.M.A.H. 1980. *Our Leaders at the Local Level*. Dhaka: National Institute of Local Government; Rahman, A. 1981. *Rural Power Structure: A Study of Local Level Leaders in Bangladesh*. Dhaka: Bangladesh Books International; Rahman, A. 1986. 'Where do the Poor Stand in the Process of National Building?' in M.A. Hafiz and A.R. Khan (eds.) *Nation Building in Bangladesh: Retrospect and Prospect*. Dhaka: Bangladesh Institute of International and Strategic Studies.
36. Khan, M.M. and H.M. Zafarullah. 1988. *The Decentralized Planning Process in Bangladesh*. Bangkok: Division of Human Settlement Development, Asian Institute of Technology, pp. 61–68.
37. Blair, H.W. (ed.) 1989. *Can Rural Development be Financed from Below?: Local Resource Mobilization in Bangladesh*. Dhaka: University Press Limited, pp. 233–41.
38. Murshed, S.M. and M.A. Quddus. 1992. 'Bangladesh' in *Impact of Decentralization on Rural Poverty: An Asian Perspective*, Dhaka and Bangkok: CIRDAP and AIT, pp. 16 and 19.
39. Government of Bangladesh. 1992. *Report of the Local Government Structural Review Commission*. Dhaka: GOB, pp. 1–2.
40. *Ibid*, pp. 1–2.
41. Blair, H.W. et al. 1992. *The Bangladesh Democracy Programme (BDP) Assessment: Final Report*. Washington D.C.: Bureau for Private Enterprise, US Agency for International Development, p. 13.

# 4

# Decentralised Governance and its Impact on Rural Society in Bangladesh

ZARINA RAHMAN KHAN

The current structure of local government in Bangladesh is once again in the process of undergoing a change. As the history of this country shows, each change in government was accompanied by a move for discarding the previous system of local government and initiating a new one. This legacy of experimentation with decentralisation, if closely scrutinised, also reveals that with each attempt at reform in the structure and the functions of the locally elected administrative bodies, the stated objectives also changed, at least at the level of rhetoric.

Although the most highlighted objective in each case has been the decentralisation of administration, the actual extent of devolution of powers and financial autonomy, which make the local institutions self-governing, has remained open to question. The second major objective of making these 'decentralised' units participatory and representative  also remained limited to the process of voting only.[1] The nature of functioning of these institutions indicates that they are still far from being people's organisations. Thus there has always been a gap between the stated objectives and actual achievement; indeed, it may be claimed that the processes that evolved through the reforms were actually different interpretations of decentralisation.[2] Decentralisation has meant the deconcentration of certain very specific administrative functions to locally elected representative bodies. The jurisdiction of functions and the resource endowment required for independent planning and operation was not devolved to the local government units under any of the reforms. Nor were these elected bodies given any constitutional guarantees.[3] Above all, under the given socio–economic structure of rural Bangladesh, the vast majority of the populace remained unrepresented in the local bodies, just as the scope for people's participation in their functions continues to be limited.

The purpose of this paper is to enquire into the objectives of decentralisation and participatory local self-governing bodies by analysing the composition, functions and the processes of their operation at the lowest level of the local government hierarchy. The main intention of this enquiry is to assess the extent of popular participation in such governance and its impact on the general populace. In order to do this, I have used two sources of information. First, all available written material on local government institutions was consulted. This included reports of various surveys and empirical studies, government ordinances and notifications. Secondly, I have looked into the functions and activities of one union parishad in its relationship with the villages and the next higher tier of administration in the local government system. This was done basically by collecting information from records at the union parishad and the related thana offices and through interviewing the union parishad chairman and its members, and five government officials at the thana level including the thana nirbhavi officer (TNO). Responses and opinions of a cross-section of villagers from different socio–economic backgrounds were also recorded. Five villagers each from the high, middle and low income groups including five women were interviewed. They were selected on the basis of the categorisation of villagers that I had done in my earlier study. In addition, I held detailed group discussions with several villagers. These discussions focused on issues such as the different local government systems, the villagers' role in these, the extent to which these bodies functioned in their interest, and the impact of the different forms of local government on their lives.

Because of time and resource constraints, the collection of empirical information at the local level had to be limited to one area and one union parishad. This may preclude me from making generalisations on the basis of the conclusions of this case study. However, it can be said that if the constraints that inhibit the 'popularisation' of the local government units are held to lie in the formulation of the system itself, then the problems can be identified at the operational level of even a single unit. Therefore, it is hoped that a study of even one local government unit will enable us to pinpoint the areas of departure from the stated purposes of decentralised local government. Again, because of time and resource constraints, I chose a region and a union parishad where I had previously worked. Since I was familiar with the region and had kept in touch with the local government units and the government representatives, I was able to elicit information from the relevant offices in the very short period of a month. My earlier rapport with the villagers of this particular union helped me to get good responses.

## Background of Local Governments in Bangladesh

Structurally, all the experiments in local government in Bangladesh retained a tier or hierarchal system, the difference being a shift of focus from one level to another. Administratively, the country is divided into divisions, districts, thanas (upazillas 1986–1991) and unions. Bangladesh started with a two-tier system at the district and union levels, with no devolution of adequate authority by the national government to any level. In the next period, a three-tier system was adopted with an emphasis on the lowest level. Later, a lower unit at the village level—envisaged as an elected organisation— was added in the form of a gram sarkar. With the next change in government, a three tier-format with the upazilla parishad wedged between the union and the district parishads was formulated. Here, for the first time, a directly elected chairmanship was introduced at the upazilla level. In every model adopted, all members (except women) and the chairman were elected directly only at the lowest level. In most cases there were elected, nominated and official members in the higher bodies with the officials holding controlling powers. In the case of the upazilla parishad alone did chairman have controlling authority over the government officials. With the abolition of the upazilla parishad in 1991, at present there are only two tiers of local government, one at the district and the other at the union level.

As far as the devolution of authority and the jurisdiction of powers are concerned, none of the local government systems evolved so far held out a promise for the emergence of an independent self-governing institution. From the very beginning, only some limited activities of the government were transferred to the local bodies; regulatory functions such as those of the police, magistracy, judiciary, revenue and land management etc. were retained by the centre. The local bodies were given the authority to collect local taxes from bridges and houses, to issue licences, to maintain law and order, to keep population records, to act as local arbitration councils and to undertake development activities. However, these functions were allotted to them without assigning them with the requisite powers of enforcement!

Similarly, in all the models tried, local government institutions were left with little scope for generating funds of their own. The bulk of the resources required for developmental work and much of that needed for its maintenance have been disbursed from the centre through government officials at various levels of the field administrative structure. The regular functions of the local bodies, particularly at the lower rungs, are required to be carried out with locally generated resources, while development activities depend on funds provided by the national government and siphoned off through its sub-national administrative units by the higher rungs of the local governing bodies. This dependency of the local government units on the national government automatically limits their ability to act independently. The financial hold of the national government on the activities of local elected bodies again leads to other 'conditions' which make them independently inoperable. The projects or programmes to be initiated and implemented by the administration are in accordance with the orders received by them together with funds sanctioned by the national government. That is to say, the government administrative unit, or the local government through which the funds flow, provide guidelines on the basis of which project proposals can be submitted. There are several specified sectors or items under which development or national building programmes can be undertaken. And every year the national government administration specifies how many and under which items may project proposals be submitted. Again, where actual implementation of projects is concerned, only very low cost ones are directly and independently handled by the union parishads. Even at the thana or higher levels, no large project, particularly if related to construction work, can be undertaken

without the direct involvement of the national government departments at that level. For example, the engineering procurement
department at the thana level is an inseparable part of any construction activity initiated by local government bodies. Members
of local bodies and some citizens are given a supervisory role
through membership in a project implementation committee, but
in name only.

## The Study Area

The focus of this paper is on the Dighi Union Parishad of Sadar
Thana which falls within the district of Manikganj in Dhaka division.
Since the days of British rule, Manikganj has been serving as the
political, administrative as well as economic centre for the north-
western part of the Dhaka division. The construction of the Asia
Highway in the 1960s improved communications with the northern
part of the country, thereby raising the status of this region in the
national plans. Thus occupying a vantage location, both administratively and physically, between the capital and the outlying
northern district, Manikganj also became the focus of both governmental and non-governmental developmental programmes.

Sadar Thana has a land area of nearly 216 sq. kms and a
population of 2.1 lakhs, one half of which comprises women. It
consists of 326 villages grouped into 10 unions and one pourashava
(municipality). The rate of literacy in this thana is nearly 30 per
cent. The area is also reputed to have a large number of primary,
secondary and high schools and there are several government
colleges in the Sadar Thana region. The main basis of the region's
economy is agriculture with an increasing bias towards cash crop
cultivation. In addition to both seasonal and irrigated paddy, jute,
tobacco and vegetables are grown in this region.

## The Union Parishad: Its Composition, Functions
## and Representation

The Dighi Union Parishad located in village Muljan is one of 10
union parishads in Sadar Thana. There are 26 villages and 23

*mouza* (revenue units) under this union. The UP office employs one secretary, one dafadar and six chowkidars. All are salaried, partly by funds generated by the UP itself and partly by government grants. The chairman and members also draw a monthly salary. The parishad is composed of nine elected members from three wards and one elected chairman. There is also provision for two nominated women members, but there are none at present. Although the names of two women were sent by the deputy commissioner to the thana administration for approval, neither has been nominated so far. It should be mentioned here that while the present parishad was elected in 1992, there were no women members in the previous council either.

As has been confirmed by other studies, in most cases union parishads are dominated by the rural wealthy and powerful in the region. The socio–economic profiles of the members and chairman of this UP reveal that all of them belong to the middle and rich category. The chairman has an annual income of over Tk. 3.0 lakh, four members have incomes of between Tk. 25,000 and Tk. 60,000, while five have incomes of between Tk. 10,000 and Tk. 30,000 per annum. The few who do not belong to the high income group are young political activists of the ruling party. The present chairman, who belongs to the Jatiya Party (the party in power before the present government) had served in the same capacity for two preceding terms, as had three of the members. Six members are reported to be *matbor* (leaders) of lineage-based village groups known as *Samaj*. Three are acknowledged to be activists of the ruling political party (the BNP) and three, including the chairman, belong to the Jatiya Party. Thus, the chairman and most of the members belong to the rural wealthy and elite class. The less wealthy ones have the advantage of belonging to the ruling political party. Therefore, as far as representation of the people is concerned, the Dighi Union Parishad definitely does not represent the vast majority of the rural population, the poor and marginal groups and women. Several studies have found that villagers chose their candidates for the UP on the basis of their relationship with them—which is an economic one. Most villagers are economically dependent on the landed few in the rural areas of the country. The landed and the wealthy are the *matbor* of the *Samaj* organisations. Again, it is the *matbor* and villagers with resources who can contest parishad elections since large amounts of money have to be spent on electioneering.⁴ Villagers from the landless and marginal categories vote for candidates who have the backing of their *matbor* or patron. Their dependency on the *matbor*/patron negates all possibilities of a choice. The middle-income villagers usually vote for candidates who wield muscle power for fear of reprisal. The forms and processes evolved so far for making local governments representative in character through popular participation apparently did not take the realities of this socio–economic structure into account.

The Dighi Union Parishad appears to be very irregular in its meetings which are also poorly attended. While villagers can participate in the parishad's general body meetings, their level of attendance is generally very low, and certainly no women are present. While a regular weekly meeting is scheduled for every Thursday, no meeting was held by the Dighi Union Parishad during the four weeks of our fieldwork. Some members claimed that 'meetings' are often conducted in the chairman's home, which is in a village a couple of kilometres away from the Parishad office. Record keeping is also very poor and haphazard. The minutes and resolutions of the meetings are not recorded during the proceedings but are written up later by the secretary. No details of meetings held in the Dighi Union Parishad were available. One parishad employee confided that a meeting of the full house is exceptional and that members rarely attend unless they are interested in some specific issue to be raised at the meeting. The signatures of non-attending members are generally collected afterwards, mainly for the sake of records.

As mentioned earlier, there are two sets of activities which are undertaken by union parishads. The first is the routine administrative functions transferred or allotted to them and the other is planning and implementation of development works at the village level. The first set is undertaken by the UP on its own initiative and by using resources generated locally. For the second set of the nation-building activities, the UP has to look to the next administrative tier and the national government departments at that level. The parishad also has to depend on higher levels for funds which come as grants from the national government.

The functions that the Dighi Union Parishad listed range from assessment and collection of taxes, maintenance of law and order, recording births and deaths, constructing roads and bridges to motivating people to adopt birth control measures and settling minor disputes between villagers. It may be of interest here to discuss some of these functions and to evaluate peoples' representation and the fulfillment of their needs and aspirations.

The collection of taxes on houses and homesteads and licence fees is an important function and source of income for the UP. However, available records of tax collection and income from licence fees do not indicate that the Dighi Union Parishad has been able to mobilise resources satisfactorily. The assessment of total taxes on houses, homesteads, brickfields,etc. in the three fiscal years of 1987–88, 1988–89 and 1989–90 was Tk. 1,58,600 and the amount collected was only Tk. 90,100—the outstanding dues being Tk. 68,450. Similarly, the tax assessed for 1991–92 was Tk. 72,597 and the amount collected only Tk. 44,982. It should be mentioned here that although theoretically, the UP has some authority to enforce payment, in most cases it does not do so. The reason, as given by the chairman and members of the Dighi Union Parishad is that they cannot put too much pressure on the people because they are mostly middle and marginal farmers who often find it difficult to pay the taxes in one instalment. Some villagers, however, view the matter differently. According to them, the union parishad is discriminatory in its assessment of taxes. The taxes levied differ in amount on holdings of the same size depending on how close the landholders are to the concerned parishad official. Then again, employees assigned for levying and collecting taxes also increase or decrease amounts depending on the bribe they receive. Indignant at such blatant discrimination, many villagers retaliate by delaying or holding back payments. According to one employee, it is generally the big landowners who are irregular in tax payments.

The arbitration of small disputes is undertaken by the secretary of the UP on payment of a fee. This fee ranges from Tk. 2 to Tk. 10, depending on the financial ability of the complainant and the complexity of the case. Like the weekly meetings arbitration courts are also supposed to be held on Thursdays. We found only three cases recorded for 1989 and one for 1990, all connected with non-payment of money owed. In two out of these, the parties settled the dispute out of court, before the UP could hold a sitting. In one case, the parishad ordered the accused to pay Tk. 200 as compensation for forcibly cutting down the complainants bamboo grove.

But one parishad member, a powerful person in the same village where the main accused lives, pressured the latter to deposit the money with the parishad secretary. In the end, the complainant received only part of the compensation money; the rest was shared by the concerned member and the secretary. In another case, a moneylender complained that a debtor had failed to repay his loan. After a long-drawn-out hearing, the arbitration council ordered the debtor to pay back the loan which amounted to Tk. 3000. The latter could pay only Tk. 2000, which he deposited with the secretary. So far, the secretary has returned only Tk. 1000 to the creditor, putting off payment of the balance on some pretext or the other. The creditor is helpless since, after the commencement of the case she not only lost her husband, she has no strong male kin to take up the issue on her behalf.

These instances reveal that the Dighi Union Parishad has been unable to function as an arbitration council with any degree of sincerity. With the controlling powers of the parishad vested in a few influential persons, the weaker sections do not stand a chance of having their basic problems redressed.

## The Union Parishad: Its Planning Process and People's Participation

Popular participation is one of the main elements of the decentralised system of administration. The extent of people's participation in local government can be assessed by examining their role in the processes of planning, implementation and the evaluation of programmes. The manual and guidelines for local level planning provide that plans at the thana level have to be based on plans formulated at and sent up by the union parishad. In turn, the union plans have to be prepared on the basis of the needs of the different villages under its jurisdiction. Let us now look at how developmental plans and projects are initiated and processed at the Dighi Union Parishad.

From the limited records available at the parishad office and from discussions with the chairman and some members, we found that the UP undertakes some specified planning activities. It formulates annual budgets by listing several items along with an estimate of its yearly income and expenditures. The items of income in the budget are mostly taxes and fees for licences, while the items listed under expenditure basically cover the parishad's establishment costs, money required for its regular programmes and for the salaries of its members and employees. The items of income listed in the budget of the Dighi Union Parishad include local taxes as well as income from grants made by the national government as, for example, the one made to enable the payment of salaries to the parishad chairman, members, and other employees like the village police force.

The UP also formulates five-year plans and sends them up to the higher units. The Dighi Union Parishad recently submitted its five-year plan for 1990–95. The items listed in it are mostly for nation building and developmental activities (see Appendix). The process of formulating the five-year plan, as described by the parishad members, indicates that the general public has no role in it at all. The contribution made to it by parishad members also appears to be negligible. The plans are generally based on the guidelines received from the thana offices (before 1992, from the upazilla parishad). The secretary draws up the items and estimates costs on the basis of these guidelines and the expenditures of earlier years. The chairman's approval is the most important consideration. During the upazilla system the chairman, who belonged to the same political party as the chairman of the upazilla parishad, used to consult his counterpart at the upazilla about the areas in which projects were likely to be approved. He would accordingly instruct the secretary to draw up the items. This increased the possibility of approval at the upazilla level. The selection of items, the specific projects and the locality were not determined on the basis of the individual needs of villages. The villagers were not consulted, and in most cases the projects approved were found to be for villages or wards where some prominent member lived. It is very common for most projects to be undertaken in villages where the chairmen live. Apart from these plans from time to time the union parishad also receives instructions from the thana to submit project proposals under specific sections from among the 13 specified areas of activities that the thana is authorised to undertake. For example, in the fiscal year 1992–93, the Sadar Thana was given Tk. 11,00,000 for spending in the three specified sectors of road construction and small bridge building; in the agricultural sector for irrigation and construction of small dams, fish culture and poultry raising; and for the repair of educational institution buildings in the unions under it. The thana asked union parishads to submit project proposals under these three sections. When the instructions with guidelines inviting project proposals were received by the UPs, the chairman asked the secretary to draw up a proposal based on its five-year plan. The upazilla parishad sent the proposals received to a project selection committee comprising the upazilla parishad chairman (elected), the upazilla nirbahi officer (chief executive in the upazilla), some government officials at the upazilla and the UP chairman (elected).

The majority in this committee were elected members, including the upazilla chairman who, by virtue of his statutory authority over the official members, dominated the decision of the committee. However, as is illustrated by the experience of the Dighi Union Parishad between 1989 and 1991, in most cases project proposals from union parishads whose chairmen belonged to the same political party as the upazilla chairman, were more easily approved. (Between 1989 and 1991, both the chairman of the Dighi Union Parishad and the upazilla parishad belonged to the same political party.)

After the abolition of the upazilla parishad, the thana administration was given the responsibility to select and approve UP projects. The thana administration is instructed to form two separate committees, one for the acceptance and implementation of projects, and the other for the selection of projects and floating tenders. The project acceptance and implementation committee comprises the thana nirbahi officer (TNO) as the chairman, the thana finance officer, the related UP chairman and the thana engineer as the member secretary. The committee for floating tenders and selecting them is composed of the TNO as the convenor, the finance officer, the chiefs of the concerned government departments and the thana engineer. No elected representatives are included in the committees at the final phase of project selection. Thus, union parishad projects are now selected and funded on the basis of decisions taken by national government functionaries at the thana level. Under the upazilla system there were elected persons in this committee, even though they were found not to represent the interests of the villages. The removal of elected members from the planning committees makes the planning process even less representative.

Once a project has been approved and the resources granted to the union parishad, a seven-member project implementation committee is formed which usually comprises the UP chairman or a member as the committee chairman, some members representing the wards in which the projects are to be implemented, a school-teacher, a local villager known to be involved in social work and a woman. The lists of three such committees found in the Dighi Union Parishad records for 1989–90 includes the names of two women in two of the committees. The male members of all three committees are more or less the same persons. One woman member claimed that she was not even informed about her inclusion in the project implementation committee. The schoolteacher and the social worker confessed that they had very little to do with the committees. These committees are drawn up for the records and exist in name only. The actual handling of projects is done by the chairman and some of his 'trusted' member-cronies.

This process of project planning at the union parishad level and its processing at the thana level clearly reveals the absence of popular participation. Under the upazilla model there was some representation in project planning and the delivery system, even though it did not often reflect the people's interests. In the present system there is no local government body at the thana level and the elected representatives do not have a role in the process of programme selection. Then again, the provision of disbursing only low cost projects (within Tk. 5,000) to UPs and retaining the costly ones for implementation through the thana undermines the possibility of formulating projects that reflect the actual needs of the people. Because of this, the concern of the UP chairman and members in formulating project proposals is not so much the requirements and needs of the various villages in the union as the eagerness to ensure that a number of projects are accepted and approved by the higher authority. The result is that the parishads put forth mostly the same types of programmes every year. This can easily be discerned from the list of the projects that have been proposed and implemented in the last few years. In 1989, three projects were undertaken by the Dighi Union Parishad, two for road construction and one for filling up old wells that were no longer being used. In 1990, two projects were proposed of which one for road construction by earth filling was implemented. Similarly, an examination of the list of projects proposed by the Dighi Union Parishad in its five-year plan for 1990–95 (see Appendix) shows that most of them are small and low cost. In the 1990–91 plan, out of six projects listed only one is for the construction of a concrete bridge; the others are for road construction or renovation and the construction of a culvert bridge. In 1991–92, all seven projects listed are for road renovation and culvert construction. In 1992–93, all six are for culvert construction; in 1993–94 there are three for culvert construction, one for building a culvert bridge and two for road construction. In the 1994–95 plan, three out of six projects are for culvert construction and the rest for road renovation. Out of a total of 25 projects, only three are of high cost.

When questioned about this, the Dighi Union Parishad members and chairman said that they submit low cost plans because only these stand better chances of being approved. If projects cost more than Tk. 5,000, they have to be processed through a tender call by the thana administration and require the involvement of the thana engineering office. Such projects are thus not likely to be entrusted to union parishads. For this reason, local needs and project appropriateness do not figure in the considerations of union parishads while formulating proposals. Their main concern is to get whatever resources they can from the government. A majority of the villagers we spoke to, felt that the project implementation is unsatisfactory. They also accepted as given the fact that the chairman and members of the UP receive a share of the resources flowing to the union. In 1986, when the government introduced the upazilla system, the grant for the Dighi Union Parishad was increased to Tk. 100,000. However, this provision was withdrawn later. The thana officials informed us that in the three-year period between 1986 and 1989, an amount of Tk. 22,00,000 was disbursed to the union parishad in the Manikganj Sadar Upazilla and to date, this money has not been accounted for.

## The Local Government and the People

With regard to the villagers' views about local government bodies and their role in them, almost all said that they are not consulted on any matter by the UP. The low income group villagers, and women in particular, said that they did not participate in any of the meetings. But they had to keep parishad members happy by obeying their orders so that they could get enlisted for the earth cutting programmes or for the destitute group projects of the union parishad. All forms of local government, whether at the UP or upazilla level were the same as far as they were concerned. None made any difference to their lives. As always, when they need help, they still go to the *matbor* or 'respected' persons in the neighbourhood. The women and the poor clearly said that the NGOs looked after their needs more than the union parishad did. Most of the landless and the marginal farmers are in BRAC on Grameen Bank programmes.

The middle and the rich income groups were more specific about the nature and functions of the UP, the upazilla parishad and the thana administration. In their opinion, there is little scope for their participation as the UP is dominated by the chairman. They are never consulted in planning for any project. They do not know what projects are planned and undertaken, the amount of funds received or the extent to which these projects are implemented. They stated that the chairman and members spend large amounts of money during elections which they recover from the funds disbursed to the union parishad once they are in office. According to them, the upazilla system made the UP chairman even more powerful and less responsive to the views of the villagers. Also, under the upazilla system, less was achieved at the village level as a share of the incoming funds were 'used up' at the upazilla level as well.

According to the middle income group respondents, only the rich and the powerful could get elected and once in the union parishad they protected the interests of the wealthy elites. This handful of wealthy persons can command a large number of votes since they provide employment to the landless. These 'political' elements also keep a group of musclemen in their employ for 'enforcing' their 'rule' at the union parishad.

The rich and the middle income groups categorically said that the UP chairman and members do not hold themselves accountable for their actions. In comparison, NGOs, particularly BRAC and Grameen Bank, address the needs of the people to some extent. And although they do make 'profits' by charging a high interest rate, at least they provide the much-needed loans to the rural poor. According to all groups of villagers, very little in the form of development has been achieved through the Dighi Union Parishad in the last few years.

The views of the UP chairman and its members regarding the nature and role of the parishad are very different from those of the villagers. According to them, it is a people's organisation as its members are elected by the people and work to serve them. But since the UP has to depend for its activities on funds from the thana administration, its scope is limited. With regard to the mobilisation of resources locally, the chairman felt that taxes cannot always be collected as per the amended rules. According to him, the abolition of the upazilla parishad has drastically reduced the possibilities for popular representation in the activities of the local administration. Without a tier of local government at the thana level, UP projects are completely at the mercy of government officials. The requirement of having projects approved by the local members of parliament has also undermined the role of the elected UP representatives. The chairman feared that projects might be delayed and even rejected, as MPs tend to favour proposals from parishads dominated by members of their own party. This problem has already surfaced in the Sadar Thana project selection process where the 10 UP chairmen belong to three different political parties (two to BNP, three to the Jatiya Party and five to the Awami League) and the MP concerned belongs to the Jatiya Party.

Both the chairman and the members of the Dighi Union Parishad very forcefully claimed that a lot of development has been achieved in the area through the UP. With regard to inclusion of women in UP membership, the elected members felt that there is no need for them as they do not actively participate in its proceedings and activities. All of them agreed that the upazilla system was more people-oriented and should be revived in the interests of the people.

The thana nirbahi officer and the other government functionaries at the thana, however, were strongly against the upazilla parishad system. They insisted that the dominant role of the elected chairman at the upazilla virtually rendered it an organisation of the elected representatives of the upazilla and the UP. The system provided opportunities for the misuse and misappropriation of funds by the elected representatives and had no mechanism for making them accountable. They held that the elected members of the UP and upazilla parishads were not the true representatives of the people and did not serve the people's interests. Giving them the power to approve and distribute funds led to the use of local bodies by dominant political parties to further their own interests. In their opinion, government departments at the thana level should be given a bigger role in the developmental work in rural areas and if necessary, its offices could be extended down to the unions. This would not be difficult as the UPs already have a land revenue office and a family welfare and training centre which provides medical and birth control advice and services.

We thus have three different sets of opinions emanating from three groups of respondents—the villagers, the elected UP members and the government officials—on the nature and functions of local government bodies. The opinions recorded here reflect the distinct positions taken by them vis-a-vis the local government organisations.

## Conclusions

The analysis of the structure and functions of local government systems in Bangladesh as reflected in the operation of a present local government unit clearly indicates that so far, they have failed as people's organisations. They neither represent nor serve the interests of the general public. Popular participation in these bodies remains restricted to voting only. In the given socio–economic structure of the rural countryside, the wealthy elites dominate and this domination is reflected in the structure of the local government bodies. The elected elites tend to cater to their own or their class interests, rather than those of the masses.

Even in the functions specifically assigned to local bodies, such as taxation, settling disputes etc., they fail to meet the needs and aspirations of the people. In addition, there is little or no direct participation by the people in the operation of these units. The elected members, chairman and government functionaries play dominant roles in the planning, resource mobilisation, project selection, funding and implementation processes. These processes clearly indicate that the interests of the elected members override all other considerations that relate to the needs of the particular region. The reliance of local bodies on the national government for resources again makes them heavily dependent on government officials at the regional level, thus undermining the possibility of self-governance. What makes matters worse is that the structure and processes involved in the local bodies formulated so far do not even have mechanisms that would make the elected representatives accountable and responsive to the needs and views of the people.

All forms of local government initiated in Bangladesh have been defined as self-governing, decentralised units. Yet their functions and processes in effect prove them to be 'local branches' of the national government, with nominally elected representatives who tend to reap benefits for themselves and their own class. This contradiction in the stated objective and the actual state of affairs, and the very nature of local government bodies allows elected representatives to operate without being accountable. This, in turn, creates opportunities for the use of elected units by successive governments at the national level to maintain their power base at the grassroots level. It is therefore obvious that in Bangladesh, the popularly elected local governments have not yet emerged as decentralised, participatory, self-governing units meant to serve the interests of the populace.

## Notes

1. Rahman, H. Zillur. 1992. *Local Government Versus Local Self Government: Issues in Democratic Institution Building and Development Administration.* Dhaka: EIDS.
2. Hye, Hasnat Abdul. 1985. 'Introduction' in Hye, Hasnat Abdul (ed.) *Decentralisation: Local Government Institutions and Resource Mobilisation*, Comilla: BARD.
3. Khan, Md. M. and Habid Md. Zafarullah. 1988. *Decentralised Planning Process in Bangladesh*. Bangkok: Asian Institute of Technology.
4. Khan, Zarina R. 1992. *Women, Work and Values*. Dhaka: C.S.S.

# Appendix 4.1

## Fourth Five-Year Projects Plan of Dighi Union Parishad, Manikganj, 1990–95

*1990–91*
1. Concrete bridge construction at Romonpur.
2. Road repair from Dautia Haat to union parishad office in Muljan.
3. Road repair from Haat Kora to Channagar via the house of Raushan Master.
4. Construction of culvert bridge on Patrail road.
5. Road repair from Dautia to Susanda via Dautia Masjid.
6. Road repair from Dautia Masjid to Bhatboir.

*1991–92*
1. Road repair from Chamta to Dautia.
2. Road repair from Kagjinagar to Patrai.
3. Road repair from Kagjinagar to Notun Bari.
4. Road repair from Dulapara to Begjan.
5. Culvert building in Dautia road.
6. Road repair from Bagjan to Dautia via Kutai.
7. Road repair from Dautia to Chamta via Romonpur.

*1992–93*
1. One culvert construction on Romonpur Road.
2. One culvert construction on Koira Road.
3. One culvert construction on Dighi Road.
4. One culvert construction on Gultia Road.
5. One culvert construction on Rohadans Road.
6. One culvert construction on Kotai Road.

*1993–94*
1. One culvert construction on Chamta Road.
2. One culvert construction on Patrai Road.
3. Road repair from Channagar to Chandara.
4. Construction of culvert bridge on Chamta Canal.
5. Road repair from Bagjan to Rohadans via masjid.

6. One culvert construction on Sagrakhuri road.

*1994–95*
1. One culvert construction on Gulotia Road.
2. Road repair of Dautia Road.
3. Road repair of Bhatboir via Master's house.
4. One culvert construction on Kharagrakhuri Road.
5. Implementing a RCC pipe on Rohadans Road.
6. One culvert construction on Kharagrakhuri Road.

# 5

# Chinese Village Autonomy: Present Status and Future Prospects

WANG ZHENYAO

Economic, political and social relations in the Chinese countryside are presently undergoing a profound transformation. Unquestionably, this transformation in the foundation of rural society has produced far-reaching changes in basic, or grassroots, level organisational systems. In this new evolving social climate, how to develop direct democracy at the grassroots while at the same time guaranteeing stable development in the rural areas has become increasingly an imperative issue for the central government.

After the abolition of the people's communes system in 1983, China established a system of township governments under the level of the county government. Below township level, village committees were formed. By 1991, 55,109 township governments were responsible for 1,018,593 village committees. Over the past 10 years, the nurturing of autonomy at the village level with the village committee as the core has been an exceptionally intricate operation, one which is still in the process of development. Attempting to implement autonomy in a domain of 900 million peasants with a long-standing tradition of enduring autocratic rule is indeed a task of huge international significance. Assessing accurately the course of building village autonomy and advancing scientific principles on which to base plans for future development requires a systematic analysis of the historical account of the village committees and contradictions they face.

## Evolution of the Village Organisation

In ancient China, the clans, neighbourhoods and squires established their own forms of self-government. This form of autonomy, which highly resembles the village commune system, continued for several thousands of years. In contemporary times, the drive for modernisation broke open the formerly closed, isolated countryside, cleavages among the peasantry widened, and warring in rural areas resulted in a comprehensive mobilisation of the rural masses. The Chinese Communist Party's (CCP) assumption of power in 1949 began a process of national administration permeating down to the village level, thus setting the stage for the implementation of rural autonomy. A brief account of such transformation is therefore in order.

### *Self-government by Clans, Neighbourhoods and Squires*

For a long period of time in ancient China, officials and powerful citizens alike jointly held posts in grassroots organisations below the county level. In the Qin Dynasty (221–206 BC), the social administrative system had a structural hierarchy in which five families made up a Wu, 10 families made up a Shi, 100 families made up a Li (neighbourhood), 10 Lis made up a Ting, and 10 Tings made up a Xiang (township). At the outset of the Western Han Dynasty (206 BC–24 AD), the country had 6,622 townships and 29,635 Tings. But, by the time of the Eastern Han Dynasty (24–220 AD) the numbers were reduced to 3,681 townships and 12,443 Tings. During this period, the township acted as the local administrative branch under the Xian (county).

In the year 486 AD, during the Northern Wei Dynasty (386–534 AD), the system was altered. In the three leader system (San Zhang Zhi), as the new administrative hierarchy was called, five families made up a Lin (neighbourhood—smaller than a Li), five Lins made up a Li, and five Lis made up a Dang, with a designated leader at each level. The leaders were basically responsible for checking housing registrations, collecting taxes, and calling up peasants for corvee labour and military service.

During the Sui Dynasty (581–618 AD), under the county was the township and under the township was the Li. A township consisted of five Lis, each of which was made up of 100 families. Each Li had two leaders, who were either government officials below the sixth grade or members of rich families.

During the Song Dynasty (960–1279), Emperor Song Shenzong established the Baojia system. It was organised in a hierarchy such that 10 families made up a Bao, 50 families made up a Da Bao, and 10 Da Bao made up a Du Bao.

In the Yuan Dynasty, under the county level 50 families made up a She and 20 families made up a Jai. The leader of She busied himself with the tasks of advising on agricultural and civil matters while also collecting taxes and assigning peasants to corvee labour.

In the Ming and Qing dynasties, a Li comprised 110 families and had 10 leaders. Each leader served a 10-year term, acting as the principal leader for one of the 10 years. The remaining 100 families not represented in the Li leadership were divided up into 10 Jias and were responsible for local civil affairs, education and tax collecting.

From the end of the Qing Dynasty up through the Republican period (c. 1912–1949), local autonomy became the order of the day. Townships established autonomous organs, and the township commissioner answered to the county magistrate in carrying out the affairs of his locality.

Over time, the township gradually became acknowledged as a genuine unit of administrative control. Strata below the township level, on the other hand, never graduated into the official administrative framework. Throughout the period of evolution from the Ting-Li system of the Qing Dynasty to the Baojia system dynasties later, grassroots control below the township was accomplished through autonomous organisations. Village level autonomy lacked democratic mechanisms and tended to rely on clan autonomy and community cohesiveness. Since leaders of Baos and Jias were selected in an undemocratic fashion, powerholders, uncurtailed by the need to appease an enfranchised constituency, became autonomous chieftains. Peasant apathy toward political participation further enabled squires to dominate positions of leadership.

Social, economic and political arrangements in the villages of the old society only allowed for peasants to manage rural production for their own subsistence. Hence, work done by the village for the greater public good was virtually nonexistent. Peasant contributions came in the limited form of paying taxes in kind and providing manpower for national defence, neither of which could facilitate the development of public works. The resolving of most contradictions in the village largely depended on stipulations of clan agreements or the harmonious relationships between friends and family. Here, the most important determining factor lay in the structure of ancient rural society. In the firmly rooted patriarchal clan system, blood relationships determined the code of ethics and the content of law. Public law was indelibly marked with the brand of 'private' law.

## The Village Organisations as Administrative Bodies (1947–1957)

After the founding of the People's Republic of China in 1949, the new government replaced Baojia organisations with peasant associations and set up district and township (administrative village) governments. At that time, townships were quite small, comprising between 1,000 and 3,000 residents. In areas such as north-east China and the Hebei province, village governments were established under the district level.

By 1952, the Chinese government had mapped out 18,330 districts and 284,626 townships (administrative villages) below the county level, not including Tibet. Then, after officially limiting the scope of local government administration down to the district and township levels in 1954, these numbers contracted somewhat. By 1956, China had 15,459 districts, 194,858 township governments and 4,487 small towns. This continuing trend of consolidation, brought on by collectivisation, accelerated the expansion of townships. By 1957, the number of districts, townships and small towns was reduced to 10,289, 117,081 and 3,672 respectively, and by the end of the year the number of townships was further reduced to around 98,000. On the eve of the movement to create people's communes in 1958, the number of townships dropped further to just above 80,000.

After 1955, township cadres implemented a fixed wage salary system, whereas village cadres implemented a type of subsidies/ration system. This marked a departure from past policy in which the government ration system prescribed a more or less universal treatment for both levels. This change in policy caused the start of a growing rift between the township and village levels.

Between 1954 and 1957, the government's new administrative village system encroached upon the constituencies of the people's congresses, thus denying them any substantial freedom to act on their own. As an auxiliary organisation under the direct control of the township government, the administrative village was responsible for calling together the township's people's congress and the working community for work conferences, where discussions on how to implement township government resolutions would take place. It also supervised the implementation of township policy and assisted in administrative matters.

The administrative village had a representative director selected by its own village representative committee. Under the administrative village, resident groups were formed by the individual villages, each with a leader selected from within. This type of system can be seen as a preliminary attempt at direct democracy at the grassroots level. However, the subsequent storm of the agricultural collectivisation movement resulted in the gradual incorporation of the administrative village into cooperatives. From this period onwards, village level organisations began to become an important economic and social unit.

### Village Organisations Under the People's Communes (1958–1982)

From their inception in 1958, the people's communes replaced township governments, taking on administrative as well as social, political and economic functions. At first, the government converted 94 counties around the country into people's communes. Village level organisations were thrown into confusion. China's 750,000 agricultural cooperatives were later combined into 23,630 people's communes by the end of 1958. The merger into communes involved a population of over 128,610,000 households (an average of 5,442.6 households per commune). Later, the government engaged in a large-scale restructuring of the commune system.

In September 1962, *The Revised Draft on the People's Communes Work Regulations* stipulated that the basic accounting unit of the people's communes was to be the production team; the organisation of the people's commune could be divided into two levels, i.e. the commune and the production team, or three levels, i.e. the commune, the production brigade and the production team. In 1962, China had 74,771 people's communes, 703,000 production brigades and 5,580,000 production teams. The executive committee of each production brigade was in charge of managing the production and administration of the production teams within its sphere of jurisdiction. This entailed:

1. assisting in the production planning of each production team;
2. guiding, inspecting and supervising the production, financial administration, and distribution of the production teams to help improve their overall operations;
3. initiating and leading the construction of water conservation projects and other basic agricultural construction projects and organising the necessary cooperation between various production groups within the production brigade;
4. managing and maintaining all of the production brigade's large- and medium-sized farming equipment and transportation vehicles;
5. administering and supervising all of the production brigade's mountain villages, forest areas, enterprises and joint enterprises;
6. supervising mandatory state grain purchases (based on quota) and purchases of other produce and sideline products, and helping production teams regulate the life of their members;
7. managing civil affairs, the militia, public security, education, public health and sanitation within the production brigade;
8. carrying out ideological and political work and implementing and enforcing the central government's policies and laws.

As the basic accounting unit of the people's communes, each production team adopted a system of independent accounting, making it solely responsible for its own profits and losses. It possessed the right to directly organise its own production and allocate its net proceeds howsoever it pleased. All land within the production team was owned and operated by the team as a legal administrative entity.

The draft law promulgated in 1962 required the production brigade to form a representative body made up of commune members, with elections held on an annual basis. The function of the commune representative council was to decide on important issues facing the commune and to elect certain officials such as the leader of the production brigade, management committee members, supervision committee members, and directors, accountants and committee members of each production team for terms of one year.

In 1978, a law was passed empowering the commune revolutionary committee, the production brigade and the production team-management committee to act as the people's commune's management organisation. All directors, deputy directors and members of these committees were to be selected for terms of two years by general election in the commune representative council or the commune council. Incumbents could be re-elected.

It is important to point out, however, that the people's commune system never really got fully off the ground. Unending political movements made it difficult to convene commune representative council conferences. Many cadres fell from grace in the confusion of political rectification campaigns and not through the democratic mechanism of representative election.

The people's communes system had a severe streak of militant communism, which encouraged the determination of the basic accounting unit to rise to the level of the production brigade. In 1980, China had 42,429 production brigades calculated by their respective communes as the basic accounting unit. Among these, Shandong had the most at 9,098 and Shanxi ranked second with 7,582.

The people's communes left an abundant historical legacy to the village level organisations:

1. From the beginning, village level organisations had a strong economic cohesiveness; land, mountains, forests, natural resources and production materials became the collective property of the peasants. This kind of cohesion was unprecedented in Chinese history.

2. From the beginning, village level organisations possessed a significant amount of non-agricultural capital; villages starting up enterprises thus acquired a substantial economic power base. By the end of 1980, village enterprises had accumulated gross fixed assets worth up to 12.6 billion Yuan (RMB), which translated into net fixed assets worth up to 1.053

billion Yuan (RMB). This established a foundation for rural industrialisation.

3. As a result of mobilising the masses to live and work together in an environment of sharing and striving toward common goals, familial ties and feelings of strict devotion to the clan began to disintegrate. Peasants started to more actively participate in the economic and political activities of the village.

In analysing the history of village level organisations, it is evident that although a tradition of autonomy exists, these organisations lacked a real democratic social structure. Perhaps communism's greatest influence on China's countryside was the installation of a democratic mechanism at the grassroots level which served to galvanise the masses. In China, however, this did not prove enough to create a modern system of democratic self-government at the grassroots level. While cultivating a democratic social structure, the conversion from a democratic system of self-government based on the mobilisation of the masses to a more modern form of autonomy necessitates a fundamental transformation of the rural economic system.

## Village Committee System

The turning point in the development of grassroots democracy came with the advent of the household responsibility system in 1979. Individual rural households began to contract out plots of land, which they were permitted to cultivate and manage to a large degree as they saw fit. This new arrangement dealt a fundamental blow to the commune system. Therefore, while phasing out the people's communes the government set up village committees to replace production brigades and production teams. This policy opened the door for autonomy at the grassroots level.

### Policies and Laws Regarding Village Autonomy

The drive for village autonomy was an outcome of the national democratisation process begun in the aftermath of the cultural revolution. In June 1981, a CCP Central Committee document entitled *On the Party's Resolution of Certain Historical Problems Since the Founding of the People's Republic of China* emphasised the gradual expansion of direct democracy at the grassroots level as an integral step in the construction of a highly democratic socialist system. The new constitution in 1982 reinstituted the system of township, minority nationality township and small town governments. It also created the village committee as the primary grassroots mass-based organisation of self-government, with its director, deputy director, and committee members to be elected by *popular* vote within the village. In this manner, the name, nature and principle of direct elections of village level organisations were, for the first time in history, defined by the national constitution.

The central government decreed the dismantling of the entire people's commune system in 1983. Most districts set up township governments to replace the people's communes, village committees to replace production brigades, and village groups to replace production teams. In provinces such as Guandong and Yunnan, township governments replaced the production brigades and village committees replaced production teams (or what in these regions had been sometimes referred to as natural villages). The dismantling process reached its full conclusion by 1985. By that year, China had formed 91,138 township governments and the nation's 940,617 village committees could claim a total membership of 3,795,958 people.

Before the separation of economic and administrative organs in 1983, production teams were given production targets which figured in the national statistics. But after the conversion of the majority of production teams into village groups, they ceased to be calculated in statistical indices. This phenomenon indicated a weakening in the economic function of the village groups vis-a-vis the production teams. Also, the main economic functions of the production teams evaporated with the arrival of the household responsibility system. Initiating public projects on the village level became the duty of the village committee.

After the village committees were set up all over the country, areas such as Beijing, Tianjin, Hebbei, Tibet, Ningxia, and Xinjiang began to design village committees to meet the unique demands of their local situations. The promulgation of these legislation packets laid the foundation for a national village committee organisation law.

Heated debate between the years 1986 and 1987 culminated in the official promulgation by the Standing Committee of the National People's Congress of The Village Committee Organisation Law of the People's Republic of China (for trial implementation) on 24 November 1987. It was also decided that the law would take effect throughout the country, on a trial basis, on 1 June 1988. The law expressly stipulated that the village committee was a grassroots autonomous organisation that would be run by the people and be responsible for local administration, public projects, mediation of disputes and public security, and would serve as the vital communication link between the people and the government. Each village committee was to be established based upon local residential conditions, population size, and other factors which best served the principles of village self-government. In the case of smaller or larger natural villages, committees could be established to administer more substantially depending on the requirements of the situation. The director, deputy director and all committee members were to be chosen for an unrestricted number of three-year terms through direct popular elections. In addition, the village committee was to host all village conferences and was obligated to call special sessions if a minimum of one-fifth of the village population so requested.

## Spontaneous Self-Government Activities (1984–1987)

During this period, the formula for grassroots autonomy still lacked concrete procedural guidelines. So despite its legal status as expressed in the constitution, it did not receive much attention. However, due to the transformation of relationships in the Chinese countryside following the advent of the household responsibility system, peasants had already set out on the road to develop self-government on their own accord.

During the establishment of village committees, villages in many areas adopted a variety of crude, unorthodox election processes. Some were merely elections of village representatives with the same number of candidates as positions available. In addition, debate and consensus activities in the villages had begun to appear. For instance, as early as 1984 Nanlou village in Zhengding county, Hebei province, established a village representatives council to deliberate on and resolve the relevant issues of the day. However, at this early stage of representative democracy, Nanlou village was a more or less isolated case. In most areas, a tense atmosphere dominated relations between cadres and peasants. As a result, the central government found it increasingly difficult to manage affairs at the grassroots level. Most peasants objected to the lack of democracy in the administration of village life.

### Implementation of the Village Committee Organisation Law (1988–1990)

The answer to why the problem of grassroots democracy did not immediately disappear with the promulgation of the Village Committee Organisation Law in 1987 lies in the imperfect nature of the Chinese legal system. In China, very often a long interim period stretches out between the passing of a law and its subsequent implementation. Moreover, if a new law encounters any local opposition, a whole new batch of difficulties will arise while putting it into effect.

At the outset, the Village Committee Organisation Law met with substantial popular resistance. Most people believe that this resistance stemmed from a lack of education among the peasantry. Peasants as a group claimed there was no need for democracy, nor would they be well enough equipped to exercise their democratic rights. They felt democracy violated the basic premises of China's national character and would hamper the progress of the countrywide modernisation effort. They advocated that the village committee should be transformed into an agency of the township government.

In contrast, supporters of democratic reform argued that grassroots democracy is the embodiment of mass participation. Its development would foster the wholehearted support of the peasantry, which would in turn lay a strong political and social foundation for modernisation.

During this period, 14 provinces, autonomous regions, and municipalities under the direct jurisdiction of the central government began to enforce the election process to create village committees. In other provinces, experimental areas in proximity to county seats took the lead in aggressively and successfully carrying out these reforms, i.e. Laixi county in Shandong province, Qinggang county in Heilongjiang province, and the Zhumadian region in Henan province.

The following trends have already appeared in putting village level autonomy into practice:

1. Village committee elections have become a key link in fully implementing the Village Committee Organisation Law. Holding elections for the village committee has become a barometer by which to measure the level at which villages are upholding the law. In the first seven months of 1989, all the 4,480 village committees under the Beijing municipality held elections for the second time. By the end of 1989, of the 5,040 villages in the Ningbo area of Zhejiang province due for second term elections, 2,282 (45.3 per cent) villages had already cast their ballots. And in the spring of 1990, 98.2 per cent of the villages in Fujian province successfully held village committee elections, reflecting an increasingly prominent nationwide trend at that time.

2. Campaigning during village committee elections also became common. In some places, village committee elections have witnessed an unprecedented emergence of democratic campaigning, i.e. candidates holding public speeches to express their views on issues, present their agenda if elected, and accept questions from the voters. The most impressive examples of this form of democracy can be found in the area under the jurisdiction of the city of Tieling in Liaoning province, Qingang county in Heilongjiang province, and the city of Nanping in Fujian province.

   Competitive elections give expression to peasants' democratic rights, kindle their enthusiasm for active participation in village administration and promote honesty among the cadres. According to statistics, in areas which launched the election process, around 80 per cent or so of the village cadres have been re-elected to office.

3. The villager councils emerged in the villages. In the course of implementing the law, many villages established a villager council which holds regular conferences to facilitate wider participation by peasants in village affairs. Hebei province's Zhengding county and Xinji municipality have provided sound examples of these organisations. In most cases, on average every 10 or more families choose one member to act as a representative in the council. The villager council convenes to deliberate on major issues of the village and has a party branch and the village committee. A case in point can be found in Hanjianzhuang village (in Hebei province's Zhengding county). The village party branch and the village committee jointly decided to appropriate public funds for the construction of an office building. This edict conflicted with the villager council's decision to allocate the money for building an elementary school in accordance with the decision of the villager council.

4. The formulation of certain regulations initiated the process of systemisation and regularisation of village self-government. The government of Laixi county in Bhandong province designated the following 10 regulations to the reality of its local situation.

(a) Regulations on the organisation of the village committee of Laixi county.

(b) Regulations on the administration of the village committee of Laixi county.

(c) Regulations on villager supervision of the village committee cadres of Laixi county.

(d) Regulations on the village council and the village representatives council in Laixi county.

(e) Regulations on the township government's role in guiding the village committee in Laixi county.

(f) Regulations on the village committee elections in Laixi county.

(g) Regulations on village financial management in Laixi county.

(h) Outline of guidance on the villagers' pledge in Laixi county.

    (*i*) Regulations on the rural cooperative service in Laixi county.

    (*j*) Outline of the villagers' education plan in Laixi county.

5. The launching of the model village campaign furthered village government autonomy. In order to amass genuine experience in the operation of village self-government, in 1989, 26 model areas were set up in the suburbs of the city of Shenyang in Fujian province. Later, the provincial government required that all counties set up at least 10 model villages based on specific criteria as a spring board to universalising village autonomy throughout the province. By July 1990, there were already a total of 712 model villages in operation in Fujian.

## Results of the Drive for Village Autonomy (1991–1992)

After 1990, the drive for village autonomy entered a new stage. During this period, misgivings about the wisdom of grassroots democracy were dispelled as cadres and peasants gained significant amounts of personal experience in the democratic process. A whole series of regulations on local self-government began to be passed into law. However, as different regions of the country advanced at unbalanced rates, gaps in the level of development among the administrative bureaus in the government began to appear. Peasants in many regions where grassroots autonomy was just getting under way still lacked adequate experience.

The most outstanding achievements in implementing grassroots autonomy since 1990 are as follows:

1. The focus and direction of central government policies became increasingly clear. The Civil Affairs Bureau clearly defined village autonomy as a threefold process: democratic elections, democratic decision-making and democratic administration. In the villages, the manifestation of this process came in the form of direct elections for the village committee, the establishment of a villager council which holds general conferences of village representatives, and a systematised structure for administration.

2. The vast majority of village committees held direct elections. At the beginning of 1992, villages in Fujian, Beijing, Liaoning and Jilin held elections for the second time. Between the end of 1992 and the spring of 1993, villages in another 10 provinces, autonomous regions and municipalities held second elections for terms which began after 1988. In addition, the standing committees of the people's congresses in both Fujian and Jiangsu formulated sets of village committee election procedures. Day by day the village committee election process became an increasingly standardised, formal system in village level politics.

3. The village committee's organisational structure became increasingly sound. As the village committee was endowed with more and more powers, it was able to organise peasants to initiate welfare projects, road construction projects, and improve public health and education. Village committees in different areas also began to start up enterprises, launch trade activities, and organise peasant households for responsibility farming. Within the village committee, sub-committees for the mediation of disputes, public security, public health and family planning were set up and standardised, as were village groups. During the process of rural economic and social development, the village committee experienced a significant rise in status as an administrative organ.

One interesting fact to note is that the movement to strengthen the foundations of village autonomy in China received only nominal financial support. With the exception of minute working funds allocated by county and township governments to carry out village committee elections, any increase in village funds or improvements in working conditions came about as a result of organisational reform and the development of grassroots democracy. At the rural grassroots, democracy and development went along hand in hand, and areas which successfully implemented village self-government reforms enjoyed considerable economic and social gains.

## The Election Process of the Village Committee

In China, the difference in size among areas administered by village committees can be quite substantial. A large constituency can consist of over 10,000 people, whereas smaller villages might only have several hundred. On average, village committees in the north serve around 2,000 people, while in the south the number drops to anywhere between 1,000 and 1,500. Most of the richer villages are situated in the east—the richest one to date reported a total production output of over 100 million Yuan (RMB). The majority of the poorer villages are usually found in the west, many of which rely on government aid.

The movement to promote village autonomy based on elections and democratic local policy formulation inevitably created disparities between different areas. For these same reasons, the village committee itself differs greatly from administrative bodies at other levels of government. The basic features of the village committee democratic elections are as follows:

1. The elections are direct. In China, cadres in positions at all levels of government above the township level are selected by general election in the people's congress of the same level. Citizens can vote for county and township level people's congress representatives, but people's congress representatives at each level of government above the county are elected by the corresponding people's congress one level below in the hierarchy.

   In contrast to this form of indirect democracy, elections to the village committee allow for the direct expression of the voice of the people. After directly nominating candidates for director, deputy director and regular members of the village committee, every villager over 18 years of age has the right to vote for the candidate of his/her choice. Peasant enfranchisement has thus weakened township and county governments' absolute control over village cadres' activities. According to statistics, an average of between 5 and 10 per cent of village committee incumbents will be voted out of office. Corrupt and incompetent officials often find that they lose the mandate of the people when running for second terms. In some areas, upwards of 30 per cent of village committee cadres failed to be re-elected.

2. Unlike government posts above the township level which can only be filled with professional administrators, village committee positions are open to all villagers. Prospective candidates are not encumbered by prohibitive age, gender, level

of wealth, occupation, education level or other sorts of restrictions. In addition, elected officials receive a salary drawn from the village coffers for their services. This arrangement allows the average peasant to aspire to a prestigious and influential position of leadership in the village, if he/she gains the support of the people.

3. Village committee elections are extremely competitive. Positions on the village committee carry with them decision-making power, so they naturally hold a strong attraction for more capable peasants. One example is Wang Chenghui, a private businessman working in the city of Linfen in Shanxi province. When Wang Chenghui heard news of the election proceedings he promptly returned to his hometown of Shenliu village to run for village committee director. His village management platform received much support from the local electorate, and after his subsequent election the policies he helped to implement transformed the entire village. Examples like this can be found throughout the country.

Generally speaking, competitive elections proceed in one of two fashions. In areas with more suitable political climates, competitive campaigning is carried out in the public arena. Peasants have attempted to imitate the American presidential election process. Candidates give public addresses to express their plans and goals if elected and accept questions from the voters. Afterwards, the peasants vote to elect the village committee director. The newly elected village committee director then nominates candidates for positions as regular members on the village committee, who are subsequently voted upon in a second round of elections.

The second type of competitive elections do not involve public campaigning. In most cases, competing clans or factions engage in activities to amass a voter base for candidates they support. In some areas, candidates even purchase votes with money or gifts, but they are prevented from running if discovered. As such, many legal disputes have arisen during the election process. Cases are known of peasants travelling to the local branch of the Civil Affairs Bureau or even the State Civil Affairs Bureau, to file suits against people who have violated election law.

Villagers take their local elections of village committee members more seriously than elections for the county and township people's congresses. Obviously, such an enthusiastic attitude stems from the fact that villagers can *directly* determine who the cadres of the village committee will be (without the added input of peasants from other townships or villages). This makes for a very vital and dynamic atmosphere in grassroots politics.

## Village Committee Policy-Making Process

In the people's communes, all decisions at the grassroots level were made jointly by the village party branch and the production brigade management committee. After the abolition of the people's commune system, the village committee took over the role of the production brigade management committee (continuing its predecessor's function as a policy formulation body in conjunction with the party branch). However, the implementation of village self-government saw the adjustment of traditional relations. The authority of the village committee expanded daily, eventually leading to the growth of the villager council system.

The villager council is comprised of village representatives, villagers who are representatives in people's congresses at various levels, village group chiefs, and village committee members. The number of members participating in a villager council conference can range anywhere from 20 to 80, with an average of usually around 50. Generally speaking, conferences are held twice a month, unless something important comes up during the interim period, in which case special sessions are convened. Matters generally discussed at these conferences include:

1. strategy for village collective economic and social development;
2. management of social welfare and public works;
3. major issues in the village;
4. establishment of village regulations and agreements;
5. deliberation on village financial matters;
6. proper execution of compulsory national assignments.

The formation of the villager council led to a large-scale transformation of the village committee policy-making system. In the new climate, neither the village party branch nor the village committee can enact policy without the approval of the villager council. If, for instance, the villager committee decides to raise money from among villagers for allocation to public welfare projects, its plan must first go to the villager council for ratification before being acted upon. In many villages in North China, rules clearly stipulate that any expense exceeding 1,000 Yuan (RMB) must receive villager council approval.

Today, the resolution of most issues requires consultation and consensus among a wide section of the local community before the execution of concrete action. Under these circumstances, one person's outspoken objection can generate substantial resistance. The dynamic of public debate is unprecedented in rural China. As Chinese peasants attach special importance to relations with neighbours, in the past open displays of discontent or objection were avoided at all costs. But in this new era, consultation and consensus have become the hallmark of grassroots democracy. Therefore, in the process of village committee policy-making, very rarely does the majority reel under the domination of an empowered minority. Also, unlike traditional chieftains, the director of the village committee does not claim absolute authority.

The village committee is an organisation with its roots in the local society. Village committee cadres make every effort to place themselves among the villagers and learn from them. Since village policy-making involves the villagers on a personal level, each household has a vested interest in influencing its outcome. The schedule of village committee meetings varies from village to village. Most meet once a week, but some once every month or so.

## An Evaluation

At present, a favourable trend has emerged in the blossoming of village autonomy in China. In the midst of China's political development, the advent of village autonomy has produced the following impacts:

1. Village autonomy has effected fundamental change in the direction of rural political development. Traditional rural

politics lacked democratic inputs. Solutions to contradictions among the peasantry came either in the form of Qing court mediation or peasant uprisings. After the founding of the People's Republic of China in 1949, political contradictions in the countryside were handled through mass political movements. Class struggle at this time aimed at rectifying political maladies which had accumulated in rural society. However, political movements were unable to solve the basic underlying problems. After the development of a commodity economy, political movements lost their effectiveness. Apart from promoting democratic self-government, no other weapon remained in the government's arsenal to combat corruption in the countryside. Relying on the ability of the peasants to employ democratic and legal measures to resolve rural contradictions, propelled Chinese political development into a new direction.

2. Village autonomy provides the peasants with the best form of training in democracy and has laid out a sturdy, mass-based foundation for Chinese political reform. As China lacks a tradition in democracy, the populace has no experience or frame of reference through which it can understand its basic principles and procedures. Therefore, when conflicts or important issues arise, rather than rely on their own ability to furnish a solution peasants instinctively look to higher levels of government to resolve the situation. This is a major problem in China. In this atmosphere, a sudden transfer of power down to the lower levels might cause widespread havoc or even break up the country. In order for reform at the upper levels to obtain substantial results, the most important strategy lies in the rigorous training of 900 million peasants. If the peasants can learn how to directly elect grassroots leaders, how to properly participate in village policy-making to determine their own destinies, then China will have achieved the necessary requirements for long-term political stability.

3. Village autonomy closely integrates the problems of democracy and development. In China's drive for modernisation, a major consideration is how to accelerate the pace of economic development while maintaining political stability. Since the movement for village self-government got off the ground,

peasants have continuously placed the finest of their ranks in local office to shoulder the task of rejuvenating the countryside. As a consequence, rural development has sky-rocketed.

China's experiment with village autonomy proves that implementing political reforms which call for decentralisation in a nation with a long-standing tradition of centralised authoritarianism, requires two important steps: First, real power must be transferred downward to lower levels and the remaining division of power between the central and local governments must be clearly defined. Second, real power must be handed over to the people to expand their genuine rights as citizens. This empowerment of the people, normally overlooked by most, entails multifaceted political training. Only when the people enjoy a wider scope of democratic rights can a foundation exist for the central government to transfer power down to the local level. People are empowered only when they are able to exercise their democratic rights more fully. If peasants learn to use democratic self-government to protect their own interests, it can be an extremely efficacious means to facilitate the smooth decentralisation of political power.

Notwithstanding the above points, there are problems in fully implementing village autonomy in the present context. Ever since the appearance of an unprecedented upsurge in economic activity in China, especially after the Tiananmen Square incident in 1989, people have not devoted much attention to grassroots democracy. At the same time, village autonomy still faces many real contradictions which must be resolved. In this phase, the guidance of appropriate policy is of critical importance. In the case of China, full implementation of village autonomy is confronted by the following contradictions:

1. The development of village autonomy is unbalanced throughout the nation. Some more conservative areas have yet to hold direct elections for the village committee. And in some other areas, where elections have been held, peasants have been unable (for whatever reason) to fully exercise their democratic rights.
2. To date, many peasants are still unaccustomed to the unfamiliar democratic process. Some villagers simply have no idea how to go about exercising their democratic rights, to

the extent that some even harbour doubts about the government's sincerity in promoting village self-government. Often villagers do not realise the effectiveness of voting until after they cast their ballots. Then they say regretfully, 'If I had known earlier it was this type of election, I wouldn't have voted this way. Wait till next time!'

3. The structure of grassroots governance in the countryside is still unclearly defined. Beneath the township level, all the villages have a party branch, and some even have cooperatives or agricultural workers and merchants' companies which handle administrative tasks. It is difficult to know how to divide executive powers between these other organisations, especially the party branch, and the village committee. Improper management of these contradictions threatens to seriously hinder the village committee's ability to effectively exercise its authority.

In China's experience, democracy is not only a noble ideal, but the practical relationship between different interests. How the peasants will integrate the procedure of democratic self-government and their own personal interests is not a simple matter. Democracy demands a complete set of specific legal norms which the Chinese society presently lacks. Establishing these norms will take meticulous effort over a relatively long period of time. Democratic self-government also requires cultivation and training, especially in developing countries. Yet, as Chinese peasants already have the right of economic self-determination and China's commodity economy continues to prosper, the motivation for grassroots village autonomy is already in place. Government policies which support village autonomy will certainly have a far-reaching impact on Chinese agricultural production and rural society.

# 6

# The Villagers' Self-government in Lishu County, Jilin Province of the People's Republic of China

CAO GUOYING

ZHANG HOUAN

Situated in the southwest of Jilin province, the heart of the Northeastern Plains, Lishu county finds itself in the north temperate zone with a monsoon climate. The total area of the county is 4.209 sq. kms with 186,000 hectares of arable land. The land is fertile with a relatively heavy rainfall every year. The economy largely depends on agriculture with maize, rice and wheat as the main crops, making Lishu county a major grain-yielding county in China. Animal husbandry in the county is also well developed. Out of the total population of 852,000 nearly 682,500 are engaged in agriculture. Under the county government there are 32 townships and towns, 336 villages and 2,846 villagers' groups. The per capita income of the farmers in 1991 was 830 Chinese Yuan (approximately US$ 138).

We selected this county for our research on villagers' self-government because, for one thing, the villagers' self-government here embodies the principles of democracy. and the local people regard elections as just and fair. This is significant in a county which needs to strive hard to attain a high level of democracy. Also, the villagers' self-government in this county has enhanced economic development, increased villagers' income and improved their living conditions.

The economic condition for implementing villagers' self-government is that farmers should gain the rights of using land independently and should obtain income from land use so that the rural economy can develop to a significant extent. However, if the rural land ownership remains in the hands of local collectives then, as far as their own interests are concerned, farmers are in dire need of an authoritative organisation formed by themselves to solve such problems as the right to use collective property, to rationally allocate the proceeds from the use of collective property, to set up rural public welfare facilities concerning the welfare of all the villagers and to rationally raise funds from among themselves for such affairs. On the other hand, the government management goal also requires that the farmers establish a kind of self-government organisation to protect their own interests, to function as a link and coordinator between farmers and the government, as well as to maintain the vitality of rural economic development and the stability of the rural society. The self-government in Lishu county had emerged under such circumstances.

Villagers' self-government was started in 1988 in Lishu county with the implementation of the Organic Law of Villagers' Committees and direct democratic elections for members of the villagers' committees in the whole county. In 1990, the democratisation of villagers, self-government was initiated step by step. Since the end of 1991, the county government has required all villages to democratically make rules of villagers' self-government so as to popularise and institutionalise villagers' self-government.

As to the individual villages, each has experienced the following stages. First, the villages publicised the state laws and local regulations to the villagers. Then democratic elections were held in accordance with state laws to produce villagers' representatives, villagers' group leaders and members of villagers' committees. Also, rules of villagers' self-government and other relevant regulations were democratically drawn up so that villagers' democratic decision-making over village affairs, villagers' self-government and the corresponding democratic supervision have all been realised.

## The Organic System of Villagers' Self-Government

In Lishu county, each village has a villagers' representative conference democratically elected by villagers, as a standing organ of power on villagers' self-government responsible for villagers' assembly. According to the Organic Law of Villagers' Committees, the villagers' assembly should be formed by villagers of 18 years and above to discuss and decide major problems concerning the interests of all the villagers. In practice, however, villagers' assemblies are only reserved for the election of members to the villagers' committee according to law and to take decisions on exceptionally important issues. Other key problems are referred to villagers' representative conferences. The reason is clear. Though the villagers' assembly system is of more legal authority, it is not only difficult to assemble hundreds of farmers together but also difficult for all these people to seriously get down to brass tacks. Comparatively speaking, the villagers' representative conference serves better the double purposes of democratic decision-making and easy management while adhering to the principle that the villagers' assembly is the highest organ of power in terms of villagers' self-government. In Huojiadian village, for example, there are 787 households, 2,119 villagers and 63 villagers' representatives, each one of whom is elected from every 10 to 15 households. Each villagers' representative conference is elected for a term of three years and the representative can be re-elected for more terms. The function and powers of the villagers' representative conference is to listen to and discuss the annual work report of the villagers' committee and to advance its opinions and suggestions. It also discusses and decides on the village's economic and social development plan, the work plan for the next year, as well as the village financial budget plan. In addition, it considers other important issues concerning the interests of all the villagers, lays down and amends the rules of the villagers' self-government and other regulations, supervises and examines village finance and examines and revises improper decisions, if any, of the villagers' committee. The decisions of the villagers' assembly and the villagers' representative conference are passed by a majority vote of all the villagers and villagers' representatives respectively.

The villagers' committee is an executive body of the villagers' assembly and the villagers' representative conference, for both of which it is responsible. It also reports its work to both of them. The villagers' committee generally consists of three to seven members, namely, the chairman, the vice-chairman and the members in charge of economic management, public security and conciliation of civil affairs respectively. Members of the villagers' committee are elected from villagers who are 18 years of age or above for a term of three years, with a provision for being re-elected for more terms.

The villagers' committee is meant to self-govern villagers in accordance with state laws and local regulations by carrying out the resolutions of villagers' assembly and villagers' representative conferences, supporting and organising villagers to develop the economy and promote the social welfare of the village, reporting to the local people's government the opinions and requirements of the villagers, fulfilling any tasks given by and accepting the leadership and guidance of the township government.

After the abolition of the people's commune system, property formerly belonging to the production brigade is now collectively owned by the village. The village as a collective is actually represented by the villagers' committee both organisationally and financially. The village earns its revenue mostly from profits of village enterprises that are turned over to the higher authorities and the reserves submitted to the village by households farming the land of the village. In different kinds of villages, the difference between the proportion of the types of revenue can be distinct. The villages whose collective economy, is developed generally depend on the former type of revenue, while the village with little or no village enterprises mainly depend on the later type.

The capital of the village is mostly used to set up and promote village enterprises and improve farming conditions, or to set up and operate social welfare facilities. However, the fund used for either purposes varies according to the actual conditions of the particular village.

The villages in Lishu are all relatively large, mostly with a population of more than 2,000. Each administrative village usually is composed of several natural villages, all with their own villagers' group. Each villagers' group is generally made up of 200 to 350 persons. The difference between the administrative villages and the natural villages strengthens the independence of villagers' groups from administrative villages. The villagers' group leader is elected from the members of the villagers' group and is therefore the natural representative of the villagers in charge of maintaining electricity for the group, building roads, popularising science and technology, conciliating civil affairs, and collecting the agricultural taxes paid in grain. The funds for such activities and the administrative expenses are borne by the farmers who benefit from these facilities.

## The Relationship Between the Institutional Framework of Self-Government and Other Organisations

One important element of the Chinese social–political system is the branch of the Chinese Communist Party established in various primary social units. The primary self-government organisations in rural and urban China function under the leadership of the party branch at the same level, which is how the villagers' committees of Lishu county work too. In practice, however, the party branch leaders mostly are concurrently members of the villagers' committees and *vice versa*. The chairman of the villagers' committee generally is the deputy-secretary or member of the party branch committee. As the nucleus of political leadership in the countryside, the party branch carries out the policies and guidelines of the Chinese Communist Party, safeguards state laws, proposes suggestions to the villagers' committee on such important issues as villagers' self-government and the village collective economy but it cannot make decisions about them without the approval of the villagers' representative conference. The party branch supports and assists the villagers' committee in its work but cannot replace it in its function and position of independent responsibility. It may recommend candidates for membership of the villagers' committee or make suggestions regarding the appointment or removal of members but it is not entitled to actually appoint or remove members of the villagers' committee. The replacement of and by-election for members of the villagers' committee must be approved by the villagers' assembly or the villagers' representative conference.

As mentioned earlier, the villagers' committee in Lishu county actually functions as the villages' collective economic organisation; it therefore shoulders the management of the village's collective economy. The combination of these two organisations promotes the efficiency of work and lowers the costs of management.

Under the villagers' self-government, the township government, instead of exercising leadership over the villagers' committee, gives guidances to it in respect of villagers' self-government and the management of the collective economy such as the village's financial budget and ways of fund-raising, the methods of contracting land, orchards and village enterprises, the capital construction on farmland and the village's public works. The administrative work like conscription, birth control, levying taxes to be paid in grain and collecting overall construction funds for the township government is assigned to the township government and carried out with the help of the villagers' committee. The different organisations cannot act in excess of the authority assigned to them and meddle with others' affairs. The villagers' representative conference may discuss methods of carrying out the work assigned by the government, report to the government villagers' opinions on the government's work and assist the villagers' committee in its fulfillment of tasks assigned by the government. But it has no right to change the government's regulations or expand the scope of its functions and powers by trespassing the limits of self-government prescribed in state policies and laws. At the same time the township government is not entitled to appoint or remove any member of the villagers' committee and cannot deprive the village collective economic organisation of its right to property and rights of management. For instance, a certain chairman of a villagers' committees in Lishu county disagreed with the secretary of the township party committee over building roads. So he led many people on a petition procession in automobiles without the previous approval of the authorities concerned. As a result, he was removed from his post as chairman of the villagers' committee by the township government. Aware that the township government did not have the power to do this, he and some villagers lodged a complaint with the county government and had the county government declare his removal invalid. From this example it can be seen how villagers' self-government rights are exercised in Lishu county.

The various committees under the villagers' committee are in charge of conciliation, public security, public hygiene and social welfare work under the leadership of the villagers' committee. The militia, the Communist Youth League and the Women's Federation support the villagers' committee in its work under the political leadership of the party branch.

## Democratic Election

The democratic election of the members of the villagers' committee is of vital concern to the villagers. In Lishu county it is carried out in the following way:

1. Special leading groups in charge of election at the county and township level are formed to organise the election, to publicise it and train cadres so that the villagers understand the significance and requirements of the election.
2. All candidates are registered in each village, and their names are announced to the public.
3. The voters in each village recommend people to form the village leading group in charge of election to preside over the election.
4. The candidates are recommended in a democratic way. The village's party branch, the villagers' groups, and 10 or more villagers with the right to vote are entitled to nominate primary candidates. People with the highest number of votes from among the voters can count as primary candidates as well. It is up to the villagers' representative conference to decide which of these two methods to adopt in the election of a particular village.
5. At the preliminary election held at the villagers' representative conference, the people with the highest number of votes become the official candidates.
6. Five days before the general election, the list of the official candidates is announced to the villagers, subject to supervision and accusation.
7. All the villagers with the right to vote caste their votes to elect members of the new villagers' committee.
8. The number of votes each candidate receives and the result of the election is announced to the villagers.

The problems faced in the first democratic election of the members of the villagers' committees in 1988 were as follows:

(*i*) Some township governments appointed candidates for villagers' committees, irrespective of the wishes of the local people.

(*ii*) In some villages, instead of all the villagers, the villagers' representative conference voted to elect members of the villagers' committee.

(*iii*) In other villages, villagers voted to elect members of the villagers' committee; then members of the villagers' committee voted to elect the chairman and vice-chairman.

Therefore, when the time came for electing members to the villagers' committee for the second term, five things were required to be made public: the names of the voters, the number of people to be elected and the qualifications of the candidates, the list of candidates and their basic qualifications, the election procedures and the specific rules, and the number of votes each candidate receives and the election results. In the meantime, it was required that voters directly recommend people to form the leading group in charge of the election, so that the recommendation, nomination and selection of candidates were not influenced by the former village cadres, and that the election was carried out entirely through legal procedures. All these conditions were stipulated to minimise the malpractices that surfaced during the first elections.

In the election at Shijiazi village of Shengli township, a certain Zhang Zhijun was listed as the candidate for vice-chairman of the villagers' committee without being nominated by the preliminary election at the villagers' representative conference. Following objections raised by the villagers, when an enquiry was conducted it was found that he had been nominated by the township government. The nomination was immediately invalidated as it had diverged from the law.

The election was conducted by holding the villagers' general assembly. Before the election, the chairman of the villagers' committee of the previous term gave a report on the work his administration had done. Then the special leading group in charge of the election gave a briefing on the candidates. Next, the new term members of the villagers' committee were elected by way of secret ballot. After the election results were made public, the newly elected chairman of the villagers' committee delivered the inaugural address.

Often, fierce competition appears in the elections. An unscrupulous farmer in Bapannianzi village canvassed his candidature in several natural villages by riding around in a hired jeep. However, he failed to get the support of the villagers and lost the election.

Another farmer in Qianjiuba village, the chairman of the villagers' committee of the previous term, had been very conscientious in his work. Someone tried to defeat him in the election by using any and all means he could command. Yet the farmer won the re-election on account of his high popularity among the people.

The second democratic election in Lishu county elected 2,270 members of villagers' committees, among which 76 per cent were re-elected for the second term while 24 per cent were newly elected. All in all, 41 former chairmen of villagers' committees accounting for 12 per cent lost the election.

It is interesting to note that in Lishu county, equally fierce competition characterised the election for villagers' group leaders. This, to some extent, reflects the importance of the post of the group leader and the farmers' sense of democracy. In the election for the leaders of the nine villagers' groups of Xibada village, there was severe competition for the leadership of two villagers' groups. The villagers' committee nominated a candidate for No. 6 Villagers' Group; however, he lost the election since he had been unfair in his handling of village affairs during his previous term as the group leader. On the other hand, the candidate who won the election was honest, fair, skillful and capable of promoting the development of his constituency.

## Democratic Decision-Making, Democratic Management and Democratic Supervision

Democratic decision-making in the villagers' self-government of Lishu county is conducted along the following lines: The village party branch and the villagers' committee together put forward their proposals on major problems, after carefully studying them, to the villagers' representative conference. Once they are adopted, it is the job of the villagers' committee to carry them out. The motion of one-fifth of the total villagers' representatives or villagers is sufficient to call the villagers' representative conference or villagers' assembly. In Huojiadian village, it is prescribed that problems concerning the following issues be discussed and settled at the villagers' representative conference:

(*i*) The annual plan and main measures for developing the village collective economy;

(*ii*) The perfection of the various production responsibility systems;

(*iii*) The signing of important economic contracts;

(*iv*) The budgeting and final accounting of the village annual revenue and expenditure;

(*v*) The expenditure of 500 Yuan or more for non-production projects and the expenditure of 30,000 Yuan or more on production projects;

(*vi*) The projects for industrial and sideline production and the project for capital construction on farmland;

(*vii*) The establishment of various public welfare facilities;

(*viii*) The collection, arrangement and use of a portion of the taxes reserved for the village out of the levies imposed on the farmers to raise funds for governments, compulsory labour for state construction and accumulated labour for village development;

(*ix*) The management of collective property and the supply of the means of production;

(*x*) The implementation of the birth control program;

(*xi*) Drafting the village construction plan and the arrangement of the area of the villagers' household residence;

(*xii*) The assignment of the purchase of grain by the state and levy of agriculture tax on the specific households and the means of allocating relief funds.

In Xibada village, the project of transforming electricity distribution lines required each household involved to hand in 400 Yuan. On the one hand, this sum was too large for the villagers; on the other hand, the distribution lines could no longer be used without a thorough transformation. Faced with this dilemma, the villagers' representative conference assembled and it decided to transform the electricity distribution lines of the whole village. The funds finally raised from each household were centralised for use without being misappropriated. This method was effective and satisfactory. At the villagers' groups, corresponding rules of democratic decision-making were formulated.

Villagers must abide by the village pledge and other rules passed by state law. Years ago, in Xibada village, early marriages were frequent due to ineffective leadership of the village cadres. Later the villagers' representative conference decided to impose a fine of 2,000 Yuan for early marriage and a fine of 1,000 Yuan for early child bearing. When they learned of the new rule, 10 couples postponed their date of marriage. It can therefore, be said that democratic management under the villagers' self-government carries more authority than the decisions of the village cadres.

Under the villagers' self-government, Lishu county persists in having the village affairs of all villages open to the public and subject to people's supervision. In Xibada village, the rules of the villagers' self-government stipulate that the following be made public: (*a*) the public affairs of the village; (*b*) the rating of the village cadres' wages; (*c*) the allocation of the village proceeds; (*d*) the revenue, expenditure and use of various kinds of funds, goods and materials collected from the village collective economic organisations and villagers; (*e*) the implementation of birth control and the reward or punishment involved; (*f*) the examination and approval (or disapproval) of the villagers' applications to build houses; and (*g*) the use of funds for village capital construction.

The financial accounts of Xibada village were not made public earlier and the villagers had complained about this. In October 1991, the village financial accounts were announced, clearing all doubts entertained by the farmers. What is more, in every village the villagers' representatives form financial affairs management groups to audit and supervise those financial affairs and projects which carry substantial outlays.

## The Economic and Social Effects

The system of decentralised governance at the grassroots level produced some favourable results:

1. The democratic election of village and villagers' group cadres had brought talented people into the limelight and raised the people's sense of responsibility as masters of New China. For centuries, village cadres were appointed by the higher authorities. Now, with the implementation of the villagers' self-government, farmers can choose a person they trust to be the village head. In 1991 the farmers of the whole county forwarded altogether 519,313

suggestions to the villagers' committee, of which 72 per cent were adopted. In Shuangmajia village of Huojiadian township, the original school buildings were in a dilapidated condition. At the suggestion of the farmers, the villagers' committee took up this issue at the villagers' representative conference and constructed a new building by investing 550,000 Yuans on it.

The democratic election has provided excellent opportunities for qualified people to show their talents, and has brought vitality to the team of village cadres. In Pengjia village of Madian town, Zhang Furong, a high school graduate, volunteered to be the electrician of the village. Recognising his good work as electrician, during the election he was nominated as the candidate for the chairman of the villagers' committee. Though he lost the election by two votes, Zhang succeeded in winning the position of director of the village birth control office following his nomination by the newly-elected villagers' committee and the approval of the villagers' assembly.

The cadres elected by the villagers enjoy a great deal of prestige. Concerned about their fellow villagers, the cadres take their responsibilities seriously, and do their best to accomplish the tasks entrusted to them by the villagers. Using his skills, Lan Xianlin, a farmer from Huojudian village, helped the farmers in his neighbourhood to raise pigs and plant vegetables in greenhouses after he became the villagers' group leader. As a result, the number of households specialising in raising pigs increased from three to 25, with an average of three to four pigs per person in the group; this helped develop the courtyard economy of the group.

2. The democratic election process helped the farmers to become true masters of the county and enhanced the development of the rural economy and the various undertakings. The rural economic and social undertakings needed to be developed, but it was a difficult problem to ask the farmers for money. This was because the decisions of the village were not open to the public. Under villagers' self-government, since decisions made democratically carry the authority of collective consent, the farmers are willing to pay for their own benefits. The economy of Xibada village had remained underdeveloped for a long time for lack of transport facilities. Following the approval of the villagers' representative conference, the villagers' committee raised 180,000 Yuan to build a road. The villagers' committee also met the expenses incurred on

the building materials and freight in instalments. Thanks to the new road that was constructed, in the spring of 1992 alone the earnings of the village increased by 60,000 Yuan.

In Huojiadian village, some 15 hectares of land had been rendered unfit for cultivation by brick makers. The village party branch and the villagers' committee held several discussions on ways to reclaim this wasteland but had to give up for lack of funds. In 1991, the villagers' representative conference passed a resolution for its reclamation, making it mandatory for every household to contribute either manpower or carts or money. After two years of hard work, 12 hectares (80 per cent) of the area were reclaimed.

3. Democratic election also facilitated the performance of other tasks assigned by the higher authorities. For a long time birth control, administration of residential areas and collection of fees for overall development were activities that were regarded as being the most difficult to tackle. The villagers' self-government required that the rules and village finance be made public, that everyone be equal under the law and abide by the state laws, and that the rules be laid down democratically. Dengjia village as a collective had an external debt of 300,000 Yuan and the money in respect of sale of grain could not be paid. Consequently, the farmers refused to turn in the grain previously ordered by the state. The town government was unable to solve the problem. During the second term election the chairman of the villagers' committee, Ding Xuewen, a fair and an honest villagers' group leader for the past two years, was elected chairman of the committee. With the approval of the villagers' representative conference, Ding Xuewen cleared off the debt and solved the problem to everybody's satisfaction. In 1990, assigned the task of afforestation by the township government, Yanhe village of Jinshan township called a villagers' representative conference to seek the help of the representatives. Headed by the villagers' representatives, all the farmers of the village participated in the afforestation campaign, planting over 100,000 saplings. With a survival rate of 98 per cent, the whole stretch of plantation has now become a 5 km green belt.

## General Reaction and Comments

Based on the reactions of the people and our own field observations, certain points emerge regarding the functioning of the villagers' self-government in Lishu county. For the sake of convenience, we have classified these into points relating to successful measures and those to which further attention must be given.

## Successful Measures

1. In keeping with the importance attached to villagers' self-government, local bodies took certain measures to ensure its effective functioning:

(a) In order to implement villagers' self-government, a special group was set up. This group was headed by the deputy county magistrate and an official in charge of villagers' self-government at the Department of Civil Affairs of Lishu county.

(b) They publicised the related state laws and policies for the benefit of individual farmers by means of such mass media as broadcast, blackboard newspapers and pamphlets.

(c) They trained village cadres to improve their understanding of villagers' self-government, with the secretary of the county party committee personally acting as the teacher.

(d) They laid down strict election procedures to ward off malpractices and prevent the elections from becoming a mere formality.

(e) They formulated rules of self-government and other detailed regulations to ensure villagers' rights of democratic decision-making in strict accordance with the law.

(f) In terms of guidance, the local government leaders insisted upon demonstrating the value of villagers' self-government by setting their own examples before developing it on a large scale.

(g The local government leaders carried out periodical inspections after assigning self-government work to the villages.

The solid work done by these bodies has brought success. The farmers have now realised that if they want good results they need to elect the right type of village cadres and take on the responsibility for resolving the problems facing their village society and polity.

2. The local leading bodies took up specific local cases and strove to solve many practical problems.

(a) By exercising the conventional power of the villagers' assembly, the villagers' representative conference adhered to the principle of democratic decision-making which was quite appropriate to resolving local problems.

(b) The combination of the village collective economy and the villagers' committee not only performed a double function but also reduced administrative personnel and the burdens of the farmers.

(c) The elected villagers' group leaders had the local economic and social orientation necessary for administrative personnel at this level.

(d) The strict and detailed stipulations regarding the nomination of candidates for membership of the villagers' committee have guaranteed democratic election.

(e) The establishment of the system of self-government also solved these problems which worried farmers the most: finance, management of residential areas, and family planning.

3. The promotion of democratic politics also initiated economic and social development:

(a) Most villager cadres elected democratically are economically oriented, capable of management, fair and just in their dealings, and have a strong sense of responsibility. This has helped pave the way for rural economic development.

(b) Through discussions at the villagers' representative conferences new ways have been found for every village to prosper, to introduce science and technology, to promote education, and to tap the natural resources of the villages.

(c) Institutionalisation of the 'five publics' regulations and the establishment of a relationship of mutual trust between the cadres and the farmers have created a suitable social environment for the development of various undertakings in the countryside.

Thus the system of villagers' self-government has brought to the countryside a fresh air of democracy in politics and a good opportunity for rural economic and social development. Farmers can now obtain material benefits by actively participating in self-government.

## Problems that Require Further Attention

1. Candidates for the villagers' committee in Lishu county can be nominated in four ways: by the village party branch, by the villagers' group, jointly by more than 10 villagers with the right to vote, and through direct election by voters. It is up to the villagers' representative conference to decide which method to adopt. All these methods have their limitations. There should be a stipulation that all the methods be tried: the nomination of a candidate by any of the first three ways is valid; if an insufficient number of candidates are nominated by these methods, votes ought to be mobilised by direct election. The official candidates are best decided at the villagers' representative conference through primary election.

2. During the official election of Lishu county, in 60 per cent of the villages the number of candidates nominated equalled the number of positions to be filled. This ratio is too high. We believe that the number of candidates nominated should be more than the positions to be filled, so that farmers can have some choice. It may also be a good idea to elect the chairman, vice-chairman and members by one ballot and members of the villagers' committee by several ballots instead of electing the chairman and vice-chairman from the members of the villagers' committee.

3. In the election of villagers' representatives, some villagers' group leaders handed out the ballots to the households and had them turn in the ballots back to them. Without announcing the number of ballots and the person elected, they took the ballots to the villagers' committee. This was illegal since the villagers' representative conference, as the organ of power for villagers' self-government, is composed of villagers' representatives. The qualifications and legitimacy of the representatives are directly related to the legal authority enjoyed by the villagers' representative conference. Therefore, it is necessary to count the number of ballots in the presence of the people and to announce the names of representatives elected. It is all right to elect villagers' representatives from each villagers' group rather than from a meeting of all

the villagers since it guarantees the wide and reasonable distribution of villagers' representatives.

4. In many villages, the candidates for the villagers' group leaders are nominated by the villagers' committee. Unless they are strongly opposed to the nomination, the villagers generally accept these nominations. This practice has its limitations and farmers ought to be encouraged to nominate candidates for the villagers' groups as they do for villagers' committees.

5. In some villages, villagers' representative groups are formulated with one group head and two group commissioners at the level of the villagers' group to discuss all important issues of the villagers' group. We feel that in villagers' group that are small, it will be less effective to set up such an organisation. The villagers' group assembly should decide if it is necessary to set up villagers' representative groups in the villagers' groups of large sizes. All important problems concerning households in the villagers' group ought to be decided at meetings attended by the representatives of all the households in the villagers' group rather than by the villagers' representative group. It should not be difficult to assemble the none-too-many representatives of all the households of the villagers' group. What is more, the important problems in the group such as setting up an enterprise, building houses in an area, the entry of new households etc. concern every household, and ought to be discussed and decided by all household representatives of the villagers' group collectively.

## Conclusion and Some Useful Lessons

The following conclusions can be drawn from the practices of villagers' self-government in Lishu county.

1. Rural economic and social development is basically motivated by the farmers' desire to pursue their own interests. Only when farmers are determined to build their homeland into a better place will there be hope for the promotion of rural development. That people's activities are all related to their own interests is a simple truth of economics. People hate to work fruitlessly, and if forced to do so, it is unlikely that they will work well. The system of the people's communes, which was implemented for over 20 years in China, has already taught us this lesson. Farmers will be more

concerned about rural development, if they directly benefit from it. The problem is whether our economic and political systems and other policies are capable of arousing farmers' enthusiasm to pursue their own interests. The theory that only the township and village cadres are most concerned about the overall development of the rural economy and that only coercive appropriation from government finance can set up various undertakings in the countryside, has not been proved empirically. On the contrary, given enough rights to govern themselves by choosing their own administrators and deciding the construction and development of the various undertakings in the countryside, farmers can do better than the leaders since they know where their interests lie. The problem now is not whether farmers are willing, or able, to self-govern themselves but whether the local government leaders will return the rights of self-governance to the farmers and guide them in the work in the light of the state laws.

2. The common Chinese farmers are generally law-abiding. Thus, the preferential treatment given to relatives and friends by the government machinery, the miscellaneous fines and charges imposed upon farmers and the unscrupulous embezzlement of collective property have aroused their resentment of governmental work. The solution to these problems lies in perfecting the democratic and legal systems which can be applied in rural administration, providing effective supervision over the execution of governmental work and enabling farmers to fulfill their own legal obligations on the one hand and resist the infringement upon their rights and interests on the other. Such activities as establishing and perfecting a system and decision-making through democratic procedures so that farmers willingly accept and abide by them are the stuff that villagers' self-governance is made of. However, some cadres at the primary organs of the state wrongly believe that they have already so much work to do in terms of rural administration that they have no time to implement villagers' self-government. Some even fear that the implementation of villagers' self-government will make rural administration more difficult. But in villages where villagers' self-government has been in practice, it is observed that the cadres are honest, the farmers are united, the economy is developed, and rural administration is smoothly carried out.

3. In the long run, any new system must ultimately win the people's confidence. The successful implementation of villagers self-government system depends largely on the extent of farmers'

participation. This, in turn, depends on whether the villagers' self-government has any practical substance in it and whether society truly gives farmers the rights of self-government. In Lishu county, it took some time for the farmers to understand the philosophy and mechanism of villagers' self-government. At first, most farmers were sceptical, and did not take the election of villagers' representatives seriously. The villagers' representatives still had doubts when they were discussing the important village affairs. But gradually they realised that the new system was true and valid. When village cadres were elected through democratic election and the decisions of the villagers' representative conference were carried out, they became more serious about the system when the election for the second term of the villagers' committee was held. In Shijiazi village of Shengli township, the farmers stayed awake all night to see the results of the election. How enthusiastic farmers were towards politics! The cadres at the basic level too have realised the value of villagers' self-government and have become its enthusiastic supporters. They helped the villagers' representatives to shoulder the responsibilities of solving important problems and to explain the decisions of the villagers' committee to the farmers. History has proved that it is always difficult to implement a new system, and even more difficult to make the system last. The longer the villagers' self-government system lasts, the more successful it will be. The success of villagers' self-government today is the result of years of unstinted efforts by the farmers. But only when the new system becomes a social norm whose existence no longer depends on the degree of the leaders' integrity will the social progress brought about by the system become irreversible. The experience of Lishu county also shows that after they obtained decision-making powers in economic matters, the farmers have exhibited a strong desire to exercise their democratic rights in political matters. This, they feel, will be an effective means of protecting their interests. When farmers show no interest in the democratic election of cadres and the democratic settlement of village affairs, it is time for local government leaders to re-examine themselves and determine whether they really have returned the legal rights back to the farmers.

4. The key to the success of villagers' self-government is to improve the ways of realising the party's leadership and to standardise government behaviour. The implementation of villagers'

self-government is an important step in the reform of the political system in China. Therefore, it inevitably involves the readjustment of the distribution of power and interests in the countryside. Since this affects the vested and expectant interests of some people, there emerges a strong resistance to villagers' self-government from some quarters. This makes reforms a difficult task.

The leadership of the village party branch representing the Chinese Communist Party as the ruling party has a specific but a restricted role to play. The problem is not whether such leadership exists, but how such leadership is realised. If the village party branch has the final say in important problems in the countryside in the traditional manner, villagers' self-government will undoubtedly become a farce. In Lishu county, however, they have blazed a new trail in this respect. The party's leadership is first of all reflected in its guidelines and policies. The leadership of the party branch in village affairs is primarily to ensure the smooth implementation of the party's guidelines and policies in the village. The villagers' committee ought to report its work to the party branch periodically. The party branch should stop the self-government organisation from violating state laws and regulations. It may nominate or recommend candidates for members of the villagers' committee but cannot prevent farmers from nomination, nor can it appoint village cadres and villagers' representatives, or deprive farmers of their right to democratic election. The village party branch may advance its proposal on the important village affairs, but may not take any decisions on them. In fact, the party branch must recognise the villagers' committee elected democratically in accordance with state laws and must respect any decisions made by the villagers' assembly or villagers' representative conference in the light of state laws.

According to the stipulations in the Organic Law of Villagers' Committee, the relationship between the township (town) government and the villagers' committee is that of guidance, which affords an important guarantee for the implementation of villagers' self-government. In these circumstances, the villagers' committee ought to persistently assist the township (town) government in its work, fulfill the tasks assigned by the township government, respect the guidance of the township (town) government, and conscientiously abide by state laws and regulations. However, the township (town) government cannot appoint or dismiss at will the cadres of the villagers' committee, nor is it entitled to veto any decisions made by the villagers' assembly and villagers' representative conference, or to force villagers to do anything within the scope of villagers' self-government against their will. Only in this way can villagers' self-government be realised in a free social environment, and be developed and perfected with the support of the farmers.

# 7

# Panchayats: The Local Self-government System in India

## GEORGE MATHEW

Local governments in rural India are known as panchayats. The word 'panch' means five and panchyat denotes the forum of five village elders which decided the affairs of the village in ancient India. In recent times panchayati raj (PR) has come to mean the system of elected government below the state (provincial) level. In a country of India's size and immense diversity there has been no uniformity in panchayati raj. The story of PR in different states has been one of ups and downs, successes and failures, heavily weighted towards the latter. This paper is an attempt to critically examine the contours of this not too successful but necessary social development and political institution which has a direct bearing on all citizens of India. This critical assessment has been conducted in a historical perspective, tracing the development of panchayati raj from the colonial period.

## Before Independence

It is widely recognised that village committees which were characteristic of agrarian economies have existed in India from the earliest times. These panchayats were the pivot of administration, the centre of social life, an important economic force and, above all, a focus of social solidarity. So much so that Sir Charles Metcalfe, acting British governor-general in India in the 1830s, had called these village committees 'little republics'.[1]

This does not mean that these 'republics' were ideal centres thriving on the democratic participation of all people. Given the caste-ridden feudal structure of village society of those days, they left much to be desired. In fact, Dr. B.R. Ambedkar, viewed village society in extremely negative terms when he remarked in the Constituent Assembly in 1946: 'What is the village but a sink of localism?' He went on to say that these village republics had been the ruination of India. One may not agree with Ambedkar in his depiction of the 'village republic' but it is equally important to guard against a romantic view of the ancient village system, especially in relation to the values of equality and democracy.

It is a historical fact that local self-government in India, in the sense of representative institution accountable to the electorate, was the creation of British rulers. The government resolution of 18 May 1882, during Lord Ripon's viceregal tenure, providing for local boards consisting of a large majority of elected non-official members and presided over by a non-official chairman, was considered the Magna Carta of local democracy in India. By 1925, eight provinces in British India had passed Acts for the establishment of Village Panchayats Acts.[2] By 1948, 20 native states had Village Panchayat Acts.[3] However, these statutory panchayats covered only a limited number of villages and generally had a limited number of functions.

Village panchayats were central to the ideological framework of the national movement for political freedom. Mahatma Gandhi categorically described his vision of village panchayats in a 1942 issue of the *Harijan*:

> My idea of village Swaraj is that it is a complete republic independent of its neighbours for its own vital wants and yet interdependent for many others in which dependence is a necessity . . . . The Government of the village will be conducted by the Panchayat. These will have all the authority and jurisdiction required.

It is a sad commentary on India's national commitment to democratic decentralisation that even with our history of the village as basic unit of administration, the national movement's commitment to panchayats and Gandhiji's unequivocal propagation of the ideal of the village *swaraj*, the first draft of India's Constitution did not find a place for it. When Gandhiji heard that panchayats were not included in the Constitution, he said: 'It is certainly an omission calling for immediate attention if our independence is to reflect the people's voice.' The Gandhians considered panchayati raj both as a means and as an end and sincerely believed in its immense potential for democratic decentralisation and for devolving power to the people. Of course, Ambedkar's objection was not to democratic decentralisation or to the concept of giving power to the people which would emerge as a result of an ideal panchayati raj system. He was speaking from his experience of what a village in India meant to him and to millions like him.

## After Independence

### The First Phase

The argument of those who pleaded for the inclusion of village panchayats in the Constitution finally prevailed albeit in modest measure. A provision in the Directive Principles (Article 40C) which, however, is not justiciable, reads:

> . . . the State should take steps to organise village panchayats and endow them with such power and authority as may be necessary to enable them to function as units of self-government.

In independent India, after the community development programme was inaugurated in October 1952, those at the helm of affairs realised that real progress in rural development could not come about without an agency at the village level 'which could represent the entire community, assume responsibility and provide the necessary leadership for implementing development programmes'.[4] The recommendation of the Team for the Study of Community Projects and National Extension Services, headed by Balwantrai G. Mehta (1958), that 'public participation in community works should be organised through statutory representative bodies'[5] was a watershed. Later, the National Development Council affirmed the basic principles of democratic decentralisation and left it to the states to work out the structures suitable to each state. Thus, panchayati raj was born 12 years after India gained independence. It was first inaugurated in Rajasthan on 2 October 1959 by Jawaharlal Nehru, who hailed it as 'the most revolutionary and historical step in the context of new India'.[6] S.K. Dey, another architect of panchayati raj, visualised it as an organic and intimate relationship between the gram sabha and the Lok Sabha, and was optimistic that PR would become a way of life for the people and represent a new approach to governance.

By 1959 all the states had passed Panchayat Acts and by the mid-1960s panchayats had reached all parts of the country. There was enthusiasm in rural India and a feeling had gripped the people that they had a say in the affairs affecting their lives. Those were the promising days of panchayati raj institutions (PRIs) in India, when rural folk hoped that they would lead to gram *swaraj*. A report of the Ministry of Community Development in 1964–65 stated that younger and better leadership was emerging through the PRIs and there was a fairly high degree of satisfaction among the people with the working of the PRIs.

A study team appointed by the Association of Voluntary Agencies for Rural Development for evaluating PR in Rajasthan a year after the programme was launched, made the following encouraging observation:

It was reported that the people felt that they had sufficient powers to enable them to mould their future . . . . They are fully conscious of the fact that such privileges and favours which were formerly under the control of the Block Development Officer (BDO) are now under their control. In this sense, full advantage of democratic decentralisation has been secured.

The report then went on to say that the conferment of power on people's representatives had improved the attendance of teachers in primary schools, the block administration had become more responsive, people voiced their grievances before the pradhan and obtained relief through him and, above all, petty corruption both among the subordinate staff as well as newly elected leaders had declined—the former because the block staff had come under the panchayati samithi and the latter because their public reputation was crucial to their getting elected.

I consider panchayati raj in the Nehruvian era as its first phase. That was the period between 2 October 1959, when Jawaharlal Nehru inaugurated PR in the country, and his death in 1964.

### The Second Phase

For about 13 years between 1964 and 1977, panchayati raj was the whipping boy of all those who wanted to ensure that it be discredited. For them, PR was the incarnation of all the evils in villages. Perhaps an exception of sorts during this period was the panchayat system in Maharashtra and Gujarat.

The appointment of the Ashok Mehta Committee in 1977 marked a turning point in the concept and practice of panchayati raj. The second phase of local self-government in India began when the West Bengal government took the initiative in 1978 to give a new life to its panchayats along the lines of the Ashok Mehta Committee recommendations. The Karnataka government followed West Bengal's lead and soon Andhra Pradesh too opened a new chapter in panchayati raj governance. Later, this 'new generation' was joined by Jammu and Kashmir (J & K). In April 1988 a new Bill was introduced in the J & K Assembly, replacing the 1958 J & K Panchayati Raj Act. It was passed in March 1989 and the Governor gave his assent in July 1989. Subsequently, however, socio–political events in the state have made it redundant.

The states of West Bengal, Karnataka, Andhra Pradesh and J&K either revised their existing Panchayati Raj Acts or passed new ones, theoretically accepting the Ashok Mehta Committee report. They adapted the recommendations to suit their conditions and learnt from each other's experience in bringing forth new legislation or amendments.

The most important underlying thrust of the second phase was the transformation of panchyats from being mere development organisations at the local level to being granted the status of political institutions. A beginning had been made in giving pre-dominance to political elements rather than to the bureaucracy—which was a welcome trend.

Initially, there was considerable opposition to making PRIs 'political'. For instance, in West Bengal there was marked resentment against the involvement of political parties in the panchayat elections. But the CPI(M) and its allies preferred official recognition of parties in panchayats. They believed that the direct involvement of political parties in the working of PRIs would make the panchayati leadership more disciplined and responsible in managing these institutions of rural democracy and would put an end to the age-old tradition of rural coteries reaping benefits by promoting narrow, sectarian and caste interests.

Other noteworthy features of the second phase were: (*a*) a high level of political perception among the rural voters with the lessening influence of caste; (*b*) the emergence of a new, youthful, literate rural leadership; (*c*) a substantial devolution of powers and resources to the local bodies; and (*d*) the participation of political parties creating large-scale enthusiasm among the villagers.

It must be admitted that the functioning of the second generation of PRIs in West Bengal, Karnataka and Andhra Pradesh had a perceptible impact on people's lives. The Congress(I) (the ruling party) leadership at the centre, which was not favourably disposed to decentralisation, began to recognise the growing popularity of the non-Congress(I) governments in these states as well as the national attention they received for actualising the devolution of power in their respective states. Most of the Congress(I) state governments, on the other hand, were objects of censure, accused of keeping local bodies in hibernation either by not holding elections for decades or by superseding elected bodies and putting the grassroots level organisations in the charge of civil servants.

The second phase of panchyati raj disturbed the earlier 'balance' between officials and non-officials. Consequently, a process of trial and error and of adjustment was inevitable in order that the viewpoints of the official and non-official sides be appreciated by the other. In Karnataka, for instance, serious questions were raised regarding the possibility of the bureaucracy throttling PR initiative. There was a feeling that the bureacrats were hurt because the rural folk had become their masters under the new dispensation.

## Constitutional Amendment

All states that took the business of local self-government seriously began to realise that state governments could not establish a full-fledged Panchayati Raj without adequate constitutional safeguards. For instance, Abdul Nazir Sab, the Minister for Panchayati Raj in Karnataka and architect of the new PR system in the state, said in 1985:

> Soon we realised that within the limitations imposed by the Constitution, the ideology of the 'Four Pillar State'—village, district, state and centre—could not be implemented *in toto* by the State Government . . . without a Constitutional amendment guaranteeing the 'Four Pillar State', our efforts may not be as fruitful as we desire. In my opinion this is the major question the intellectuals of this country must ponder over. They must create a public debate on the necessity of a Constitutional amendment.

All those concerned with decentralised democracy have been pleading for a specific constitutional provision for Panchayati Raj so that PRIs can be invigorated by regular elections and made financially viable.

It was against this background that in May 1989 the government introduced the 64th Constitutional Amendment Bill in Parliament to confer statutory status on panchayati raj. The Bill was introduced without sufficient spade work and it raised several questions about federalism. The underlying issue was that any move to revitalise the local bodies and introduce a new system of governance below the state level could be effective only if accompanied by genuine federalism, both in theory and practice, at the national level. In the absence of it, critics argued, such measures are merely form without content.

The 64th Amendment Bill was passed by the Lok Sabha (Lower House) but defeated in the Rajya Sabha (Upper House) in October 1989. Then the 74th Amendment Bill was introduced in Parliament in September 1990 by the National Front Government. But before it could even be taken up for discussion, the National Front Government went out of power. When the present government headed by Prime Minister P.V. Narasimha Rao came to power in

June 1991, the 72nd Constitutional Amendment Bill was introduced in September 1991. It was sent to a Joint Committee of Parliament for consideration of various clauses. The Bill was passed as the 73rd Constitutional Amendment Bill on 22 December 1992 and on 23 December 1992, the Bill for Municipalities was passed as the 74th Amendment by both houses of the Parliament. It requires ratification by 13 State Assemblies and the assent of the President of India before it becomes an Act.

The main features of the Bill are: (*i*) formation of gram sabhas (the assembly of all adults in the village/s; (*ii*) uniform three-tier system at village, block and district levels with the exemption of the intermediate level in states with a population less than two million; (*iii*) direct election to all seats at all levels; (*iv*) indirect election of chairmen at the intermediate and apex levels with mode of election for the lowest level being left to discretion of the state; (*v*) voting rights to MPs and MLAs; (*vi*) 21 years as minimum age for members as well as chairmen; (*vii*) reservation on rotational basis for the Scheduled Castes (SCs) and Scheduled Tribes (STs) in proprotion to their population both for membership as well as chairmanship of the panchayats; (*viii*) reservation of not less than one-third of the seats for women; (*ix*) five-year terms; (*x*) in case of supersession or dissolution, fresh elections within six months; (*xi*) devolution of powers and responsibilities by the state to districts and blocks in the preparation and implementation of development plans; (*xii*) sound financial arrangement through tax, grant-in-aid, levies, fees, etc.; (*xiii*) setting up a finance commission to review, every five years, the financial position of the PRIs and to make suitable recommendations to the state on the distribution of funds among panchayats; (*xiv*) provision for the maintenance and auditing of accounts; (*xv*) holding of elections under the superintendence, direction and control of the chief electoral officer of the state.

A major drawback of the Bill is that it has adopted a uniform three-tier system below the state level. It might have been more appropriate to let the states decide, on the basis of their specific socio–historical milieu the number of tiers that would be required. It seems artificial to create a fixed number of tiers for all states irrespective of their history and tradition. The AIADMK and DMK, the two opposition parties of Tamil Nadu, spoke vehemently against this three-tier uniformity but theirs was a lone voice. Even the dissenting Marxist voice, which spoke against uniformity in legislation, finally gave in. The only concession that has been given is that panchayats may not be constituted at the intermediate level in states which have a population of less than 20 lakhs.

When introduced, the present Bill provided for direct elections to the post of chairman both at the village and intermediary levels. At the district level, the decision was to be left to the legislatures. The Joint Committee considered this issue but advocated direct elections only at the village level. The Marxist members of the Joint Committee had objected to direct elections at any level. But in order to achieve a consensus, the Marxists suggested that the election of the chairperson at the village level be left to the state legislatures. Finally, the left position prevailed. Without arguing the pros and cons of indirect or direct elections, it may be said that direct elections for chairman are more in consonance with the presidential form while indirect elections are in conformity with the cabinet system which we have adopted.

Another lacuna in the Bill is the contradictory and inconsistent position given to the idea that panchayats are institutions of self-government. The Bill has rightly defined panchayats as institutions of self-government but later, when it defines their functions, these have been narrowed down to developmental ones in Article 243(a) and (b). Without policing (law and order) as a function at each level, no institution of self-government is worth its name. When the 1983 Karnataka Act was discussed at a meeting of the Institute of Social Sciences, Swami Agnivesh, a well-known human rights activist, asked Nazir Sab; 'Who will wield the *lathi* (stick) in the villages? Whose orders will the police take to use force?' Nazir Sab's answer was; 'It is our intention that the police should come under the control of the zilla parishads. But we cannot do all these things simultaneously. We will do them step-by-step when the district government is constituted.' Now that the 'district government' idea has been established, this crucial point is sadly missing. Nirmal Mukarji, former Cabinet Secretary, who is a strong advocate of panchayats from vast experience in administration, termed this dilution of the concept of institutions of self-government as flawed thinking and drafting.

Wherever panchayats have not taken root or have been uprooted after a brief spell of success, it has been observed that MPs and state legislatures have not been too friendly towards these institutions. Not only have they been indifferent to local governments, at times they have been openly hostile. No one would like to see another centre of power emerging as a challenge, nor would they like to see their existing powers being diluted. Had state legislatures not been created along with the Parliament, it is possible that the MPs would have prevented the creation of the former after a few years of tasting power. They would have argued: 'We can look after the interests of all those whom we represent, why have another tier like the state legislature with all its nuisance value?' Similarly, MLAs and MPs have been arguing against strengthening or revitalising panchayats. And it is perhaps to assuage their feelings and to pre-empt any trouble from them that a statute has recently been passed giving membership with voting rights in panchayats. This, to my mind, will only undermine the panchayats which we are now aiming to strengthen.

In the context of states being asked to give more powers and departments to panchayats, an oft-repeated question that the centre has to face is, when will the centre itself devolve more powers to the states? Sooner or later this question will have to be answered.

It must be pointed out that flawed though the Bill is, with it we have taken a major step forward. Amendments are always possible, even after the Act is implemented.

## Electoral Process and Panchayats

The Santhanam Committee (1964) on panchayati raj elections had stated that one of the most controversial issues they had to deal with related to whether and to what extent political parties should participate in PR elections. At the time, there were two prominent though sharply divided schools of thought on the subject. One school advocated apolitical panchayat bodies while the other was against the 'woolly idea of having local bodies' elections on an apolitical basis'.[7]

Inspired by Gandhiji, the Sarvodayees argued that PRIs should be 'non-political', meaning that political parties should be kept out. Consensus was considered the best way of arriving at decisions. Jayaprakash Narayan believed that political parties corrupted the panchayati raj programme and used decentralisation for selfish party interests. The Sarvodayees wanted to rebuild Indian democracy with the gram samaj at the bottom and upper tiers at the samiti, district, state and all-India levels with a representation at each level through indirect elections. They believed that through this, if not unanimity, then at least the principle of consensus would prevail at all levels of the administration and electioneering and party politics would be eliminated. Of course, this argument has a fine moral appeal. Since the vast majority of our people are illiterate and ignorant, the protagonists of this school of thought sought 'to save them from becoming pawns in the contest for power by political parties and ambitious pressure groups'.[8]

The liberal democrats opposed this concept and wanted political participation in panchayat bodies. S.K. Dey, the Union Cabinet Minister for Community Development and Panchayati Raj during Nehru's time, for instance, characterised democracy without contest as that of dead people:

A self-sufficient village republic consisting of god-fearing people thinking, believing and acting all alike, is a village dead before it is born. Life cannot spring from such an inanition. Democracy demands ideology and ideals in a perpetual but healthy clash. Only dead people do not compete.[9]

C.P. Bhambri, a political science Professor, and others argued that the involvement of political parties in the panchayati raj system was both necessary and desirable. The parties would act as tools of modernisation in the villages:

The PR institutions provide a base for progressive parties to operate and fight against the forces of backwardness and tradition. The village people are to be politicised . . . political parties have to act as a great instrument for the politicisation of the rural masses.[10]

The use of party symbols in panchayat elections was not permitted in any of the states except Kerala, but even here such symbols were not being used at the time of the Santhanam Committee review. The Santhanam Committee felt that while it was not possible to legally ban political party influences, it was wrong and unnecessary to encourage their entry into the villages by the provision of party symbols. However the Ashok Mehta Committee unequivocally said that political parties should be allowed to participate effectively at all levels of panchayat elections.

West Bengal was the first state to put the Ashok Mehta Committee recommendation into practice. Nineteen years after the
inauguration of PRIs in the country, for the first time in 1978
political parties were officially recognised in local elections in that
state. In 1987, the Karnataka elections to PRIs were officially held
on party lines. For the first time, individuals who ruled the village
by virtue of their caste and family status, money power and bullying
tactics, were challenged by candidates put up by national or regional
parties. Villages which had for several decades been dominated by
one particular family or caste, now had the opportunity to challenge
this domination. Families, and even members of a single family,
began to align themselves with different parties, causing serious
rifts to occur within the family unit. Discussions and debates that
took place in teashops and other public places became more politically ideological, assessing the balance sheets of political parties
and the track record of political leaders. Elections became a churning
pot of ideas and action, creating a high level of political awareness
among the villagers.

There is no point in making a fetish about village harmony. As
the late Abdul Nazir Sab, the then Karnataka's Minister for Panchayati Raj who worked tirelessly to usher in a new era of PRIs in
the state, used to say: 'Anyway in the villages there is *Ramanna–
Bhimanna* politics. It is a reality. Isn't it healthier that they align
on democratic party lines rather than on the basis of caste, religion,
etc?'[11] A study undertaken by Institute of Social Sciences' on the
working of PRIs in Karnataka since the 1987 election showed that
the involvement of political parties down to the mandal panchayat
level generated healthy discussions and debates on definite policies
and programmes. Following Karnataka's example, the Andhra
Pradesh and Kerala governments also permitted political parties to
participate directly in local elections in their states.

In our particular social and political situation there is a tendency
for ruling parties to adopt an ostrich-like attitude towards the
official contest of parties in local elections. They view these elections as a verdict on their performance and popularity and, more
often than not, prefer to shy away from this test. The 1989 panchayati raj elections held in Uttar Pradesh without the official
participation of parties is a case in point. In such contests, independent candidates of any hue and shade and without any internal
control or accountability can jump into the fray. But it is an open
secret that these independents are in truth not all that independent.

If a party finds that it has no base, it may support an 'independent'—as was the case in the recently concluded Punjab panchayat elections.

Only official party participation in local self-government will prevent lumpens from taking over politics. Therefore, the PRIs and their elections should be seen as nurseries for political leadership. Young blood will be attracted if elections are based on political ideology and inspired by state level as well as national political leadership.

There is, no doubt, a dearth of political leadership at the lower levels. When national parties had to put up candidates for the mandal panchayat elections in Karnataka, they found it difficult to identify enough party activists. The organic link from gram sabha to Lok Sabha can be effectively realised only if political parties work with the people. The absence of such a link has brought about a pathological decay of our democratic system. Wherever official parties have been involved in PRIs, the enthusiasm of the local people has been high and the level of polling unprecedented.

The elections to panchayats are hotly contested. In many cases money and muscle power are involved, resulting in violence that is reminiscent of State Assembly or Parliament elections. For instance, in the recent Orissa gram panchayat and panchayat samiti elections, 17 persons reportedly lost their lives; several candidates contested for each post and the percentage of voting was 75 to 85 per cent. In the recent Punjab panchayat elections, the voter turnout was about 82 per cent.

## Structure of Panchayats

In India, the structure and arrangement of panchayats vary from state to state. In general, gram panchayats form the lowest tier; panchayat samitis or mandal panchayats constitute the middle level and the zilla parishads (districts) are at the top. There are four states/union territories (UTs) which go by the traditional council of village elders, while eight states/UTs have only a one-tier panchayat system. Five states have a two-tier system and 14 have three tiers. The average population covered by gram panchayats, the average number of villages per gram panchayat, the average number of gram panchayats in a panchayat samiti and the average number of panchayat samitis in a zilla parishad (district) vary across states and union territories. Table 1 and Table 2 show the distribution of states/UTs by the number of tiers (of the panchayati raj system) and the average size of PRIs at various levels.

With the passing of the Constitutional Amendment Bill 1992, panchayats in all states except those with a population of less than two million have a uniform three-tier system.

## Decentralised Planning

Any discussion of local self-government in India will not be complete without a look at decentralised planning in the country. Professor D.T. Lakdawala, noted economist and former Deputy Chairman, Planning Commission, had said:

> The logic of decentralisation is so powerful that it has been almost universally accepted. It is now a well recognised dictum that since local resources are to be harnessed, local needs to be consulted and local knowledge is needed, a large degree of decentralisation is essential for ,the success of developmental efforts. This is especially so for those developmental efforts which aim, at transforming the lives of the people or where the masses are involved.[12]

Then he went on to say: 'It is no use transferring functions and powers unless we also transfer the wherewithals with which to discharge the functions.'[13]

A democracy working for social ends has to base itself on the willing assent of the people and not the coercive power of the state. Means have therefore to be devised to bring the people into association both at the level of formulation of the plans and at every stage of their implementation.

This position has been reiterated in one form or another in all the subsequent plan documents, including the Seventh Plan. The Planning Commission issued guidelines for district planning as far back as 1969. In 1977, the Planning Commission appointed a working group under the chairmanship of M.L. Dantwala to draw up guidelines for block level planning. In 1983 the Economic

**Table 7.1: Tiers in States/Union Territories**

| States/UTs Having Traditional Council of Village Elders | State/UTs Having only One-tier System | States/UTs Having Two-tier System | State/UTs Having Three-tier System |
|---|---|---|---|
| 1. Meghalaya | 1. Goa | 1. Haryana | 1. Andhra Pradesh |
| 2. Mizoram | 2. Jammu & Kashmir | 2. Kerala | 2. Arunachal Pradesh |
| 3. Nagaland | 3. Tripura | 3. Manipur | 3. Assam |
|  | 4. Andaman & Nicobar | 4. Sikkim | 4. Bihar |
|  | 5. Dadra & Nagar Haveli | 5. Lakshadweep | 5. Gujarat |
|  | 6. Daman & Diu |  | 6. Himachal Pradesh |
|  | 7. Delhi |  | 7. Karnataka |
|  | 8. Pondicherry (only at block level) |  | 8. Madhya Pradesh |
|  |  |  | 9. Maharashtra |
|  |  |  | 10. Orissa |
|  |  |  | 11. Punjab |
|  |  |  | 12. Rajasthan |
|  |  |  | 13. Tamil Nadu |
|  |  |  | 14. Uttar Pradesh |
|  |  |  | 15. West Bengal |
|  |  |  | 16. Chandigarh |

**Table 7.2: Average Size of PRIs at Various Levels**

| State/UTs | Average Population per Gram Panchayat | Average No. of Villages per Gram Panchayat | Average No. of Gram Panchayat per Panchayat Samiti | Average No. of Panchayat Samiti per Zilla Parishad |
|---|---|---|---|---|
| 1. Andhra Pradesh | 2108 | 1.5 | 17.9 | 48.6 |
| 2. Arunachal Pradesh | 665 | 4.3 | 14.3 | 5.4 |
| 3. Assam | 7000 | 10.0 | 10.0 | 4.0 |
| 4. Bihar | 5251 | 6.0 | 19.8 | 15.1 |
| 5. Goa | 10032 | 4.2 | – | – |
| 6. Gujarat | 1764 | 1.4 | 73.1 | 9.6 |
| 7. Haryana | 1744 | 1.2 | 53.6 | – |
| 8. Himachal Pradesh | 1639 | 7.3 | 38.3 | – |
| 9. Jammu & Kashmir | 3218 | 4.7 | – | – |
| 10. Karnataka | 10081 | 10.7 | 14.7 | 9.0 |
| 11. Kerala | 20512 | 1.4 | – | – |
| 12. Madhya Pradesh | 3000 | 4.1 | 41.0 | 10.2 |
| 13. Maharashtra | 1653 | 1.7 | 82.8 | 10.3 |
| 14. Manipur | 3651 | 4.0 | 18.4 | – |
| 15. Meghalaya | Traditional system exists. | | | |
| 16. Mizoram | 794 | 1.0 | | |
| 17. Nagaland | 5000 | | | |
| 18. Orissa | 5343 | 11.5 | 14.0 | – |
| 19. Punjab | 1108 | 1.2 | 92.8 | 9.8 |
| 20. Rajasthan | 3680 | 5.0 | 31.0 | 8.8 |
| 21. Sikkim | 1920 | 3.2 | – | – |
| 22. Tamil Nadu | 3837 | 1.3 | 32.8 | 15.4 |
| 23. Tripura | 2621 | 1.0 | | |
| 24. Uttar Pradesh | 1230 | 1.5 | 82.6 | 14.2 |
| 25. West Bengal | 11945 | 11.5 | 9.8 | 22.6 |
| 26. A & N Islands | 2318 | 4.2 | | |
| 27. Chandigarh | 1381 | 1.0 | 21.0 | 1.0 |
| 28. D & N Haveli | 10300 | 7.2 | | |
| 29. Delhi | 2366 | 1.4 | | |
| 30. Daman & Diu | 3724 | 2.4 | | |
| 31. Lakshadweep | Traditional system exists. | | | |
| 32. Pondicherry | There are only commune panchayats at block level. | | | |

Source: *Panchayati Raj Institutions in India*, Ministry of Rural Development, 1991.

Advisory Council to the Prime Minister presented its 'Report on Decentralisation of Development Planning and Implementation in the States'. The latest in the series of such reports was that of the Working Group on District Planning, submitted to the Planning Commission in 1984, which formed the basis of the Seventh Plan proposals on decentralised planning.

According to noted economist C.H. Hanumantha Rao, 'barring a few exceptions, the performance in respect of decentralised planning has been dismal.'[14] Rao lists three main reasons for this: political and bureaucratic resistance at the state level to sharing power with the local level institutions. The political–bureaucratic nexus not only did not share power, they did not share resources and prevented planning from below. Secondly, given that the rural elite often dominates PRIs and appropriates a major share of benefits from development, those who view decentralised planning as a means for improving the socio–economic condition of the weaker sections are sceptical about its prospects unless structural changes are brought about to ensure the rise of the rural poor to a position of dominance in these institutions. Thirdly, the lack of political will is equally responsible for the failure of decentralised planning.

In addition to statutory provisions, Rao suggests five major areas of action that would make decentralised planning effective. These are: (*i*) suitable modifications in the centrally sponsored schemes so as to impart greater flexibility to local level planning; (*ii*) measures for planning at the regional level, particularly in the bigger states; (*iii*) electoral reforms to ensure adequate representation for the poor in the local level institutions; (*iv*) structural changes to release the initiative of the rural poor by freeing them from various forms of socio-economic exploitation; and (*v*) strategies to ensure people's participation, which would, among other things, involve voluntary organisations.

The Constitutional Amendment Bill goes a long way in meeting some of these. But the excellent results achieved in states like West Bengal must be published and publicised so that they may serve as models for the rest of the country.

## Why have Panchayats not been Successful?

Why has the panchayati raj system not been successful in India? It is well known that panchayats have not blossomed into 'units of self-government'. Of course, their resources have been meagre. But that could have been set right had there been adequate political will. The critical problem is the domination of the PRIs by the economic and socially privileged classes. This is essentially a socio-political problem and could have been tackled to a great extent by holding elections at regular intervals. The resulting political education of communities who have been oppressed for ages would certainly have changed matters significantly. But panchayats were left to the mercy of states, who thought it expedient not to hold elections to local bodies. For instance, in Tamil Nadu elections to local bodies were held in 1986 after a lapse of 16 years! In 1985; the Committee set up by the Planning Commission under the chairmanship of G.V.K. Rao, said in its report:

> Apart from inadequate resources, elections to these bodies have not been held regularly. In fact, elections have become overdue for one or more tiers of the Panchayati Raj Institutions in 11 States and in 8 States even elections to Gram Panchayats are overdue. Elections have been put off on one pretext or another . . . and the term of the existing bodies has been extended or the bodies have been superseded.[15]

Evidence suggests that there has been a deliberate attempt on the part of the bureaucracy, local vested interests and their elected representatives in the state legislatures and in Parliament to cripple and eventually discard panchayati raj, the ascendancy of which they fear.

In 1966–67 the Ministry of Community Development was reduced to the status of a Department and brought under the Ministry of Food and Agriculture. In 1971, the very title 'Community Development' was dropped and replaced by 'Rural Development'. According to L.C. Jain, 'This was not just a cosmetic change. It marked the end of both the "community" and "Panchayats" as agents of change and agencies of development.'[16] It should be emphasised here that all the development programmes became bureaucracy–centred with hardly any element of participation by the people. Thus the bureaucracy gained the upper hand in a grand alliance with the state and central level political elite. The role of the bureaucracy in bringing PR to its present plight was sharply brought out by the Ashok Mehta Committee in its report.

This has not been the experience just of independent India. As pointed out earlier, Lord Ripon made an earnest effort to introduce local self-government, but failed. Why? The Indian Statutory Commission of 1929 had stated that whatever self-government might have been at that time, it was not free from *official control* and 'no real attempt was made to inaugurate a system amenable to the will of the local inhabitants'.

Why did the political elite dance to the tune of the bureaucracy? The reason is not far to seek. No politician would care to see his power base eroded by a breed of new local leadership. It is thus reasonable to conclude that the bureaucracy, commercial interests, the professional middle class, the police and the political elite colluded with each other against democratic decentralisation. A thesis was developed and popularised by these vested interests that a centralised bureaucracy could benefit the rural poor better than local elected 'vested interests'. The result was that we ended up creating an impregnable alliance of urban officialdom and the rural rich which excluded the rural poor.

By the second half of the 1980s, at least a few at the helm of affairs in the ruling party at the centre began to realise the evil ramifications of concentrating power. The political and social implications of centralised power were becoming transparent. On the economic front, for instance, former Prime Minister Rajiv Gandhi had to admit that out of every rupee earmarked for development, only 15 paise reached the target group. Without the proper functioning of local bodies, the growing frustration of the people could not be stemmed.

## Conclusion

The basic problem of Indian democracy has been its inability to provide the local self-government system with a firm base. Not only was the concept of local governance not allowed to take root, the very idea of panchayati raj was denigrated. It is heartening to know that both the people and the politicians have finally begun to realise the folly of this neglect and subversion and that concrete measures are being taken to give PRIs constitutional status. Of course, by itself, no constitutional amendment will be able to bring about a meaningful devolution of power or vibrant panchayats. Without land reforms and universal education, panchayati raj in India will end up becoming an instrument of oppression in the hands of landlords, the dominant castes and the rich. Therefore, the central and state governments must simultaneously and determinedly take steps to implement land reforms and universal education. Only a strong political will can usher in real panchayati raj. In the last few years state governments have realised that panchayats are a *sine qua non* for people's participation in their development and their prosperity. Success stories of panchayats in West Bengal, Karnataka and some other states have been talked about across the country. The demand for panchayats has been gathering momentum and has taken on the force of a people's movement. The constitutional status accorded to panchayats can turn PR into a success story only with a strong people's movement to give it the necessary momentum.

## Notes

1. *Imperial Gazetteer of India*, 1909, Vol. IV, pp. 278–79.
2. The eight provinces in British India which passes Acts for the establishment of village panchayats were: Madras (Panchayat Act of 1920); Bombay (Village Panchayat Act of 1920); Bengal (Self-Government Act of 1919); Bihar (Self-Government Act of 1920); Central Provinces and Berar (Panchayat Act of 1920); I.P. (Village Panchayat Act of 1920); Punjab (Panchayat Act of 1922); and Assam (Self-Government Act of 1925).
3. A Quarterly of Local Self-Government Institute, Bombay. No. 128, pp. 452–53. According to this quarterly, the native state enacted legislations were:

   (*i*) Cochin Panchayats Regulations Act, 1919.
   (*ii*) Holkar State Panchayat Act, 1920.
   (*iii*) Travancore Village Panchayat Act, 1925.
   (*iv*) Baroda Village Panchayat Act, 1925.
   (*v*) Kolhapur Panchayat Act, 1926.
   (*vi*) Mysore Village Panchayat Act, 1926.
   (*vii*) Bikaner Village Panchayat Act, 1928.

(*viii*) Karauli Village Panchayat Act, 1939.

(*ix*) Hyderabad Village Panchayat Act, 1940.

(*x*) Mewar Gram Panchayat Act, 1939.

(*xi*) Jasdan Village Panchayat Act, 1942.

(*xii*) Bhavnagar Village Panchayat Act, 1943.

(*xiii*) Porbandar Village Panchayat Act, 1943.

(*xiv*) Bharatpur Village Panchayat Act, 1944.

(*xv*) Marwar Gram Panchayat Act, 1945.

(*xvi*) Wadia State Village Panchayat Act, 1946.

(*xvii*) Dharangadhara State Village Panchayat Act, 1946.

(*xviii*) Morvi State Village Panchayat Act, 1946.

(*xix*) Sirohi Village Panchayat Act, 1947.

(*xx*) Jaipur Village Panchayat Act, 1948.

4. *A Study of Panchayat Government of India*, May 1958.

5. The Team for the Study of Community Projects and National Extension Service was constituted under the Committee on Plan Projects (popularly known as the Balwantrai Mehta Committee) in 1959. The recommendations of the Committee for Democratic Decentralisation Through Setting Up of PRIs accelerated the pace of constituting PRIs in all states through Panchayat Acts.

6. Quoted in the report of the Committee on Administrative Arrangements for Rural Development (CAARD), Department of Rural Development, Ministry of Agriculture, December 1985.

7. Subrahmanyam, K. 1989. 'Panchayat Reform: A Few Pitfalls Can Be Avoided', *The Hindustan Times*, 18 May.

8. Jayaprakash Narayan. 1961. *Swaraj for the People*. Akhil Bharat Sarva Seva Sangh, Rajghat, Varanasi.

9. S.K. Dey, 1960. *Community Development: A Movement is Born*. Kitab Mahal, Allahabad, p. 173.

10. Quoted in Mats Kihlbers, *The Panchayati Raj of India*, New Delhi.

11. George Mathew. 1987. 'Panchayat Poll in Karnataka', *The Hindustan Times*, 9 February.

12. D.T. Lakdawala. 1986. 'Decentralisation of Economic Power' in *Panchayati Raj in Karnataka Today: Its National Dimensions*. Concept Publishing Co., New Delhi. pp. 26–31.

13. Ibid. p. 27. 1989.

14. C.H. Hanumantha Rao. 1989. 'Decentralised Planning: An Overview of Experience and Prospects', *Economic and Political Weekly*, 25 February, p. 411.

15. Report of the Committee to Review the Existing Administrative Arrangement for Rural Development and Poverty Alleviation Programme (CAARD). 1985. Planning Commission, Government of India, New Delhi. p. 143.

16. L.C. Jain et al., 1985. *Grass Without Roots*. Sage Publications, New Delhi. p. 44.

# 8

# Power to the People: The Karnataka Experiment

ABDUL AZIZ
CHARLES NELSON
DEVENDRA BABU

Decentralised governance derives its rationale from the fact that it gives power to the people and ensures their participation in decision-making. As people's participation is enlisted under this system, not only is decision-making attuned to resolving local problems but the implementation of such decisions becomes more effective. However, the extent to which the fruits of decentralised governance are realised depends upon the nature of the politico–administrative institutions created, the extent of power and finances delegated to local governments, the pattern of power distribution among different interest groups of the rural society, and people's perceptions about decentralised governance. While addressing the broader issue of the performance of decentralised governments, this paper seeks to relate it to the very nature and structure of the basic tier of decentralised governments in Karnataka: the mandal panchayats. More specifically, the objectives of this paper are to sketch the nature and structure of mandal panchayats and assess the extent of power delegation and its distribution; evaluate the performance of mandal panchayats; and suggest future courses of action for improving the system of decentralised governance.

The paper is based on field data collected from selected mandal panchayats in Kolar and Mysore districts. From each district two mandal panchayats were selected on the basis of their distance from district headquarters—one is very close to and one very far away from district headquarters and situated in the interior. Data were collected using two schedules—one for collecting quantitative information about the mandal society, economy and polity, and one for interviewing official and non-official members, and selected citizens of the mandal panchayats under study. What follows is an account of the preliminary results of an ongoing survey on the subject.

### The Study Region: The Economy, Polity and Society

The state of Karnataka came into being in 1956 following the reorganisation of states on a linguistic basis. To the erstwhile princely state of Mysore was added the Coorg state and the Kannada (the state language) speaking areas from the former Bombay and Madras presidencies, and the princely Hyderabad state to form what is present-day Karnataka. With 20 administrative districts, Karnataka has a population of 44.8 million (1991). It is one of the largest Indian states accounting for 5.31 per cent of the population and 5.83 per cent of the country's area, and ranks eighth in population and area. With rich mineral deposits (gold, iron ore, manganese, copper, bauxite, zinc), surplus electric power (although not any longer), and a good measure of infrastructure, the state attracted private industrial capital and union government undertakings. Its vast number of skilled farmers promoted agriculture, horticulture and animal husbandry in the rural areas. The people of Karnataka largely comprise Scheduled Castes and Tribes (SCs and STs), minorities, dominant caste groups like the Lingayats and Vokkaligas, backward classes and upper castes, making it a pluralistic society like other parts of India. With 28.9 per cent urban and 56 per cent literate population (against 52 per cent in the country), Karnataka can be regarded as a typical state of the Indian subcontinent.

Except for 1983–88, when the Janata Party ruled the state, Karnataka has been returning the Congress Party to power. Up to 1956, the state government was controlled by the Vokkaligas; in 1956 power passed into the hands of Lingayats who ruled the state until 1971 when it was taken over by non-dominant caste groups.

Since 1971, state power has been in the hands of the so-called backward classes except during 1990 when it was captured by the dominant caste groups for a brief period.

Like other states in the country, Karnataka too has its share of political parties who vie with each other in a bid to claim power. But it is either the Congress Party or the Janata Party (consisting largely of ex-Congressmen) which has generally succeeded in capturing it. The left, communal, linguistic/region based political parties have also been in the fray, but they never managed to acquire any significant power base.

## The Mandal Panchayat System

With the passing of the Karnataka Zilla Parishads, Taluk Panchayat Samithis, Mandal Panchayats and Nyaya Panchayats Act in July 1985, the earlier three-tier panchayati raj (PR) institution structure comprising the district development council, the taluk development board and the village panchayat was replaced by a new system consisting of the zilla parishad, the taluk samithi and the mandal panchayat (Government of Karnataka, 1989). Figure 8.1 illustrates the place of mandal panchayats in the system of decentralised governments created under the Act referred to above.

The mandal panchayat (MP) is the first elected tier of the panchayati raj system comprising a cluster of villages with populations of between 8,000 and 12,000, with an elected people's representative for every 400 population. There are a total of over 2,500 mandals in the state for which over 55,000 members are elected. There is a provision according to which 25 per cent of the mandal panchayat seats are to be reserved for women and 18 per cent for SCs and STs. Wherever members of the backward communities are not elected to the MP, the zilla parishad (ZP) nominates two persons representing the backward classes. A pradhan and a up-apradhan are elected from amongst the members to preside over the meetings of the MP. The panchayat secretary, who is assisted by bill collectors, is the administrative head of the mandal panchayat.

The functional areas assigned to MP relate to sanitation and health, public works and amenities, agriculture and animal

**CHART 8.1:** NEW DECENTRALISED GOVERNMENTS

---

ZILA PARISHAD

---

| People's Government | Development Administration |
|---|---|
| Adhyaksha | |
| Upadhyaksha | |
| Elected Members and Ex-officio Members | Chief Secretary |

| Deputy Secretaries | Chief Accounts Officer | Chief Planning Officer |
|---|---|---|

---

TALUK PANCHAYAT SAMITHI

---

| Chairman | Block Development Officer |
|---|---|
| Ex-Officio Members | |

---

MANDAL PANCHAYAT

---

| Pradhan | Secretary |
|---|---|
| Upapradhan | |
| Elected Members | |

---

GRAM SABHA
College of Eligible Voters

husbandry and the welfare of SCs and STs and backward classes.
The MPs are expected to prepare plans for the development of the
mandal areas, maintain records relating to the survey of village
sites, public and private properties and organise and mobilise the
village youth for constructive and productive purposes.

The mandal panchayat is expected to build a fund from out of
which expenses are to be met. This fund is to comprise of amounts
allotted by the ZP, grants from the state government and its
agencies, proceeds from the sale of dust, dirt, dung etc, income
from its property, proceeds from taxes on entertainment, vehicles
other than motor vehicles, mineral rights, water rates, and fees on
markets, bus stands and MP grazing lands etc.

For its functioning, the MP is expected to get feedback from the
gram sabha. The gram sabha (village council), which is the basic
tier of the PR system, comprises of all eligible voters i.e. persons
above the age of 18 years of the village in question. Each of the

over 27,000 villages in the state has a village council which is required to meet not less than twice a year to (*a*) discuss and review all development problems and programmes of the village, (*b*) select beneficiaries for the beneficiary-oriented programmes, and (*c*) plan for the development of the village economy and its people, which includes minimum needs, welfare and production-oriented programmes. Apart from the voters, the meeting is attended by people's representatives, government officers and officers from the bank which provides loan assistance to beneficiaries under various government schemes. Thus, though the people's representatives voice their needs and aspirations in the mandal panchayat, it is the gram sabha that actually provides the basic mechanism for people to directly participate in decision-making.

The taluk panchayat samithi, which comprises of ex-officio members such as all the pradhans of mandal panchayats in the taluk, all MLAs, MLCs and ZP members representing the taluk, and the five co-opted members, representing SCs and STs, backward classes and women, is a purely advisory and coordinatory body—advising on and coordinating the activities of mandal panchayats.

The zilla parishad (ZP), which is the second directly elected tier of the PR system and is constituted at the district level, is expected to supervise, coordinate and integrate development schemes at the taluk and district levels and to prepare and implement district development plans. It has elected members with reservations for women, and SC and ST population who in turn elect a president and a vice-president for carrying out the ZP functions under their supervision and control. The chief secretary is the administrative head of ZP and he is assisted by administrative and technical personnel.

## Power Structure

A long-standing criticism of the local governments is that their power structure is weighted in favour of the stronger sections of the society—meaning that these bodies are dominated by landlords and members of the upper castes and dominant communities. To meet this criticism, as it were, the recent legislation on the PR system in Karnataka provided opportunities for the weaker sections such as the SCs and STs, backward classes and women to enter the PR bodies through reservation. The new PR bodies are therefore expected to be more representative in the sense that their membership would be fairly distributed among all sections of the society.

Available data for all mandal panchayats in the state show that on the whole, women members (25.4 per cent) slightly exceed their quota of 25 per cent. SC and ST male and female members together account for 26.2 per cent as against their reserved quota of 18 per cent (Department of Rural Development, Government of Karnataka). Data relating to mandals under our study present an even better picture in the sense that the share of women (25.5 per cent) and SCs and STs (36.2 per cent) is quite high (Table 8.1).

Thanks to the policy of reservation, women and members of SCs and STs have entered local governments in a big way, both accounting for well over half the MP membership. This is a welcome development considering that these sections had hitherto not enjoyed access to local governments, at least to this extent. However, a point to be noted is that the dominant castes—the Vokkaligas and the Lingayats—have managed to capture the office of pradhan in all the mandals under study; in two out of four MPs, Vokkaligas function as upapradhans. Though it is not correct to generalise from the experience of four MPs, it appears that even though the presence of dominant community members has reduced, the key positions still remain with them. This means that the PR bodies in rural Karnataka continue to reflect the same dominant caste-oriented power structure that prevailed earlier, and that though the reservation principle provided the socially backward communities access to PR bodies, it did not give them access to positions of power.

### Political Autonomy

The nature of power structure apart, the degree of political autonomy enjoyed by the decentralised governments can also influence the manner of their functioning. It may be stated that under the Act, mandal panchayats are independent political units in the federal structure of decentralised governments subject, of course, to final control by the state government. They enjoy a good deal of autonomy in respect of day-to-day functioning. But an irritant

**Table 8.1: Percentage Distribution of Mandal Panchayat Members by Caste and Sex**

| Name of mandal panchayat | Vokkaliga | | Lingayat | | Minorities | | SC/ST | | Others | | Total | | Caste of Pradhan | Caste of Upa-pradhan |
|---|---|---|---|---|---|---|---|---|---|---|---|---|---|---|
| | M | F | M | F | M | F | M | F | M | F | M | F | | |
| Hunasenahalli | 6.9 | 6.9 | 3.4 | – | – | – | 37.9 | 10.3 | 27.6 | 6.9 | 75.9 | 24.1 | V* | SC* |
| Julapalya | 26.1 | 8.7 | 4.3 | – | – | – | 26.1 | 4.3 | 21.7 | 8.7 | 78.3 | 21.7 | V* | V* |
| Hinkal | 34.6 | 15.4 | – | – | – | – | 19.2 | 7.7 | 19.2 | 3.8 | 73.1 | 26.9 | U*1 V*2 | V* |
| N. Belthur | 4.2 | 4.2 | 4.2 | – | 4.2 | 4.2 | 29.1 | 8.3 | 29.1 | 12.5 | 70.8 | 29.2 | L* | N* |
| | 17.6 | 8.8 | 3.0 | – | 1.0 | 1.0 | 28.4 | 7.8 | 24.5 | 7.8 | 74.5 | 25.5 | | |

Note:  V – Vokkaliga
SC – Scheduled Caste
L – Lingayat
N – Nair
U – Urs
1 – First half of the term
2 – Second half of the term

which can surface any time is the dubious practice on the part of the state government to exercise its power of supersession. Thus, in the present case, the first five-year term of the MPs expired in January 1992 but instead of holding elections, the state government placed these bodies under the charge of administrators. The elections to these bodies were held after a lapse of some time, that is, December 1993, but not before the state government amended the Panchayati Raj Act. Among other things the amended Act replaced the mandal panchayat by a smaller unit of 5,000 to 7,000 population called the gram panchayat. The tendency on the part of every new government to design and redesign the size and structure of the decentralised government bodies speaks volumes about the political autonomy ensured to them.

## Performance of the Mandal Panchayats

In principle, mandal panchayats are expected to identify and articulate the needs and aspirations of the people, formulate projects on the basis of these needs and implement them. In doing this, they are expected to involve people and non-government organisations, and take decisions in the highest tradition of democracy. The following pages present an account of the MP planning process and its outcome.

### Planning Process

The MP planning process is expected to follow a set procedure. Towards the end of July every year the State Planning Department indicates to ZPs and MPs the financial ceilings within which their annual plan should be formulated for the following year. Having received this information, the mandal panchayat issues notices and distributes pamphlets about the impending biannual meeting of eligible voters, indicating the date, time and venue of the gram sabha meeting. Apart from the voters, the MP functionaries and people's representatives, the bank and block development officers, the MLA and the ZP member of that region are also expected to attend the meeting. It has been found that in the first two years gram sabha meetings were held regularly, but in due course their number and that of villages where the meetings were held gradually declined. In fact, it is reported that in 1992 hardly any gram sabha meetings were held in the mandals under study.

Where, however, meetings *were* held, attendance was not very high. Interviews with MP members and select citizens reveal that only 10 to 15 per cent of the citizens assembled in such meetings. Of those who assembled, only a few participated in discussion; most of those who spoke happened to be either informal leaders, or were very close to the mandal members, or had the opportunity to visit the mandal headquarters and taluk headquarters frequently. Participation by women citizens was found to be minimal, as indeed was their presence in the meetings.

Suggestions from the citizens in the gram sabha relate mostly to location of amenities, and grant of loans, house sites, houses and lighting. The community amenities sought are health centres, drinking water, drainage, road construction and repairs. Besides this, prospective beneficiaries under the Indian Rural Development Programme (IRDP), Jawahar Rojgar Yojana (JRY) and mandal panchayat programmes are identified in consulation with the citizens.

The development programmes for the villages and beneficiaries identified in the gram sabhas are listed and the consolidated list of projects and beneficiaries is discussed in the MP meeting. Since the number of projects suggested by the people and the names of the beneficiaries identified in gram sabha meetings is generally very large, a process of sifting and choosing takes place in the MP meeting. Thus MP members can commit themselves to only a few projects and beneficiaries. This leads to complaints of favouritism and negligence being levelled against MPs. To avoid this situation, the MPs have effected a compromise by (*a*) giving some project or the other to each village in the current year and deferring others to a future date and (*b*) allotting a quota of beneficiaries to each member so that conflict and acrimony are reduced to the minimum. While this method may not conform to the accepted norms of project identification, the MP functionaries and members argue that this is the best way of meeting people's needs and aspirations considering the fact that the whole exercise has to be carried out within the framework of a political process. They argue that this process is also the best means of conflict resolution.

Conflict normally occurs either between spatial groups, i.e. members divided on the basis of the villages they hail from, or between economic classes like landed interests and weaker sections or even between the dominant caste and backward caste members.

Where decisions regarding the identification of projects and their location are concerned, the mandal panchayats are guided by the principle of urgency and necessity of the service required. For example, wherever the question of choosing between two projects like drainage and water supply arose, the latter was invariably selected because water rather than drainage was perceived to be the more important need of the people. Also water supply has a better reach to the people than drainage, which may be restricted to a particular ward of the village. Therefore, it was good logic to put the water supply project on the priority scale.

This process of identifying projects and their location is considered by MP members to be far superior to what obtained earlier when, under the taluk development board system, the decision was mainly influenced by one individual, i.e. the local MLA. It is pointed out that more often than not, the MLA would take almost all the projects to his own or the villages of his close associates and hangers-on. As a result, projects were not equitably distributed across villages or regions of the taluk. In the present system which allocates some project or the other to each of mandal panchayat member, there is wider dispersal of projects which in fact meets the equity criterion. Whether this also meets the economic and technical criteria is, however, a different question. But so long as this practice is followed in a democratic framework and in the spirit of give and take, perhaps the purpose of decentralised governance is served.

From the list of projects taken up and completed by the MPs (Table 8.2), it can be seen that both community amenities such as roads, drainage, water supply, school and anganwadi buildings, street lights and bus shelters, as well as group specific projects like house sites, houses, electric light connections under Bhagya Jyothi and Mandal Jyothi schemes have figured in all the mandals. In the list of projects either proposed or deferred, slightly higher level community amenities such as health centres, youth centres, veterinary hospital buildings and asphalting of roads figure prominently. If the projects taken up by the MPs under study are juxtaposed with the functional areas assigned to them, it is clear

**Table 8.2: Projects Completed and Projects Proposed (Deferred) to be Taken up in the Mandal Panchayats, 1987–1992.**

| Name of Mandal Panchayat | Projects Completed | Projects Proposed |
|---|---|---|
| Hunasenahalli | Construction of houses, roads, school and anganwadi buildings, drainage, piped water supply, Bhagya Jyothi lighting, street lighting. | Primary health center and veterinary hospital buildings, group houses, youth centres, water tank, and drainage. |
| Julapalya | Construction of houses, school building, roads, irrigation tank, bus stand, pitching works, free sites, street lights, water supply, drainage, Bhagya Jyothi lights. | Public latrine, MP building, temple building repair, house sites for poor, road repairs, drainage. |
| Hinkal | Piped water supply, drainage, toilets, road repairs and asphalting, houses under JRY and Nazeer Awas schemes, free sites, bus stand, school buildings, anganwadi building Bhagya Jyothi, Mandal Jyothi, repair of Ram Mandir, street lights. | Water tanks, group houses, asphalting roads, health centre, street lights, road construction, drainage. |
| N. Belthur | Water supply, street lights, drainage, school building, road repairs, street lights. | Water supply, asphalting roads, houses to poor. |

that they have concentrated on amenities and public work-oriented projects and neglected production-oriented projects such as those in respect of agriculture, animal husbandry and fisheries. Table 8.3, which presents the expenditure pattern of the MPs (consolidated figures for five years), brings out this point more sharply. It is evident that if we leave out expenditure in respect of salaries etc., almost the whole of the MP resources was devoted to projects related to amenities and public works. Only in the case of Hunasenahalli, a fraction was devoted to developing fish seedlings. But otherwise, spending on agriculture and animal husbandry—the mainstay of the rural economy—is zero.

**Table 8.3: The Expenditure Pattern of Mandal Panchayats under Study, 1987–1992**

| Items of Expenditure | Hunasenahalli | Julapalya | Hinkal | N. Belthur |
|---|---|---|---|---|
| Civic Amenities | 5,21,498.98 (64.71) | 2,86,704.38 (59.89) | 21,57,700.86 (17.22) | 2,72,100.00 (22.57) |
| Public works | 42,682.00 (5.30) | 61,239.00 (12.79) | 82,21,941.53 (65.61) | 4,84,100.00 (40.15) |
| Works under 20% program | 8,820.00 (1.09) | 3,000.00 (0.63) | – | 2,13,600.00 (17.72) |
| Fish seedling | 15,772.00 (1.96) | – | – | – |
| Staff salary, stationery, furniture, etc. | 1,72,323.95 (21.38) | 1,000.67 (20.90) | 18,17,374.23 (14.50) | 1,40,020.00 (11.61) |
| National festivals and sports | 7,841.00 (0.97) | 1,900.00 (0.40) | – | 500.00 (0.04) |
| N.S.C., IVP, miscellaneous | 37,015.00 (4.59) | 25,782.40 (5.39) | 3,34,365.24 (2.67) | 95,360.00 (7.91) |
| Total | 8,05,952.93 | 3,79,626.45 | 1,25,31,381.86 | 12,05,680.00 |

Note: Figures in parentheses are percentages.

**Table 8.4: Income Pattern of Mandal Panchayats under Study 1987–1992 (in Rs.)**

| Items of Income | Hunasenahalli | Julapalya | Hinkal | N. Belthur* |
|---|---|---|---|---|
| Taxes and rates | 1,81,635.01 | 79,699.65 | 62,37,544.52 | 2,56,000.00 |
| | (20.46) | (15.18) | (59.89) | (21.50) |
| Non-tax revenue | 26,950.00 | 10,933.00 | 22,36,591.50 | 2,52,500.00 |
| | (3.04) | (2.08) | (21.47) | (21.21) |
| Grants | 6,46,237.65 | 3,68,759.26 | 12,76,981.35 | 4,84,152.00 |
| | (72.79) | (70.25) | (12.26) | (40.66) |
| Miscellaneous such as deposits, balances, etc. | 32,971.97 | 65,540.00 | 6,64,445.44 | 1,98,000.00 |
| | (3.71) | (12.49) | (6.38) | (16.63) |
| Total | 8,87,794.63 | 5,24,931.91 | 1,04,15,562.81 | 11,90,652.00 |
| | (100.00) | (100.00) | (100.00) | (100.00) |

**Note:** Figures in parentheses are percentages.
* Data for this Mandal relates only to 4 years.

What are the possible reasons for this pattern of resource allocation? Our discussion with the official and non-official members
brings out the following points:

(a) The extremely important nature of production-oriented projects in the micro plan has not been realised and appreciated
by them. This is so partly because the feedback from the
people has been such that almost everybody who registered
his needs and aspirations invariably preferred amenities
and public works. Hardly anyone suggested a community
project that would strengthen agriculture and animal husbandry.

(b) The limited nature of mandal resources on the one hand,
and the long list of projects that would meet the basic needs
of the people on the other, is another important point to
reckon with. In view of the dilemma of limited resources,
even those members who appreciated the importance of
production-oriented projects had to change their stand.

Income constraint has been a major problem with mandal panchayats. From Table 8.4, which presents the mandal income
aggregated for five years, it is evident that only two mandals cross
the one million rupee mark. Leaving out of account the exceptionally rich mandal—Hinkal—which is situated in an industrially rich
belt, the annual average income of the remaining mandals is about
Rs. 180,000. On the assumption that the average population size
of a mandal is 12,000, this income provides an annual per capita
resource of Rs. 15. Of this, Rs. 10 is a per capita grant received
from the zilla parishad and the balance of Rs. 5 (which is a third of
the total resource) is obtained by way of tax and non-tax revenue.
The agony of functioning with such meager resources perhaps
prompted the mandal panchayats to submit memoranda to the
State Finance Commission requesting an enhancement of assistance
from the state by way of a share in state tax revenue and an
increase in grants-in-aid. Though the State Finance Commission
has in its report recommended enhancement of state assistance,
the Karnataka government is yet to act on this recommendation.

## The Village Community and Economic Development

In the system of decentralised governance envisaged, the mandal panchayat has been conceived as an agent of initiating and promoting village community and economic development. As part of shouldering this responsibility, the MP is expected to mobilise financial and human resources, build development-oriented infrastructure, take up production-oriented projects in the agriculture, animal husbandry, forestry and fisheries sectors, and provide amenities such as street lights, drainage, drinking water, health and education facilities. An unwritten responsibility of the MPs, implied in the directive that people should be involved in decision-making, is one of inspiring people, by its own example, to develop an interest in and awareness about decentralised governance. What is the role of MPs in these spheres? From the analysis of the planning process presented in earlier paragraphs, the following implications to village community and economic development may be drawn:

1. During their first term, the MPs established a good record in respect of provision of village amenities such as drinking water supply, street lights, bus shelters, school and anganwadi buildings, drainage, street pitchings, roads and culverts. What is more important, some of these amenities, particularly drainage and street pitchings, have been provided in colonies where the weaker sections (SCs and STs) live. In addition, free electric lighting connections (under the Mandal Jyothi Scheme) are provided to these sections. The special attention bestowed on the weaker sections has undoubtedly improved their living conditions which, in turn, has gone to improve their social status.

2. Apart from promoting social development, amenities also help promote development of the village economy. However, it cannot be denied that measures which promote development more quickly are production-oriented projects that directly strengthen agriculture and non-agricultural activities. It is in this sphere that the mandal panchayats have faulted. It has already been pointed out that production-oriented projects have not received the attention they deserve. We would like to add here that while some MPs have taken up social forestry projects, this has been under the

Jawahar Rozgar Yojana which is sponsored by the union government. The MPs own resources are not involved. It is thus reasonable to assume that mandal panchayats still have a long way to go in initiating and supporting the development of the village economy.

3. The picture that emerges vis-a-vis the role of mandals in inspiring people to develop an interest in and awareness about decentralised governance, is also not very encouraging. The following account of people's perception and awareness regarding decentralised system of governance bears testimony to this.

Generally speaking, in the interior village women, SCs and STs did not know who the pradhan and the upapradhan of the mandal panchayat were. In villages which are far off from the MP headquarters, some citizens did not know where the MP office was located.

Not many villagers knew about the functions of the MP but those of the small number of persons who did, mentioned that it was supposed to improve the condition of the village economy. While many were not sure about the rationale of decentralised bodies, the more knowledgeable ones felt that they were meant to inculcate the democratic spirit among people. It is in this perspective they perceived the importance of the MPs in the polity.

A large number of citizens recalled the names of the major political parties which fought MP elections but only a few could mention the names of the individuals who contested elections from their village. A large number of respondents voted in the elections. Minorities, SCs and STs admitted that they voted on a party basis; the dominant communities said they voted on the basis of the qualification of the individual, irrespective of his party affiliation. Women also exercised their franchise but many of them admitted that they voted on instructions from their husbands and for a candidate of latter's choice. The majority of respondents approved the reservation of membership for women, SCs and STs but felt that the proportion should be smaller. Those who opposed the idea of reservation for women, did so on the ground that women would be ineffective as mandal members!

The mandals are expected to mobilise voluntary labour and other resources for implementing community development projects in the areas of their jurisdiction. None of the mandals under study had done so and none of the citizens who were interviewed had contributed anything to the mandal fund. The explanation offered for this by official and non-official members is disturbing. They stated that in recent years, the people have got used to getting financial and other help from government and non-government bodies, so much that they found the idea of making contributions to these bodies quite alien!

## Some Suggestions

The analysis of the working of decentralised governance in Karnataka shows that:

1. The decentralised politico–administrative structures and participatory mechanism created are appropriate for people's participation in decision-making.
2. Though reservation of seats for women and socially backward classes has given them access to the mandal governments, the same dominant community-oriented power structure that obtains in rural Karnataka seems to prevail in the mandal governments too.
3. The political autonomy enjoyed by the mandal panchayats leaves much to be desired.
4. Financial inadequacy is another constraint under which the mandal panchayats have to work.
5. Community development projects have received utmost attention which helped promote social development among weaker sections.
6. Production-oriented projects have received the least attention. As a result, the contribution of MPs to the development of the village economy is minimal.
7. The degree of awareness about the mandal panchayat system is very low, especially among women, SCs and STs, and among those in the interior regions.
8. The perception of people about the utility of decentralised governance needs to be sharpened.

In view of these findings, the following suggestions for strengthening decentralised governments may be considered:

1. The offices of the pradhan and upapradhan should also be brought under reservation on the same pattern as mandal panchayat membership. This is one way of regulating the skewed pattern of power structure in rural government.
2. Holding elections to these bodies regularly and restricting the state's power to supersede these bodies will allow them greater political autonomy.
3. The state should allocate more grants of an untied nature and share tax revenues with the mandal panchayats so that the latter can enjoy financial autonomy and also have adequate funds for development projects.
4. The mandal members and functionaries should be educated to take up production-oriented projects. Perhaps spending a specified proportion on these types of projects of mandal income should be made mandatory.
5. People should be educated about the nature and purpose of decentralised governance through various media. They should also be made aware of the desirability of such a system for resolving local problems and promoting local development.

# 9

# Decentralisation and Local Self-governments in Nepal: An Overview

## SOORYA L. AMATYA

## Historical Account and the Present Political Context

Prior to the formation of the present Nepal in 1770s, the country was made up of tiny states. Even in the Kathmandu valley, there were as many as four small kingdoms. As such, decentralisation of authority was not a matter of concern in the past. With the unification of the country in 1772 the political and administrative power became centralised and with the autocratic rule of the Rana family since 1846, it became highly concentrated. The country was divided into four regions and 35 districts. The four regions were administered by the commanding Rana Generals and the 35 districts by Bada Hakims. They had absolute power and were directly accountable to the Rana Prime Minister.

The Rana regime was overthrown in 1951 and some changes were recorded in the autocratic framework of administration. The first effort was to promote rural development through the tribhuvan village development programme. This was basically a community development approach designed on the Indian model with a hierarchy of institutions at village, block and district levels. The programme was supported jointly by India and the United States of America. The philosophy of the programme was to help the village development workers in their task of mobilising the local community to participate in self-help projects. But in practice, it was heavily focused towards technical diffusion. There was little of people's participation and the programme had limited spatial coverage. However, it created a need for decentralisation of political and administrative powers for accelerating economic development in the country. In 1962, the district organisation committee was constituted. On the basis of its recommendations, the district administration was reorganised and the country was divided into 14 zones and 75 districts. For a number of years in the past, the chief district officers had dual responsibilities of maintaining law and order, and supervising the implementation of development programmes in the district. Later, in 1971, the post of local development officers (LDOs) was created with the main responsibilities of supervising and coordinating development programmes in the district.

A number of commissions and committees were constituted to evolve political and administrative decentralisation.

1. The Administrative Decentralisation Committee was constituted under the chairmanship of Bishow Bandhu Thapa in 1963. On the basis of field studies and observations, the committee presented a comprehensive decentralisation report which strongly recommended that district panchayats be empowered to formulate and execute development programmes with local resources. The report also emphasised training the district level political leaders (panchas) in the process of planning and the exercise of authority.
2. A Decentralisation Committee was constituted in 1967 under the chairmanship of Bhoj Raj Chimire to critically assess the report submitted by Thapa's commission. It recommended gradual implementation of the decentralisation scheme.
3. The Administration Reform Commission constituted in 1968 also emphasized the need for decentralisation of administrative power.
4. The Administration Decentralisation Commission of 1972 also recommended decentralisation of power for mobilisation of local resources, democratisation, enhancement of local leadership and promotion of effective district administration.
    A series of government policies and decisions were adopted for strengthening the district administration and promoting the decentralisation process in the country.

5. The District Administration Plan was introduced in 1975 with the main objectives of providing better coordination between district line agencies and district panchayats and of promoting people's participation in development programmes.
6. The Ministry of Panchayat and Local Development was created in 1981 with the main objective of providing financial and policy support to the district.
7. For better guidance, supervision and coordination, the country was divided into five development regions.
8. On the basis of a comprehensive report submitted by a high level sub-committee of the Panchayat Policy and Evaluation Committee, a Decentralisation Act of 1982 and Decentralisation By-laws of 1984 were enacted and promulgated in December 1984. The main objectives of the decentralisation scheme were:
   - to establish an effective system of planning, implementation and evaluation at village, town and district levels;
   - to ensure institutional development of panchayats at different levels;
   - to mobilise local resources and promote greater participation of local people; and
   - To devolve planning and decision-making authority to district and local panchayats.

Unlike in the past, the Decentralisation Act of 1982 and the By-laws of 1984 were implemented effectively, but there were some shortcomings. A study made in Salyan and Dang districts in 1987 brought out the following facts:

1. The political leaders at district level were found comparatively more enthusiastic in the decentralised planning process.
2. The district leaders participated actively in the decision-making processes.
3. The district line agency officers were still hesitant in delegating the decision-making power to the political leaders.

According to the decentralisation scheme, there were three tiers of planning bodies for taking final decisions regarding development programmes: the national planning commission (NPC) at the national level provided development priorities and guidelines to the district and local level panchayats. The district panchayat assembly, which is the second level of planning authority, approved all the district development programmes based on their own resources and the development grants. The local panchayats were the lowest tiers of planning authority which carried out planning tasks at the town and village panchayat levels.

In fact, the decentralisation scheme was undertaken as a political slogan. It was not backed by strong political commitment and sincere bureaucratic support. The planning exercises were done for five years at district and local levels. But in early 1990, the multi-party democratic system was restored in response to the people's popular movement. It brought far-reaching changes in the political and administrative organisations in the country. All the political organisations at district and local levels were abolished. The multi-party democratic constitution, which was drafted and promulgated in 1990, emphasised decentralisation of planning authority to the district and local political bodies and the promotion of people's participation in local governance and development activities. For about a year and a half, an interim arrangement was made for local government institutions for districts, towns and villages. A study completed by CEDA in 1991—'Strengthening Decentralised Local Level Planning Process in Nepal'—had clearly indicated an urgent need for a permanent institutional arrangement for district and local governments. The Village Development Committee Act 2048 was promulgated in 1991. On the basis of these acts, elections to the village development committee (VDCs), municipalities and district development committees (DDCs) have also been completed in 1992.

## Institutional Structure of Decentralised Government and its Role and Function

In Nepal, there is at present a system of two-tier decentralised government institutions. These comprise the district and local government institutions. The local government institutions consist of village development committees and municipalities.

## Village Development Committees

There are 3,994 village development committees in the country. These committees are uniformly divided into nine wards. Each VDC comprises 11 members, including the chairman, vice-chairman and nine ward members. They are elected directly by the people. Nepali citizens of 18 years of age and above residing in the village development area are entitled to elect the chairman, the vice-chairman and one ward member.

There is a provision for an advisory board comprising representatives of the users' committees, NGOs and different sections of the local community, particularly women, local elites, social workers and backward classes. The VDC also organises a ward committee of five persons, including the ward member in each ward. The ward member chairs the committee. The members of the advisory board, ward committees and ward members are members of the advisory assembly of the village development committee.

A government employee, deputed by HMG/Nepal works as the secretary of the village development committee. The VDC executes the development and maintenance programmes under the following heads: (*a*) education and culture, (*b*) health and population, (*c*) agriculture and irrigation, (*d*) forest, environment and energy, (*e*) drinking water, (*f*) transportation and construction, (*g*) industry and tourism, (*h*) social welfare, and (*i*) miscellaneous.

The village development committee should finalise the estimates of all available resources by the end of the month of Bhadra (mid-September) and complete the collection of the programmes of the NGOs. It should formulate development plans in the current year to be implemented in the next year. The plans need to be formulated on a quarterly and yearly basis. The Act has specified that priority needs to be given to the following aspects with a view to providing maximum benefits to the people:

(*a*) programmes that would directly benefit the people by increasing their income and employment;
(*b*) programmes to boost agricultural production;
(*c*) programmes which use local resources and skills; and
(*d*) programmes which directly benefit the weaker sections, women and children.

The Act also emphasises the need for feasibility studies and proper selection of projects. The projects thus selected should be made known to the villagers. While formulating plans, the VDC should comply with the directives issued by the national planning commission (NPC) and district development committee (DDC). The projects are to be classified into four categories:

(*i*) projects to be implemented by local resources;
(*ii*) projects to be implemented with grants and resources from the DDC;
(*iii*) projects to be implemented by NGOs; and
(*iv*) projects selected for inclusion in DDC plans.

### Municipalities

There are at present 36 municipalities in the country, including three new municipalities that were added in 1992. The Municipality Act 2048 (1991) has designated municipalities as autonomous corporate bodies. The tenure of the members of the municipalities is five years. The number of wards in a municipality range from nine to 30, depending on the population of the municipality. The municipal body comprises of a mayor, a deputy-mayor and ward members. Quite a large number of functions (43) have been specified to the municipality. To execute these functions, the municipality is expected to constitute committees or sub-committees. The municipalities too have to comply with the directives issued by His Majesty's Government and the NPC. The mayor, deputy mayor and ward members are directly elected by the people of the municipal areas.

The municipality has to formulate town development plans with the main objective of providing maximum benefits to the people. The Municipality Act has specified that priority needs to be given to programmes that help in increasing income, employment and production, utilise local resources and skill and benefit the weaker sections, women and children. First, the municipality is expected to undertake a series of feasibility studies. Second, it should make a careful selection of the projects, keeping in view the following considerations: protection and conservation of the environment, maximum participation of the people, and expected grants from DDC and the government. Thirdly, the selected projects should be made public for the information of the town people. It has also been specified that NGOs are to be promoted for the identification, formulation, implementation, supervision, evaluation and maintenance of the projects. The NGOs are expected to function in coordination with the municipality.

In addition to grants, the municipality can raise funds and enhance income through taxes, fees, levies, charges and other sources. The government appoints an executive officer, who works as a secretary of the municipality. HMG/Nepal may also appoint other required administrative and technical staff for the municipality. The municipality may also appoint other required staff with its own funds and under its own terms and conditions. It is the responsibility of the executive secretary to prepare an annual budget with the guidance of the mayor and present it for the approval of the municipality. A unique feature of the Municipality Act 2048 is that any balance left in the budget will be automatically carried over to the next fiscal year to complete the project works. This is indeed a welcome departure from the past practice of lapsing the budgeted fund.

## District Development Committees

The district development committees (DDC) of the 75 districts in the country are the second tiers of planning authority. A DDC is an autonomous corporate body with a chairman, vice-chairman and one member from each of the sub-districts (ilakas). The district comprises a minimum of nine sub-districts (ilakas) and can group to a maximum of 17 sub-districts. The number of members of the DDC ranges from 11 in small districts to 19 in big districts. MPs from the concerned district are ex-officio members of the district development committee. The district assembly comprises of all the chairmen and vice-chairmen of the VDCs, the mayor and the deputy mayor of each municipality within the district, the chairman, vice-chairman and members of the district development committee.

The chairman and vice-chairman of the district are elected for a term of five years by the members of the VDCs and municipalities from among themselves. The members of the district development committees are also elected in the same way from among the members of the VDCs and municipalities of the concerned sub-district. So, unlike the direct election of the village development committees and municipalities, the election of the chairman, vice-chairman and members of the district development committee is indirect and they are elected from among the elected members of the local government institutions.

HMG/Nepal appoints local development officers (LDO) for each of the 75 districts and the LDO functions as a secretary to the district development committee.

As a general rule, the DDC has to meet at least once in a month and the district assembly once a year. It approves proposals related to mobilisation of local resources, annual budget, development plans and regulations presented by the DDC. The district assembly complies with the policies and directives of the government and provides directives to DDC.

Like the VDC and municipality, every year the DDC also has to formulate district development plans. First, it has to conduct feasibility studies for the projects. Second, it has to make a careful selection of the projects on the basis of the availability of resources, environmental considerations and people's participation. However, the DDC Act 2048 (1991) has specified that priorities need to be accorded to programmes that help increase income, employment and agricultural production, use local resources and skills and protect the environment.

The development projects in the district belong to the following categories: projects based on local resources; projects based on grants and the resource of the government; and projects to be implemented by NGOs.

The DDC Act has particularly specified that the users' groups and NGOs are to be given encouragement and authority to implement development programmes. It also has highlighted that the users' groups and NGOs should maintain closer coordination with the DDC.

The government also promulgated DDC by By-laws 2049 (1993) on 18 February 1993, which specify procedures for the execution of the provisions of the DDC Act. These regulations simplify the process of working and implementing projects. The regulations provide for the formation of committees for agriculture, development works, industry, forest and environment, and health and social works.

## Planning Processes

The regulations specify the following processes for preparing plans: The DDC has to finalise the estimation of internal resources by mid-September. The concerned ministries have to provide directives and investment estimates for district level programmes by mid-November. The LDO has to convene the meeting of all the district line agency officers related to development programmes, NGO representatives, and heads of the financial institutions for preparing district development programmes for the forthcoming fiscal year. At the meeting, the district line agency officers have to submit current status descriptions, incorporating the projects selected by the VDC of the district. The DDC may issue directives to the secretary of the DDC to forward the list of proposed projects in prescribed forms to the concerned plan formulation committees.

The DDC by-laws specify four plan formulation committees: agriculture related committee; development works committee; industry, forest and environment committee; and health and social committee.

The agriculture related committee comprises of deputed DDC members, the agricultural development bank manager, the livestock officer, the chief of AIC, cooperative officer, women development officer, planning and administrative officer, and the DDC nominated representative of the users' committee. The agriculture development officer (ADO) functions as a member-cum-secretary of the committee.

The development works committee consists of deputed DDC members, the road office chief, the irrigation office chief, the watch supply office chief, the planning and administrative officer and the DDC nominated representative of the users' committee. The building and housing officer chief is the member-cum-secretary of the development works committee.

The industry, forest and environment committee comprises of deputed DDC members, the industry officer or cottage industry chief, the timber corporation branch chief, the representative of the district industry commerce association, the planning and administrative officer, and the DDC nominated representative of the users' committee. The district forest officer (DFO) is the member-cum-secretary of this committee.

The health and social committee consists of deputed DDC members, the district education officer, the women development officer, a nominated teacher of campus or school, a nominated doctor of a private nursing home or holding a private health post and a nominated representative of the users' committee. The public health officer is the member-cum-secretary of the health and social committee.

The DDC has to issue directives and determine the scope of work of these four plan formulation committees. The committees have to submit their drafted plans to the DDC by mid-February for approval. NGOs have to implement development programmes in close coordination with the DDC. According to the regulations, the DDC has also to incorporate development programmes relating to women's development and NGO-funded programmes.

The district development project coordination committee is constituted under the chairmanship of the chairman of DDC, and includes the vice-chairman of DDC, all the convenors of the plan formulation committees, development related district line agency chiefs and the LDO. The LDO acts as a member-cum-secretary of project coordination committee. The project coordination committee invites MPs, the chief district officer and the representative of regional NPC office. It reviews the selection of the projects suggested by the plan formulation committees and then, forwards its recommendations to the DDC.

The DDC then submits the development plans to the district assembly for its approval. While approving the plans, the district assembly has to take into consideration the government directives, available resources, feasibility studies and the priorities set by the DDC Act. The DDC regulations have specified that the plans for the coming year are to be submitted and approved by district assembly by mid-March of the fiscal year. Information regarding the plans that have been approved is then communicated to the concerned ministries and agencies.

With regard to the implementation of projects, the DDC regulations have incorporated the following provisions:

(*i*) The projects relating to the people's participation have to be implemented through the users' groups.
(*ii*) The projects relating to NGOs' involvement have to be implemented by NGOs.

(*iii*) The DDC can also make an alternative arrangement for implementation of the project if it is not practicable to be implemented by the users' groups or NGOs.

The DDC regulations also require that the DDC prepares progress reviews on quarterly and annual bases. These progress review reports have to be forwarded to the Local Development Ministry. The DDC has to invite all the members of the DDC, concerned project chiefs, the regional director of the NPC and the chief district officer to attend its progress review meetings.

It has also been specified in the regulations that under the guidance of the DDC chairman, the LDO will coordinate and monitor all district level development programmes. The district line agency officers have to comply with the directives issued by the DDC regarding plan formulation, implementation, monitoring and evaluation. The DDC can also constitute a monitoring sub-committee for regular monitoring and supervision of the execution of the development programmes in the district.

## The Users' Groups and NGOs

The DDC Act 2048 and the DDC By-laws have accorded much importance to the users' groups and NGOs in the process of project implementation and maintenance. It is mentioned in the regulations that the DDC has to prepare a list of the users. The users' group of nine members is to be constituted from among the users. The concerned DDC member can attend the meeting of the users' group in an advisory capacity. The users' group should invite the concerned line agency chief or his representative and the secretary of the VDC. The users' group has to convene its meeting once a month and it has been entrusted with a number of functions and duties including mobilisation of local resources and ensuring people's participation. It can also constitute a sub-committee for the maintenance of the projects.

The NGOs have also been accorded with a considerable degree of freedom in project preparation and implementation. As a general rule, NGOs have to coordinate with the DDC and in respect of projects funded by the district, they have to get DDC approval prior to implementation.

## Working of the Decentralised Governments

The present district and local government institutions were formally elected in 1992 under the new Constitution of 1990, and under the district and Local Acts of 1991. First, the chairman, vice-chairman and members of the village development committees, the mayor, deputy mayor and ward members of the municipalities were elected on the basis of adult franchise. Then, the chairmen, vice-chairmen and members of the DDCs were indirectly elected from among themselves. It has been less than a year since the DDCs, municipalities and VDCs were formed. The district and local governments have just begun the planning process for the formulation of development plans. So it is too early to critically review the working of decentralised governments in Nepal. However, it is possible to make the following observations:

1. The Nepali Congress Government has already shown its commitment to decentralise planning and devolve decision-making authority to the DDCs, VDCs and the municipalities.
2. There is relatively less bureaucratisation in the working processes of the district and local governments. It has been specified in the regulations that as regards construction, procurement and contracts, no DDC member or any member of his family be allowed to take such contracts from the DDC. DDC members are also prohibited from taking out any money for the purpose of construction work and procurement. These are good departures from the past practices.
3. The users' groups and NGOs have been accorded decisive roles in project formulation, implementation and maintenance. Under the previous decentralisation scheme, the ward member used to be the ex-officio chairman of the users' group. Now the chairman is elected from among the members of the users' group as per the provisions of current DDC Act and regulations. NGOs today enjoy relatively greater freedom to organise and execute their development activities in the districts. NGO representatives are also invited to the DDC plan formulation meetings.
4. The regulations also provide guidelines to the DDC for designating and framing plans for the development of village

settlements which are suitable for urbanisation. The DDCs are now empowered to issue building codes and prepare plans for the future development of the bazar settlements.

5. Government grants will continue to play a dominant role in district and local level planning. As in the previous decentralisation scheme, the district and the local bodies are given the authority to raise internal resources. But past experience indicates the difficulty of increasing internal resources. Nevertheless, the financial situation of the municipalities is comparatively much better because of the imposition of the octroi tax.

## Current Policy Issues and Future Outlook

The election to the district and local government institutions are held on the multi-party electoral system. The district and the local level political leaders are members of national political parties. Thus the policies and political ideologies of these parties will obviously be reflected in the decision-making processes of the DDCs, the municipalities and the VDCs. Some recent events that have occurred in a few DDC meetings are not pleasant to record in the democratic evolution of the district and local government institutions. It will probably take some years to evolve democratic norms in the planning and decision-making processes of the district and local government institutions.

The district and local government institutions in Nepal have a weak resource base. In addition to fully exploiting existing sources of revenue, new sources need to be identified. In the context, the imposition of land tax should be given priority in local resource mobilisation. The equal distribution of government grants is to be discontinued; grants are now to be distributed on the basis of project viability. So far, the district and local governments have not maintained proper financial records and relevant statistics required for the formulation of the plans.

The erosion of people's confidence in the sincerity and capability of the district and local governments in the past has to be rectified with sincere commitment and exemplary development works. This is quite essential for greater mobilisation of local resources and for enhancing people's active participation.

The resource bases of the municipalities are comparatively better than that of the DDCs and VDCs. The municipalities receive grants from bilateral and multilateral agencies for certain development programmes. There is the town development fund (TDF) which provides a modest amount of grants to municipalities for its development programmes. The management support for urban development (MSUD) has prepared structural planning for 32 municipalities and carried out financial analysis for 33 municipalities for the period 1984/85 to 1990/91. On the basis of available financial data, own source revenue of the municipalities has been increasing at an average rate of 29.34 per cent per annum. This impressive growth rate of the own source revenue is mainly due to the octroi tax, which accounts for about 80 per cent of the total revenue. Urban development through local efforts (UDLE) has continued to provide financial management support to the municipalities. Technical as well as financial management supports need to be extended to district and local government institutions as well. A district development fund (DDF) needs to be created which could provide loans to the DDCs and VDCs for the implementation of development works. HMG/Nepal should request the bilateral and multilateral agencies to extend support for creating the DDF.

The decentralisation scheme in Nepal has been in implementation for the last six years. Due to lack of funds, knowledge and skills, the scheme has not been successful. For the effective utilisation of decentralised planning and decision-making powers, a big push is needed to enhance the knowledge and planning skills at the district and local levels. HMG/Nepal should provide training to the elected leaders and officials of the district and local government institutions, focusing on skills relating to planning, implementing, monitoring, supervision, evaluation, financial management and administration. There are a number of well-established regional training institutions in the country which should be reorganised and adequately funded for shouldering the responsibilities of training and orientation programmes.

In the past, there used to be central interventions through ministers, MPs and zonal commissioners. Elected local government institutions would be dissolved on any flimsy pretext. There should be no central interventions in the working of the district and local government institutions. However, a mechanism would need to be developed through which elected leaders and officials could be made accountable to the concerned district assembly, municipalities and the VDCs.

## Select Readings

Abullaish, 1980. *An Evaluation of Administrative Decentralization in Nepal*, Kirtipur: CEDA, Tribhuvan University.

Amatya, S.L. 1987. 'Decentralization in Nepal: An Overview' in Harvey Demaine and Romana E. Malong (eds.) *Decentralization: Area Development in Practice in Asia*. Bangkok: Asian Institute of Technology, pp. 93–109.

_____. 1987. *Impact of Decentralization of Planning Process: A Case Study of Salyan and Dang Districts Nepal*. A Report Submitted to FAO/RAPA. Bangkok.

_____. 1988. 'Rural Development through Decentralized Planning: A Case Study of Nepal'. *Alumni Paper Series*, No. 17. East-West Center Association.

APROSC/FAO. 1990. *Training Manual on Decentralized Planning (District Level)* Nepal:

CEDA. 1992. *Strengthening Decentralized Local Level Planning Process in Nepal*. A Study Submitted to the Ford Foundation (New Delhi). Kathmandu.

Dhungel, D.N., G. Joshi, and S.B. Gurung. 1989–90. 'Local Government'Reforms in Nepal'. *The Journal of Development and Administrative Studies*, CEDA Vols. 11 and 12, Nos. 1 and 2, pp. 1–21.

Gurung, S.B. and P. Roy (eds.). 1988. *Planning with People: Decentralization in Nepal*. New Delhi: Orient Longman.

HMG/Nepal. *District Development Committee Act, 2048* (in Nepali).

_____. *By-laws of Decentralisation of 1984* (in Nepali).

_____. *Village Development Committee Act, 2048* (in Nepali).

_____. *Municipality Act, 2048* (in Nepali).

_____. 'District Development Committee By-laws', 2049, *Nepal Rajpatra*, 18 February 1993 (in Nepali).

_____. *Decentralisation Act of 1982* (in Nepali). Kathmandu, 1985.

Kafle, M.P. 1984. *Decentralisation Scheme in Nepal: Problems and Prospects*. Occasional Paper. APROSC.

Shrestha, M.K. 1965. *A Handbook of Public Administration in Nepal*.

Shrestha, T.N. (ed.) 1985. *District Administration in Nepal: Issuance and Ideas*. Lalitpur: Nepal Administrative Staff College.

Singh, G.R. 'Pattern of Decentralization in Nepal'. *Vasudha*, Vol. XI, Asadh, 2025.

UDLE. 1992. *Financial Analysis and Monitoring of 33 Municipalities of the Kingdom (FY 2041/42 to 2047/48)*. Kathmandu.

# 10

# Decentralised Governance and Planning Process: A Case Study of the Karnali–Bheri Integrated Rural Development (K-BIRD) Project, Nepal

## SANT B. GURUNG

## Brief Background of K-BIRD Project and Location of Project Area

The Karnali–Bheri Rural Development Project (K-BIRD Project) is a joint effort of His Majesty's Government of Nepal (HMG/N) and the Canadian International Development Agency (CIDA). The project primarily aims at uplifting the socio-economic conditions of the rural people of the project areas. The K-BIRD Project is one of the several IRDPs implemented in the country during the early 1980s. With the successful completion of the first phase (1981–1985), the second phase was initiated in 1985 with a special focus on productive sectors. These covered agriculture, livestock, forestry, cottage industry, appropriate technology, small farmers and local development, including women's development services.

The project area covers three districts: Jumla in the Karnali zone, and Surkhet and Dailekh in the Bheri zone. All these three districts lie within the mid-western development region of Nepal.

## Mid-Western Development Region

The mid-western development region is one of the five development regions of Nepal. Administratively, this region is made up of three zones, i.e. Rapti, Karnali and Bheri and there are 15 administrative districts under these zones. The population of this region is 13.03 per cent of the total population of the country. This region is comparatively the least developed.

*Surkhet district* is one of the inner Terai districts of the midwestern developed region. Birendra Nagar is the district and regional headquarters. The district is divided into one municipality (Birendra Nagar) and 50 village development committees (VDCs). Surkhet has a total population of 225,296. The total number of households is 37,723 with 39,830 families (census 1991). The number of persons per family is 5.66 (see Table 10.1). The absolute change of population between 1981–1991 is 36.0 per cent (see Table 10.2). The cultivated land area, forest area and the nonproductive land area of Surkhet district is shown in Table 10.3. The forest area of Surkhet is larger than Dailekh and Jumla districts.

**Table 10.1: K-BIRD Project Area Population: 1991 Census**

| K-BIRD project districts | No. of households | No. of families | Population | | | Persons per Family |
|---|---|---|---|---|---|---|
| | | | Total | Male | Female | |
| Surkhet | 37,723 | 39,830 | 225,296 | 111,817 | 113,479 | 5.66 |
| Dailekh | 31,294 | 34,277 | 187,820 | 93,764 | 94,056 | 5.48 |
| Jumla | 13,180 | 13,580 | 76,305 | 39,154 | 37,151 | 5.62 |
| Total | 82,197 | 87,687 | 489,421 | 244,735 | 244,685 | 5.58 |

The Mahendra Raj Marga (national east–west road) is linked to Birendra Nagar by the Kohalpur–Surkhet gravel road at Kohalpur. The airport of Surkhet is also connected to this road.

*Dailekh district* is one of the hill districts of Bheri zone in the mid-western development region. Dailekh Bazaar is the district headquarters. The district is divided into 60 village development committees (VDCs). The total population is 187,820 with 49.9 per cent male and 50.1 per cent female members. The average family

**Table 10.2: Population Change by Districts, 1981–1991**

| Project area/districts | 1981 | 1991 | Absolute change | Per cent |
|---|---|---|---|---|
| Surkhet | 165,666 | 225,296 | 59,630 | 36.0 |
| Dailekh | 97,117 | 187,820 | 90,703 | 93.4 |
| Jumla | 67,545 | 76,305 | 8,760 | 13.0 |
| Total | 330,328 | 489,421 | 159,093 | 48.2 |

**Table 10.3: Land Use Distribution in K-BIRD Project Area**

| | Surkhet | Dailekh | Jumla | Total |
|---|---|---|---|---|
| Cultivated land area (km²) | 526 | 523 | 241 | 1,290 |
| Forest area (km²) | 1,803 | 757 | 1,045 | 3,605 |
| Non-productive land (km) | 46 | 15 | 595 | 656 |

size is 5.48 (Table 10.1). The population has increased by 93.4 per cent between 1981–1991 (Table 10.2) and the land use pattern is shown in Table 10.3. The forest area and rock/waste area is less than the other two districts.

*Jumla district* is one of the most remote and mountainous districts of Karnali zone with its district headquarters at Chandan Nath. The total population is 76,305 with 51.3 per cent male and 48.7 per cent female members (see Table 10.1). The population increased by 13.0 per cent during 1981–91, which is comparatively lower than the other two districts. Being a mountainous district, the cultivated land area is also less than in the other two districts. Jumla has an air service to Nepalgunj and Kathmandu. Air transportation is expensive and cannot provide a complete alternative to roads for the movement of people and commodity flows. But Jumla and Dailekh have no road links. All movement of goods and people is either by foot or pack animals such as sheep, ponies and mules, which are in substantial use in Karnali zone and in some parts of the Bheri zone to transport foodgrains and salt.

## Local Government Bodies (LGBs)

The restoration of the multi-party democratic political order in April 1990 brought far-reaching changes in the Nepalese political landscape. The local government institutions—district, town and village panchayats were replaced by new set of local government institutions called district development committees (DDCs), village development committees (VDCs) and municipalities. The Parliament has passed and brought into implementation the DDC Act 1992, the VDC Act 1992 and the Municipality Act 1992. One of the directive principles of the new democratic Constitution of Nepal (1991) is participation through decentralisation. The present political system ensures an environment for the effective involvement of local level institutions in order to institutionalise a participative self-managed and sustainable development at the local level.

## Local Political Institutions

After the nationwide elections in May 1992, two-tier local government institutions i.e. the village development committee (VDC) altogether 3,395 VDCs, 36 municipalities and 75 district development committees (DDCs) have come into existence.

### The Village Development Committee (VDC)

The VDC is the lowest grassroots political institution. Each VDC has nine elected ward committees. The local elections based on adult franchise were completed in July 1992 at the district municipality and village levels. The chairman and the vice-chairman of the VDC are elected by the voters of the VDC. One member from each ward is elected as a ward chairman. These direct elections are held on a political party basis.

The VDC has the mandate to formulate and implement village level development plans on the basis of its own resources as well as grants received from the DDC and NGOs. The village level projects are executed and coordinated through users' committees and

NGOs. The VDC has to function in relation to the formulation and implementation of village level plans. The village secretary of the VDC is a government employee who provides administrative support under the direction of the VDC chairman.

## Municipality

Municipalities are the lower tier political institutions for urban areas. The mayor and deputy mayor of the municipality are directly elected by the voters on a political party basis. Membership also includes one elected ward member from each ward in the municipality. (The number of wards depends on the size of the municipality.)

The municipalities have the mandate to formulate town development plans and implement development projects on the basis of their own resources and grants received from the DDC and NGOs. They have to follow the directives issued by the government and the DDC about the formulation and implementation of town development programmes. They can execute and coordinate their programmes through users' groups, ward committees, concerned line agencies and NGOs. The executive secretary of the municipality is an employee of the government and provides it administrative support.

## District Development Committee (DDC)

Each of the districts has a DDC, which is an elected body responsibile for district level development. Its chairman and vice-chairman are elected by the members of municipalities and VDCs and its members are elected (indirect election on political party basis) from ilakas and can range from 9 to 17 in number. Members of Parliament of the concerned district are its ex-officio members.

The DDC has the mandate to formulate district level development programmes to be implemented by the government and semi-government organisations and to submit it to the district assembly (DA) for approval; and upon approval to implement them, to supervise the implementation process, to review their progress and to coordinate the programmes initiated by the NGOs.

The development projects under the district development programmes are classified into (*a*) projects to be implemented with
local resources, (*b*) projects to be implemented with government
grants and resources, and (*c*) projects to be implemented by
NGOs.

## Government (Public) Sponsored Institutions

*At the district level*, there are three types of government organisations involved in regulatory and development administration:

  (*i*)  the district administration office headed by the chief district
         officer (CDO);
  (*ii*)  the line agencies of sectoral ministries responsible for sec-
         toral programmes; and
  (*iii*) the local development officer (LDO) as the secretary of
         the DDC who has a special role in the planning and man-
         agement of grant-in-aid as well as in coordinating various
         development activities.

*At the service centre level* there are branch offices such as the
health post, agricultural service centre, veterinary service centre,
forest office, women development section, police office, post office,
etc.

*At the village level,* the government office is represented by the
village secretary, as mentioned earlier.

### Decentralised Planning Process

The growth and development of local level institutions in Nepal is
mainly the outcome of the decentralised planning concept and
approach. The decentralised planning process, operationalised at
different levels according to the Decentralisation Act 1982 and
Rules 1984 is presented in Figure 10.1

The DDC, VDC and Municipality working management rules
have been recently approved by the HMG/N. The trans-district
level plan is prepared after discussing the proposals in the regional

**FIGURE 10.1:** District Development Plan Formulation

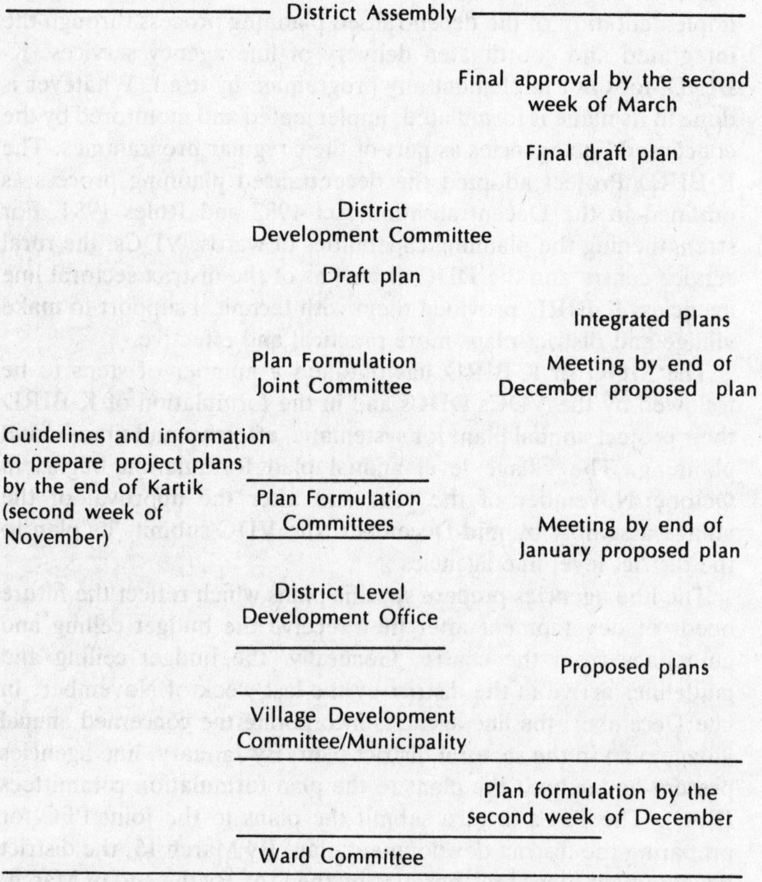

———————————— District Assembly ————————————

Final approval by the second
week of March

Final draft plan

District
Development Committee

Draft plan

Integrated Plans

Plan Formulation          Meeting by end of
Joint Committee           December proposed plan

Guidelines and information
to prepare project plans
by the end of Kartik          Plan Formulation
(second week of              Committees                Meeting by end of
November)                                             January proposed plan

District Level
Development Office

Proposed plans

Village Development
Committee/Municipality

Plan formulation by the
second week of December

Ward Committee

workshops, keeping in view the budget ceilings and guidelines
provided by the PCO.

## K-BIRD Decentralised Planning Process

The main objective of the K-BIRD Project is to increase the
capacity to implement integrated and self-sustained development
projects for the economic, environmental and social improvement

of the people in the project area. To achieve this objective, K-BIRD's stated purpose is to assist HMG/N in accelerating the implementation of the decentralised planning process through the integrated and coordinated delivery of line agency services. K-BIRD does not implement any programme by itself. Whatever is done in its name is formulated, implemented and monitored by the concerned line agencies as part of their regular programmes. The K-BIRD Project adopted the decentralised planning process as outlined in the Decentralisation Act 1982 and Rules 1984. For strengthening the planning capabilities of wards, VDCs, the rural service centre and the DDC as well as of the district sectoral line agencies, K-BIRD provided them with technical support to make village and district plans more practical and effective.

The MOU of K-BIRD has outlined a number of steps to be followed by the VDCs DDCs and in the formulation of K-BIRD their project annual plan, for systematic, effective and time-bound planning. The village level annual plan formulation begins in October/November of the year and after the approval of the village assembly by mid-December, the VDC submits its plan to the district level line agencies.

The line agencies prepare specific plans which reflect the future needs of development after they receive the budget ceiling and guidelines from the centre. Generally, the budget ceiling and guidelines arrive in the district by the last week of November. In late December, the line agencies incorporate the concerned annual village plan in the sectoral district plan. By January, line agencies present and submit the plans to the plan formulation committees (PFC). The PFCs in turn submit the plans to the joint PFC for preparing the district development plan. By March 15, the district development plans are approved by the DA. By the end of March, the DDC sends the approved district plan to the prefect coordinator's office (PCO).

Trans-district level planning is prepared in the regional workshop within the budget ceiling and guidelines issued by the PCO. Then these plans are submitted to the PCO by March for inclusion in the K-BIRD project annual plan. By April, the PCO prepares the final draft of the K-BIRD annual plan by consolidating all the plans within the given format of guidelines and budget ceilings and submits it to the Ministry of Local Government (MLG), the National Planning Commission (NPC) and Canadian International

Development Agency (CIDA) for review and comments. By May/ June, the PCO finalises the K-BIRD annual plan and again sends it to the MLG, NPC and CIDA for final approval. By June, HMG/N and CIDA approve the final K-BIRD annual plan. Finally, by July/August, the House of Representatives approves the national annual plan and budget, including the K-BIRD Project annual plan.

## Problems and Constraints

The problems and constraints related to planning and implementation of the K-BIRD Project are as follows:

### Inadequacy of Data Base at Village and District Levels

Planning activities need certain essential data which are reliable and relevant in order to prepare the annual and perspective plan. The profile or resource inventory of the village and the district may be viewed as a dynamic tool for local level planning. According to the norms of decentralised planning, the village and district profiles should be completed by September. The Decentralisation Act stipulates that by mid-October the village secretary should prepare or update the village profile, and DDC secretariat should do the same for the district profile on the basis of updated VDC and municipality profiles. Most of the VDCs and districts of the project area have failed to prepare and update their profiles. The main reason is lack of training and knowledge about the methods to be used in preparing and updating profiles. The village and district profiles are thus hardly used for preparing VDC and DDC plans. Due to lack of trained and technical staff, the data bases at the village and district levels remain inadequate.

### Budget Ceiling and Guidelines

The budget ceiling and guidelines are major parameters in the formulation of village and district development plans. In the K-BIRD project area, most of the budget ceilings and guidelines from the central ministries were not received in time by the district. The line agencies therefore had to prepare their annual plans on the basis of tentative budget ceilings which were projected in trans-district seminars. Sometimes there is a wide gap between the tentative budget ceiling and actual budget received from the ministries later. Delays in budget disbursement by three to four months is also a major problem which affects the implementation of plan. For this reason, and in order to avoid wastage of time and resources, line agencies do not schedule any programme in the first trimester. Consequently, projects are not begun on time and in all probability end up remaining incomplete.

## Lack of Political Commitment

Most of the political members of the PFC, the joint PFC and the district assembly are not well-versed or trained in the planning process. They have therefore been unable to perform effectively in district development planning. Lack of awareness and acquaintance of political leaders with the decentralised planning process and the DDC and VDC Act, 1992, indicate an absence of political commitment in the plan formulation and implementation process.

## Lack of Planning Skill in Planning Process

Most VDC members and local leaders are unaware of the Decentralization Act, 1982 and Rules, 1984, the VDC Act 1992 and the K-BIRD Planning Document. They also lack complete knowledge of the planning process and skills. Therefore, the VDCs hardly ever prepare plans either in accordance with the NPC format or the K-BIRD format. None of the VDCs formulate a calendar of plan operations and plan management. They only prepare a list of projects and send it on to the district line agencies (DLAs) to include in the district line agencies plans. Due to this, the DLAs face serious problems in including the list of projects in their district plans. VDC plans thus hardly receive any attention in the sectoral plans.

## People's Participation

Local people have hardly any part in the decision-making, planning, implementation and benefit sharing processes related to development activities. Local leaders can play an important role in motivating local people to participate in development activities, but they seem unable to convince people to do this.

In the K-BIRD Project, locals are encouraged to become members of users' committees (UCs) for the implementation, operation, maintenance and repair of development projects. But the quality of construction and maintenance of the projects undertaken by the users' committees leaves much to be desired. Also, there is a strong feeling among the UCs that K-BIRD should provide the funds for the operation and maintenance of the completed projects.

Sometimes it is very difficult to communicate with and convince the local people about the need for their participation in development activities. For example, Dailekh and Jumla are difficult areas from the point of view of transportation. Due to lack of transportation and other facilities, the people believe that the most important project would be the construction of a motorable road. Unless this project is undertaken, no matter what is done in other sectors, the people of the Jumla and Dailekh districts will not feel satisfied with K-BIRD activities. Such a situation gives rise to problems of communication between K-BIRD and its beneficiaries.

## High Staff Turnover

High staff turnover is one of the major problems of the K-BIRD Project with related line agencies in Surkhet, Dailekh and Jumla districts. Since its inception in 1981–82, K-BIRD Project has had seven project coordinators including the current one. Two of them worked for a period of one-and-a-half years; one held the position for 11 months and one for less than two months.

The same situation obtains with regard to the regional directors, DFOs, LDOs, WDOs and other district level line agency officers of Surkhet, Dailekh and Jumla districts. The frequent transfer of skilled, trained and capable LA officers hampers the effective planning and implementation of K-BIRD Project activities.

## Lack of Coordination among Sectoral Line Agencies

There has been little or no coordination or collaboration between sector line agencies. For example, irrigation programmes are formulated without taking into account the requirements of the agricultural programmes. When similar programmes are undertaken by different sectoral agencies in the same area, instead of collaborating with one another, each agency is interested only in meeting its own target.

## PCO and LA Linkages

The major function and objective of the K-BIRD project coordinator's office (PCO) is to facilitate and coordinate the line agencies in the planning and implementation of K-BIRD activities. The sectoral line agencies are responsible for the formulation and implementation of K-BIRD activities. The PCO plays no role in actual implementation. Because of this, it has to rely upon personal or informal relationships to achieve the desired results.

The linkages maintained by PCO with line agencies were found to be of no consequence due to lack of direct command between PCO and LAs. A study on PCO–LA linkages indicated that feedback given by PCOs regarding the preparation of management plans through circulars and correspondence were generally neglected by LAs. However, it now seems that the interaction between the PCO and LAs has improved a bit through the organisation of various planning meetings and workshops.

## Existing Situation of PCO and LAs Staff

Two types of staff work in the PCO for the management of K-BIRD: permanent employees of HMG/N; and K-BIRD personnel. Among the K-BIRD personnel, some are permanent for the project period and others are temporary. Out of 62 sanctioned posts, two (that of project coordinator and assistant accountant) are permanent employees of HMG/N, 40 are permanent for the project period, four are temporary and seven posts are vacant.

In other words, 85 per cent of the total staff are K-BIRD personnel and 12 per cent of the total posts are vacant. Only 3 per cent of the staff are permanent employees of HMG/N. Similarly, out of a total of 355 revised sanctioned positions in K-BIRD Project areas Surkhet, Dailekh and Jumla, 85 (24 per cent) are vacant, 251 (71 per cent) are for the K-BIRD project period, and 19 (5 per cent) are HMG/N temporary positions in the regional and district level line agencies. Apart from this, the personnel are uncertain about their job security because of the staff reduction policy recently adopted by the government and the practice of the K-BIRD Project to grant one year's extension at a time. In such a situation, it is not realistic to expect loyalty and dedication from the officials. K-BIRD personnel tend to think of their jobs as mere stop-gap arrangements.

## Recommendations

1. The central, district and ilaka level seminars conducted by K-BIRD were very productive. Hence, this practice should be continued. These seminars helped the sectoral line agencies to understand K-BIRD policies and the concept of development planning, budgeting and programming. It also helped to minimise deviations from the budget ceiling and reduced changes in the sectoral programmes and their coordination. Similarly, at the ilaka level, the seminars created an awareness among the RSC chiefs and staff about their role in supporting the VDCs in the planning process.

2. Past experience shows that it is not easy to involve all the line agencies with a large number of different components in IRDP. It will be much easier to manage, coordinate and implement projects in a few selected priority needs of the area for self-initiated and sustainable economic, environmental and social improvement in the project area.

3. A group approach would enable individuals to come together into a 'group' on the basis of their common felt needs to enhance their skills, knowledge and capability for collective efforts. This approach represents a process of working with the people rather

than for the people. The main objective of the approach is to educate, encourage and empower village communities to mobilise and manage their local resources by using sustainable technologies and techniques.

In almost all the projects implemented by K-BIRD, there are certain activities taken up by the users' groups/committees. These groups are involved in managing such community resources as forestry, irrigation, drinking water, etc. But it was found that most of the projects initiated were the subject of local disputation and the majority of the beneficiaries were not even aware of them. They were not involved in the project cycle which includes pre-planning, planning, implementation, monitoring and evaluation. As a result, most of the users' committees became defunct soon after their formation. Therefore, the major focus should be to involve beneficiaries in the planning cycle; also, members of the users' committees must be trained, particularly in effective group formation and management.

4. The overall goal of the K-BIRD project is to increase the capacity for self-initiated and sustainable economic, environmental and social improvement in the project area by assisting and accelerating the HMG/N line agencies in the planning and implementation of the Integrated Rural Development (IRD) strategy. K-BIRD is trying to tackle development problems by using both the target group approach (TGA) and the area development approach (ADA). Both are long-term processes which demand continuous efforts and readjustment of the programmes taking into account the needs and requirements of the project beneficiaries for their self-sustainability. But since K-BIRD has been implementing its programmes on an ad hoc basis and since the financial year 1990–91, on a one-year extension basis, it is very difficult to prepare a systematic and productive plan to tackle the development problems of the target groups and to achieve the projects overall goal of bettering the lot of the beneficiaries. This issue will have to be resolved as soon as possible by both the donor agency and HMG/N.

5. Transportation and communication networks play a very important role in the effective implementation and management of projects. The major constraints that K-BIRD faces in its development efforts are lack of transport, isolation and a difficult topography. The main problem is difficult access for the development of these districts. Besides these problems, the K-BIRD Project is

saddled with two zonal boundaries. To deal with two zonal administrators is not always easy for the project management. If the transportation and communication network were good, the largeness of project area would not have mattered. But transportation is a serious problem in the K-BIRD area. It will be easier to deal with project management issues if the project area is small or, alternatively, if it is in a continuous geographical and in the same administrative area (i.e. district, zone or region). This is one issue that will need to be considered for the future phase of the project by policy-makers and donors.

6. Plan projects should be identified on the basis of the interest, basic felt needs and demands of the local people for their benefit. As far as possible, the annual and periodic plans of local level should be prepared on the basis of policies, objectives and priorities followed by the national plans.

In order to effect a simple, practical and people-oriented plan formulation, the following process should be adopted:

(*i*) The related experts should visit the spots and take all the required information and data and suggestions from the local community and village secretary and local leaders.

(*ii*) The district level plan should be prepared taking into account the plans of all the VDCs/municipalities of the district and priorities should be decided by the related line agencies, plan formulation committee and the DDC.

To prepare scientific village and district profiles on the basis of Decentralisation By-laws, 1984, the village secretary should be trained, provided with opportunities of promotion and enough monetary incentives to encourage him to collect reliable data/information in time. Also, before the plan is formulated, related experts and technical personnel should undertake feasibility studies.

7. Past experience in plan implementation has revealed certain problems:

(*i*) delayed approval and release of the budget;

(*ii*) lack of supervision and monitoring;

(*iii*) lack of specialised, trained and technical manpower;

(*iv*) delegation of responsibilities to local level agencies, but vesting power/authority at the centre;

(*v*) unnecessary political pressure; and
(*vi*) equal distribution of HMG grant-in-aid among the VDCs of the district.

To make plan implementation more effective, all the responsibility and authority should be given to the district level line agencies for the implementation of plan programmes. Local level plans and programmes should be implemented through users' committees/groups. The list of approved programmes and the budget should be released before the fiscal year begins.

## Implication for Future

Decentralisation is not only a technical process dealing with planning, management and monitoring, but it also has a political dimension, i.e., the empowerment of people. The corrupt, highly centralised and top-down style of administration practised in the past cannot achieve the country's goals of democracy and development. One of the decisive aims of decentralisation is to enhance the creativity of citizens and their self-help potential, and to foster the real devolution of decision-making powers to the local level units.

Decentralisation in Nepal needs a big boost in order for it to achieve the development goals of sustainable economic growth, poverty alleviation and rural development and regional balance. For this, a self-sustainable participatory, decentralised and integrated development approach needs to be formulated and clearly understood by all the actors of development, i.e., the planners, policy-makers, NGOs, local governments, etc. In this alternative development approach, the governments (central and local), the bureaucrats and NGOs need play only a facilitating role: the mere active role should belong to the non-governmental local level institutions.

Quentin W. Lindsey has suggested 10 keys to democracy, decentralisation and development in Nepal, which are relevant to the self-sustainable participatory approach just mentioned:

(*i*) Locally elected representatives should encourage and support local groups to form users' committees, cooperatives and similar organisations including private consulting firms.

(*ii*) The users' committees and other organised units such as the DDCs, the municipality and the VDCs should have the freedom and flexibility to use additional sources of funds, and to contract for technical and other assistance in order to facilitate development at district, village and town levels.

(*iii*) Local people at ward, town and district levels should be provided with sources of public revenue independent of the central government.

(*iv*) To ensure the effective development of high quality social and cultural components of local society, and infrastructure requirements such as local roads, bridges, drinking water projects, users' committees should be given functional flexibility and all the necessary support.

(*v*) District national NGOs (especially local people's organisations) and private consulting firms should be encouraged to establish themselves in the more distant districts where none now exist.

(*vi*) It should be ensured that users' committees, schoolteachers and similar public servants are not drawn into political parties but work together as members of such committees.

(*vii*) Conferences, seminars, training programmes etc. should be developed in order to enhance understanding of how elected representatives, users' committee members and local people should function in carrying out the decentralisation process.

(*viii*) External assistance from various donor sources should be closely related to the decentralisation theme.

(*ix*) Simultaneously with the implementation of the aforementioned elements, it is essential that central ministries and departments also understand and adapt to them.

(*x*) Need to clarify central government policy with respect to democracy, decentralisation and development should be clarified.

**196 / Sant B. Gurung**

## Select Reading

Gurung, Sant B. 1991. *Effective Delivery of Human Resources Development Programmes Country Study, Nepal*. Bangkok: ESCAP.
Gurung, Sant B., D.N. Dhurgel and G. Joshi. 1991. *Local Government Reforms in Nepal*. Manila: EROPA.
Gurung, Sant B. and A.J. Shah 1992. *Decentralisation and Local Level Institutions in the Changed Political Context*. Kuala Lumpur: NASC/APDC.
Gurung, Sant B. and Prodipto Roy (eds.) 1988. *Planning with People: Decentralisation in Nepal*. New Delhi: Orient Longman.
HMG/N. 1991. *Constitution of Nepal, 1991 (in Nepal)*. Kathmandu: Ministry of Law and Justice.
————. 1992. *District Development Act: 1992*.
————. 1992. *Municipality Act: 1992*.
————. 1992. *Village Development Committee Act, 1992*.
————. 1993. *District Development Committee (Working Management Rules)*.
Inaryatullah, (ed.) 1978. *Rural Organisations and Rural Development: Some Asian Experiences*. Kuala Lumpur: APDC.
Lindsey, Quentin, W. 1992. *The Keys to Democracy, Decentralisation, and Development in Nepal*. Kathmandu: UNDP/NPC.
National Planning Commission. 1991. *Approach to the Eighth Plan (1992–97)*. Kathmandu: HMG/NPC.

# 11

# Local Governance and Decentralisation: The Philippine Experience[1]

## ALEX B. BRILLANTES, Jr.

The enactment of the Local Government Code in 1991 was a result of decades of struggle of local governments for more autonomy from the stranglehold of a highly centralised politico–administrative structure based in 'imperial Manila'.[2] Local governments in the Philippines are actually the territorial and political sub-divisions of the country that is divided into 76 provinces. The latter are divided into 60 chartered cities and over 1,500 municipalities which are further subdivided into over 42,000 barangays. Owing to the unique circumstances obtaining in some parts of the country, notably Muslim Mindanao, the Cordilleras and metropolitan Manila, variations in the local government systems were made with regional governments set up for the Cordilleras and Muslim Mindanao and with an integrated metropolitan governmental structure for metro Manila. The clamour for autonomy among the 'regular' local governments in the Philippines should be located within the broader context of the need for a more decentralised politico–administrative structure that will be more responsive to the needs of the people.

The first part of the paper provides a historical overview of the local governmental system of the Philippines and the struggle for autonomy for local governments that culminated with the enactment of the Local Government Code in 1991. It will be followed by a discussion of the various political and administrative structures at the local level, including references to local electoral, planning and decision-making processes. The paper also discusses critical issues, problems and concerns that have resulted in politico–administrative shocks in various forms and degrees for local governments.

## Historical Account and Present Political Context[3]

The movement for autonomy among local level institutions within the general framework of decentralisation has its origins as early as 1898 under the Malolos Constitution-governed first Philippines Republic that lasted until 1902. Decentralisation then was described by Jose P. Laurel as 'the most ample form of decentralisation' for local governments.[4] However, local governments were still subject to regulation based on several principles, including the 'determination in their powers in matters of taxes, in order that the provincial and municipal taxation may never be antagonistic to the system of taxation of the State'.[5]

With the arrival of the Americans in the beginning of the 20th century, centralisation of the politico–administrative system was effected in order to ensure the consolidation of powers of the colonialists. Consequently, all local governments were placed under the control of the military to ensure their effective control. The period of the Philippines Commonwealth that lasted from 1935 to the early 1940s saw a shift from 'control' over the local governments by the executive departments to 'supervision' towards the general direction of assuring some kind of autonomy for local governments.

The period from 1946 to 1972 marked the operationalisation of a supposedly independent Philippine Republic. One of the pillars of such a republic was the autonomy of the constituent local government units. In 1959, the first autonomy law for local governments (Republic Act 2264) was passed. It vested in the city and municipal governments increased fiscal, planning and regulatory powers. It broadened the taxing powers of the cities and municipalities within the framework of national tax laws. It likewise granted the cities and municipalities power to adopt zoning and planning ordinances. Finally, it granted provincial, city and municipal governments the authority to undertake and carry out public works projects that the local government itself finances. It was in the same year (1959) that autonomy to the lowest levels of government was granted through the Barrio Charter Act (Republic Act 2370). It sought to transform the barrios,[6] the smallest political unit of the local government system into quasi-municipal corporations vested with taxing powers. Barrios were to be governed by an elective barrio council that was empowered to enact ordinances and laws for the area.

Less than a decade later, the 'Decentralization Act of 1967' (Republic Act 5185) was enacted. It further increased the financial resources of local governments and broadened their decision-making latitude over administrative—mostly fiscal and personnel—matters. The Decentralisation Act declared the following policy:

It is, therefore, the purpose of this Act to grant local governments greater freedom and ampler means to respond to the needs of their people and promote prosperity and happiness to effect a more equitable and systematic distribution of governmental power and resources. To this end, local governments henceforth shall be entrusted with the performance of those functions that are more properly administered in the local level and shall be granted with as much autonomous powers and financial resources as are required in the more effective discharge of their responsibilities.

The Act therefore allowed provincial and city governments to retain financial resources previously contributed to the national government. Appointments of provincial personnel—such as the provincial agriculturist—were vested in the provincial governor.[7] The Act also enumerated a number of 'duties and powers of local chief executives not subject to direction or review by any national official'.

By any measure, the imposition of martial law in 1972, which abolished local elections and vested in the dictator the powers to appoint local officials who were beholden to him, was a great setback for the local autonomy movement in the Philippines. Notwithstanding the highly centralised dictatorial set-up, the Marcos Constitution, 1973, rhetorically committed itself to a policy of local autonomy:

The State shall guarantee and promote autonomy of local government units, especially the barrio, to ensure their fullest development as self-reliant communities.

The document likewise constitutionalised the taxing powers of local government units thus:

Each local government unit shall have the power to create its own sources of revenue and to levy taxes subject to limitations as may be provided by law.

However, the President continued to exercise 'supervision and control' over the local governments. The authoritarian government promulgated the Local Government Code of 1983 (Batas Pambansa Biland 337) which reiterated the policy of the State to

guarantee and promote the autonomy of local government units to ensure their fullest development as self-reliant communities and make them effective partners in the pursuit of national development.

However, full autonomy could not be realistically implemented under the authoritarian regime.

With the overthrow of Marcos in 1986 during the so-called ESA revolution that installed Mrs. Corazon Acquino as President of the Philippines, the Freedom Constitution was enacted. It specifically provided that 'the President shall have control and exercise general supervision over all local governments'. It was this specific provision that enabled President Acquino, through the Minister of Local Government, to remove local officials throughout the country whose loyalties were questionable, and replace them with officers-in-charge (OICs). Seen as an isolated act, the appointment of OICs may be seen as a set-back to the cause of local autonomy, but viewed in its proper historical/political context, it may be appreciated as a necessary measure in stabilising the immediate post-dictatorship transition government.

However, with the promulgation of the 1987 Constitution, specific provisions guaranteeing autonomy to local governments were included. Among the major state policies is the policy that 'The State shall ensure the autonomy of local governments'. Additionally, Article X, Section 3 of the Constitution provides:

The Congress shall enact a local government code which shall provide for a more responsive and accountable local government structure instituted through a system of decentralisation with effective mechanisms of recall, initiative, referendum, allocate among the different local government units their powers, responsibilities and resources, and provide for the qualifications, election, appointment and removal, term, salaries, powers and functions and duties of local officials, and all other matters relating to the organisation and operation of local units.

From the preceding, it can be concluded that the Philippine politico–administrative history is replete with examples of tensions between a highly centralised governmental structure and the demands for autonomy among the various component local units: at one level, there is an imperative for a dominant and assertive leadership necessarily for the consolidation and even for the very survival of the weak state; at another level, is the clamour and demand among the component local institutions for maximum autonomy from the central government in order to enable them to become more responsive to situations obtaining locally.

## The Local Government Code of 1991

This section discusses the Local Government Code of 1991 and how it responds to the tensions. The enactment of the Local Government Code of 1991 was a fulfilment of a constitutional directive to provide the framework for local autonomy for local governments. The Local Government Code:

- devolves the responsibility for the delivery of basic services (which formerly belonged to the central government) to the local governments;
- devolves the enforcement of certain regulatory and licensing powers formerly reposed in the national government, to local governments;
- increases the internal revenue allotment of local governments;
- expands the taxing powers of local governments;
- expands the LGUs structure through the creation of mandatory and optional positions in the local bureaucracy in order to make them more responsive to local conditions at the local levels;

- elevates the relationship between the national and local governments from one of patronage to partnership; and
- broadens the notion of 'governance' beyond the confines of the formal structures and processes of government by encouraging direct participation of non-government organisations and people's organisations in various special bodies, supporting joint GO–NGO collaborative undertakings,[8] and promoting local accountabilities in local governance through the mechanisms of recall and initiative.

Among the basic services whose delivery formerly was the responsibility of the national government but were devolved to local governments are health, infrastructure, agriculture, social welfare and environment. Together with the shift in responsibility for the delivery of such basic services was the transfer of personnel from the national government agencies to the local governments. Corresponding programmes, projects, records and equipment were likewise to be transferred.

The devolution of the wide-ranging set of responsibilities to the local governments was accompanied by an increase on some taxation powers of local governments. These are primarily taxes on local businesses and other local taxes, and the real property taxes. However, taxation powers are only as significant as the tax base of local governments. Appendix 2 details the taxes that may be levied by various local government units).

There is likewise the significant increase in the internal revenue allotment (IRA) share of local governments from a low of 11 per cent to as high as 40 per cent over a period of eight years. In spite of the increase in revenue share of local governments, estimates have shown that the financial resources accruing to local governments as mandated by the Code would not be sufficient to bear the 'costs of devolution'. Thus, local governments have banded together through their various leagues at different levels—led by the League of Provinces—to demand increased financial resources from the national government to pay for the costs of devolution.

The Code guarantees local government units a 40 per cent share of the proceeds of exploitation of natural resources in their jurisdiction. It allows them to obtain loans and credits and float bonds, and receive grants and subsidies from external sources they are able to tap and develop. The Code has also mandated an expansion of the organisation of the local governments in order to cope with the expanded responsibilities devolved to them. Various positions—mandatory and optional—depending on the needs and realities at the local level—may be created. For instance, among the positions that may be created at various levels of the local government units depending on the local government's thrusts are officers who would specialise in environment and natural resources, co-operatives, population, etc. (Refer to Appendix 1 for the specific mandatory and optional positions that may be created at the various local levels.)

Another outstanding feature of the Local Government Code of 1991 is that it provides the organisational infrastructure that could lead the way for the institutionalisation of 'people empowerment' through the direct participation of non-governmental organisations (NGOs) and people's organisations (POs) in local special bodies. For instance, NGOs and POs are allocated specific seats in the local development council, the local health board, the local school board, local prequalification bids and awards committee and the local peace and order council. The opportunity for empowerment is likewise given a boost by the allocation of seats in the local legislative bodies (sangguniang bayan) to sectors traditionally marginalised in the general process of local governance. Such sectors include women, labour (agriculture and non-agriculture), disabled and indigenous cultural communities.

It is within the context of the above developments that the enactment of the Local Government Code of 1991 has generated a flurry of downstream activities in all areas of public administration, both at the national and local levels. The first year of implementation has largely been instructive in terms of the surfacing of a number of issues and concerns. The following section discusses these various implementation issues and concerns.

## Issues and Concerns

The major issues and concerns as far as the implementation of the Local Government Code of 1991 is concerned can be broadly clustered into either administrative and/or political considerations. More specifically, administrative concerns as far as the implementation of the Local Government Code of 1991 is concerned can be broadly clustered into either administrative and/or political considerations. Even more specifically, administrative concerns pertain to the following: personnel; financial; organisation and management; intergovernmental relations; and relations with NGOs/POs and the private sector.

The following may be considered implementation concerns that have political implications: warlordism/bossism/refeudalisation; intergovernmental relations; and GO–NGO relations

The ensuing discussion summarises these implementation concerns.

## Implementation Concerns: Administrative

A major administrative concern pertains to the so-called 'administrative capacities' or absorptive capabilities of the local government units to assume the various functions and responsibilities that will be devolved to them under the Code.

Around 66,000 national government personnel are potentially affected by the devolution process. These national agency personnel are from the Departments of Health, Agriculture, Social Welfare, and Environment and Natural Resources whose services are devolved to the local governments. Table 11.1 reflects the breakdown of the number of these personnel.

One of the initial sources of confusion in the Code's implementation pertained to contradictory policies and statements that emerged from various national government agencies involved in the devolution process. In this case, the Civil Service Commission and the Department of Budget and Management released contradictory policy statements early in the devolution process pertaining to the status of personnel to be devolved to LGUs. At one level, the Code provides that the personnel of national government agencies devolved to the local governments shall be mandatorily absorbed by the local governments. The Code likewise provides that such personnel shall not suffer any diminution in rank nor pay. Thus the Civil Service Commission has released memoranda to LGUs to that effect. It has been generally observed that nationally employed personnel enjoy higher salaries than the locally paid employees.[9] However, at another level local governments are prohibited from allocating more than 45 to 55 per cent of their

Table 11.1: Number of Personnel to be devolved to the Local Governments as per Local Government Code of 1991*

| Department | Total No. of personnel | Total No. of personnel to be devolved to the LGUs | Percentage |
|---|---|---|---|
| Health | 73,000 | 46,000 | 61 |
| Agriculture | 41,225 | 14,335 | 34 |
| Social Welfare | 6,767 | 3,827 | 56 |
| Environment and Natural Resources | 21,687 | 895 | 4 |
| Total | 1,42,679 | 65,057 | 45 |

* Note that these are *Potentially* affected personnel since they are deployed in the various local governments throughout the country and basically report to the local chief executive of the area. There were some departments that had already identified the specific number of personnel to be devolved to the LGUs.

Source: Table constructed from data obtained from various departments.

budgets for personnel services. The Department of Budget and Management has come out with circulars to local governments communicating the ceilings. However, because of the mandatory devolution, and because of higher salaries enjoyed by the devolved personnel when they were still nationally paid, local budgets are strained with personnel services easily going beyond the 45 to 55 per cent ceiling. It is therefore imperative to reconcile such contradictions.[10]

As far as financial capacities are concerned, it is entirely possible that the amounts devolved to the LGUs may not be commensurate with the value of functions and services devolved to them because the devolution process involves the transfer of equipment, records, personnel and projects of the national departments affected.

Then, there is concern that the delivery of basic services at the local level will be disrupted largely as a result of the transition. There is anticipated fragmentation of the delivery of basic services which used to be the primary responsibility of the national government but are now devolved to the LGUs. At one point, the DOH even claimed that as many as 40,000 lives may be lost as a result of the devolution and fragmentation. Such a situation may lead to what some believe to be diseconomies of scale that will occur in the delivery of devolved services.

Largely because of the concerns raised above, there seemed to be a general hesitancy among local governments—especially among the poorer ones—to accept the responsibility for the delivery of a whole range of basic services—from agriculture to health to infrastructure to social services—that has suddenly become theirs under the Code. The fear is that they may not be able to financially support the delivery of such services. Such a situation has even led some local legislative councils to pass resolutions to the effect that they will not accept personnel who will be devolved to them. As a matter of fact, this was the general theme that emerged during the 1992 Cebu Convention of the League of Cities. However, as articulated by one mayor, he did not mind absorbing the devolved personnel provided they are assured of financial assistance.[11]

During the first year of implementation, in order to allay fears among local governments that they would not be able to bear the 'costs of devolution', there were proposals for the Department of Budget and Management to set aside a 'stabilisation fund', also referred to as an augmentation fund (described by some local officials as 'mythical augmentation funds' because such funds never seemed to materialise) to assist local governments that could not afford the devolution costs at all fronts, i.e. absorb personnel and bear the costs of operation of devolved programmes and projects.[12]

It was in this connection that the League of Provinces advocated for the passage of a bill that would amend the Local Government Code separating the cost of devolution from the internal revenue allotments of LGUs. The League has pressured the President to put his support behind the bill that allocates additional funds to the local governments to cover the costs of devolution, which mostly pertains to supporting the salaries of the personnel of the various national agencies that will be devolved to the local governments. The original idea as provided for in the Code was that the costs of devolution would be charged to the internal revenue allotment share of the local government units. But estimates have shown that the IRA share of the LGUs is barely sufficient to support the implementation of the various programmes and projects that will be absorbed by the local governments. Hence the need for some kind of an 'augmentation' fund specifically allotted to cover the costs of devolution. More specifically, the proposed bill (House Bill 6346) provides that

The costs of devolved services shall first be excluded or deducted from the total internal revenue allotment allocable to local government units and shall be equitably distributed to each of them. In 1993, the amount so excluded or deducted shall be the actual cost of devolution. In 1984 and the subsequent years the amount for devolved services shall increase or decrease in proportion to the increase or decrease of the total revenue allotment of local government units.

## *Political*

The issue of decentralisation and local autonomy is really anchored on power and how it should be dispersed from the centre and how it will be shared among the various levels of government.

As mentioned earlier, the Code encourages the active participation of non-governmental organisations ·and people's organisations in local governance. There is a danger that the term 'non-governmental organisations' might be construed and abused in its broadest and most liberal context resulting in the sprouting of all kinds of 'non-government' organisations, fly-by-night NGOs ('come and go's') and politician organised NGOs. To a certain extent, there are NGOs that have been organised by defeated politicos who see NGOs as a 'back door' to local power politics.

There is likewise the political issue of turf and the delineation of sharing of power among the various levels of government (e.g., national–local, and even national–national), and between the formal and established structures of government and the NGOs. Except for a few, government functionaries and bureaucrats have not been used to working with those not within the formal structures of the bureaucracy, e.g. NGOs. This is also true for some NGOs themselves who are not familiar with the nuances and culture of local government bureaucracy. The Code encourages some kind of a partnership between these two sectors. To say the least, problems are inevitable in the process of 'getting to know each other' and overcoming mutual suspicion and distrust.

It should be noted that there have been attempts from various sectors to subtly derail the provision of sectoral representation in the local sanggunian. In the House of Representatives, two measures have been filed that will effectively disable the implementation of sectoral representation at the local governments. The first pertains to the postponement of the election of sectoral representatives in local legislative bodies from 1993 to 1995. The second gives the elected members of the local legislative bodies the option to decide whether or not the local government should still have sectoral representatives. Both proposals are anchored upon financial grounds, i.e. local governments are cash-strapped and cannot afford the salaries of additional sectoral representatives that could cost as much as P 200,000 per year per sectoral representative.[13]

Some local chief executives have actually suggested that the local governments should be given from five to 10 years to be able to adjust to the additional expenditure of inheriting personnel devolved from the national governments. Such a perception was also shared by a number of national government agency officials. The only problem with 'delaying' the implementation is that it may provide an opportunity for some sectors to water down and— eventually—subvert the Code's provisions.[14]

Finally, there is the persistent concern of warlordism, i.e. that devolution will simply lead to warlordism, 'bossism' and refeudalisation of local politics. While this is certainly a possibility, it must be emphasised that the process of local autonomy does not only entail the devolution of powers but of accountability as well. This is a process that is given emphasis in the Code with the provision for recall and initiative at the local level.

## Concluding Remarks

The passage of the Local Government Code, while an answer to the decade-old problem of overcentralisation, has brought with it politico–administrative shocks and stresses upon the local governmental system, stresses that are quite expected when implementing radical changes in any system. Some of the major sources of local government's stresses are; stress from people's expectations about the ability of the local government to quickly respond to their demands as a result of the increased powers of local governments; stress as a result of the lack of financial resources and support to the local governments; stress from the lack of adequate technical resources, capabilities and qualified people at the local level; and stress from the affected national government agencies. Some national government agencies willfully withhold support to local governments in order to set them up for failure, and thus justify retention of powers and authorities with the national government.

However, the above transition-related problems and stresses are not insurmountable. Various sectors of society—from the national government to the non-governmental organisations—should come in and provide the necessary support that will be needed by the LGUs. If there is any pressing imperative right now, it is the need to support local governments to help them assume the various responsibilities that have now been devolved to them under the Code. Support can be mainfested in various ways:

(*i*) non-interruption of the internal revenue allotments to LGUs. Unfortunately, the anticipated LGU share from the IRA for this year went down from the anticipated P 24 billion to P 18 billion.

(*ii*) proper allocation of the augmentation fund identified by the DILG specifically in terms of demonstrating a bias for the lower income local government units who may still be unable to absorb the various functions that will be devolved to them.

(*iii*) support for various capability-building efforts of various institutions—such as those conducted by various academic and non-academic institutions—to help strengthen the various capabilities of LGUs.[15]

(*iv*) encouragement of NGO participation in the various mechanisms made available to them, including their membership in local special bodies; the conduct of joint ventures and cooperative agreements with the LGUs; their participation in local legislative bodies through the election of sectoral indigenous cultural minorities, disabled and any other sector determined by the local sanggunian.

(*v*) promotion of local accountabilities through the system of recall.

The struggle for local autonomy in the Philippines within the general context of decentralisation has been a long and difficult one for local level front-line institutions, with centrally located stockholders expected to jealously protect their turf and spheres of influence and power. The enactment of the Local Government

Code somehow marks a culmination of the struggle of the local institutions. The Code may finally provide the opportunity for the release of the potential at the local levels long restrained by a highly centralised politico–administrative system. The political will to meaningfully implement the Code is, therefore, indispensable. Choices that demonstrate a bias for local autonomy have to be made, with central officials and agencies taking a secondary role this time. Otherwise, it will remain another piece of legislation that will follow the well-trodden path to non-implementation.

## Notes

1. The author would like to express his gratitude to Terreпce George for his comments and to the Ford Foundation for the support that enabled participation in the conference. Views and opinions expressed in this paper are the author's and do not necessarily reflect the views of the institutions he is associated with. The author assumes full responsibility for any errors and shortcomings of this paper.
2. The term 'imperial Manila' has been used by various local level officials as a manifestation of their continued resistance—and contempt—for the decades-old highly centralised politico–administrative structures and processes that have been blamed for the (local government units) inability to 'take off' in their development efforts.
3. This section is based on my article entitled 'Decentralization in the Philippines: An Overview', *Philippine Journal of Public Administration*, 31:2, April 1987.
4. Jose P. Laurel was President of the Japanese-sponsored Philippine Republic during the Second World War. He was a former local official himself, having been former governor during the American occupation when local governments were still in their evolution stage. His book (*Local Government in the Philippines Islands*) from where this citation is taken, was written in 1926 and is considered among the classics in the literature on Philippine local governments.
5. Romeo Ocampo and Elena Panganiban 'The Philippines' in Chung Si Ahn (ed.) *The Local Political Systems in Asia*, (Seoul: Seoul National University Press, 1987), p. 90, as cited in Brillantes, *op. cit.*
6. The barrios were the precursors of the barangays as the smallest political unit of the local government system.
7. This notwithstanding, the national agency, the Department of Agriculture, could also appoint its own provincial agricultural officer (PAO), thus leading to the duplication of presence of agricultural officers at the provincial level. Such duplication—not only of the agricultural sector but also of other sectors such as infrastructure—is one of the concerns that the 1991 Local Government Code tries to address.
8. In an earlier article, entitled 'GO–NGO Collaboration: A New (and Encouraging) Development in Local Governance' (*Go–NGO Watch*, November 1992, p.

2). I argued that the enactment of the Code has expanded the notion of governance by going beyond the pale of formal structures and processes of government:

> Governance, as commonly understood, has always been the responsibility of the government, which after all, is mandated to govern, i.e., provide the leadership in the delivery of basic services to the people, and in the process, exercise predominating influence and legitimacy. However, because of a number of constraints—ranging from limited sources to bureaucratic problems like red tape and corruption—conventional structures and processes of government have become generally ineffective in fulfilling their tasks of governance . . . . Thus, extra governmental structures—including the private sector, NGOs and POs—have taken on the task of governance, more specifically in the delivery of basic services, active development work, and consequently increased influence and legitimacy at the local levels.

9. For instance, there are cases where a nationally paid provincial agriculturist has a monthly salary of PHP 12,000 versus his local counterpart who is paid around PHP 7,000. The Code provides that national agency officials who are devolved have to be paid either the same or higher salaries, but in no case shall the salary be lower than the amount previously enjoyed while they were being paid by the national government agency.

10. This was one of the major findings of the Rapid Field Appraisal conducted by the Associates in Rural Development on 10 August 1992.

11. Problems in the devolution of the health sector seems to be the most dramatic. A number of Bills in both houses have been filed to defer the implementation of devolving the health sector to the local governments. However, analogous situations are being drawn for other sectors such as peace and order and the devolution of the police forces, and the infrastructure sector.

12. However, initial findings of a second rapid field appraisal on the implementation of decentralisation conducted by the Associates in Rural Development seem to indicate that local government units can actually cover the personnel services cost of devolution including the area of health. What they cannot afford, the study shows, are expenses for management and operating expenses and capital outlay.

13. This perception of some members of the House of Representatives is likewise the perception of some local governments. For instance, in the municipality of San Juan in metro Manila, the move not to have sectoral representatives is gaining support based on two grounds: (*a*) the financial (in)capability of the local government, i.e., it is expensive to have sectoral representatives, and (*b*) the elected members themselves can capably represent the very sectors they come from, e.g., an urban poor woman elected legislator can represent the women or urban poor, hence obviating the need for a sectoral representative for such sectors. Such argumentation misses the whole point of sectoral representation and may even subvert the very spirit of the people empowerment provision of the Code: it is precisely the vehicle of sectoral representation that will 'make up' for the historical politico–administrative bias against the very sector (some from of affirmative action) and therefore should not be compromised. One cannot put a price on people empowerment.

14. There are also some quarters that opt for phasing and delaying the full implementation of the Code, pending the 'readiness' of the local government units. For instance, the Department of Health has identified a three-phase programme in implementing the Code over a period of five years: (*a*) the changeover phase; (*b*) the transition phase, and (*c*) the stabilisation phase.

15. Various government and non-government academic institutions have identified local government capability-building programmes among their major priorities. These include the following: the Local Government Academy of the Department of Interior and Local Government; the Local Government Centre of the University of the Philippines College of Public Administration; the various Philippine Business for Social Progress–local Development Assistance Programme-initiated Centres for Local Governance; the Local Government Development Foundation; the Evelio Javier Foundation; the Centre for Local Development of the Development Academy of the Philippines; and the Congressional Research and Training Service.

## Select Reading

Associates in Rural Development, Inc. 1992. *Rapid Field Appraisal of the Status of Decentralisation: The Local Perspective*. Manila: Local Development Assistance Programme.

*Second Rapid Field Appraisal*, February 1993.

Brillantes, Alex Jr., 1992. 'GO–NGO Collaboration: A New (and Encouraging) Development in Local Governance'. *GO–NGO Watch*, November.

————. 1990. 'Challenges to Local Government Administration'. *Local Government Bulletin*, December.

————. 1987. 'Decentralization in the Philippines'. *Philippines Journal of Public Administration*, 31:2, April.

Laurel, Jose P. 1926. *Local Government in the Philippines Islands*. Manila: Pilarica Press.

Sosmena, Gaudioso. 1991. *Decentralisation and Empowerment*. Manila: Local Government Development Foundation.

Tabunda, Manuel and Mario Galand. 1992. *A Guide to the Local Government Code of 1991*. Manila: Mary Jo Educational Supply.

# Appendix 11.1

## Mandatory and Optional Positions for Local Government Units as per 1991 Local Government Code

| LGU Level | Mandatory positions | Optional positions |
|-----------|---------------------|--------------------|
| Barangay | Secretary<br>Treasurer<br>Lupong Tagapamayapa | Community brigades |
| Municipality | Treasurer<br>Assessor<br>Accountant<br>Budget officer<br><br>Planning and Devpt.<br>  Coordinator<br>Engineer<br>Health officer<br>Civil Registrar | Administrator<br>Legal Officer<br>Agriculturist<br>Environment and<br>  Natural Resources officer<br>Social Welfare and<br>  Devpt. officer<br>Architect<br>Information officer |
| City | Treasurer<br>Assessor<br>Accountant<br>Budget officer<br>Planning and Devpt.<br>  Coordinator<br>Engineer<br>Health officer<br>Civil Registrar<br>Administrator<br>Legal officer<br>Veterenarian | Architect<br>Information officer<br>Agriculturist<br>Population officer<br>Environment and Natural<br>  Resources officer<br>Cooperatives officer |

|  | Social Welfare and Devpt. officer General Services officer |  |
| --- | --- | --- |
| Province | Treasurer Assessor Accountant Engineer Budget officer Planning and Devpt. Coordinator Legal officer Administrator Health officer Social Welfare and Devpt. officer General Services officer Agriculturist Veterenarian | Population officer Environment and Natural Resources officer Cooperatives officer Architect Information Officer |

**Source:** Based on materials prepared by the Department of Interior and Local Government.

# Appendix 11.2

## Local Taxes That May be Levied by Local Government Units as per Local Government Code of 1991

- Higher ceiling for tax rates
- Mineral and forest products now taxable by LGUs
- Gross receipts of banks and other financial institutions now taxable by LGUs
- Tax on business of manufacturers, wholesalers, retailers and contractors.

  - graduated fix rates
  - percentage tax for gross receipts exceeding specified levels
  - Authority of LGUs to adjust tax rates

    - Once every five years
    - Authority not to exceed 10 per cent of rates prescribed in the Code

  - Authority of LGUs to grant tax exemption privileges
  - Withdrawal of tax exemption privileges to government-owned and controlled corporations
  - Tax bases transferred from provinces to municipalities

Source: Based on materials prepared by the Department of Interior and Local Government.

# 12

# Local Self-governance: The Case of Itogon Municipality in the Philippines

Since the Local Government Code (LGC) of 1991 has only been in effect for the past 12 months, it is too early to attempt a thorough evaluation of the impact of decentralised governance on the socio-economic dynamics of rural society in the Philippines. Instead, this paper looks at the process of initial implementation of the Code in a municipality and the various problems and issues that have arisen as a result of its implementation.

## Study Region and its Resource Endowment

Itogon is one of 13 municipalities[1] in the province of Benguet in the mountainous Cordillera region which is situated in the northern region of Luzon—the largest and the most populous island in the Philippines. It is approximately 26 kilometres from the provincial capital of La Trinidad and 269 kilometres from the national capital of Manila. The land area of Itogon is 498 sq. kms, which is 18.7 per cent of the provincial land area.

Itogon is the centre of the country's principal mining district. The country's largest mining firms are concentrated in this tiny municipality, which has traditionally accounted for its being the premier municipality in Benguet in terms of tax revenue collection.

Mining has drawn many people to Itogon from the poverty-stricken areas around it. The population increase in Itogon since the post-war period has been nothing less than remarkable. Population doubled from 1948 to 1960 (from 16,970 to 32,742): since then, the population has increased by 20 per cent to 30 per cent every decade.[2] It has been observed that periods of high population growth have generally coincided with peaks in mineral production of the corporate mines in the municipality.[3] According the the latest census data gathered in May 1990, Itogon has a total population of 61,773—a part of which consists of in-migrants.

The largest mining firm operating in the municipality—indeed, in the country—is Benguet Corporation which started its Benguet gold operations involving underground and tunnel mining as early as 1903. However, more than 80 years of intensive mining operations has all but depleted the underground high-grade gold ores, resulting in declining revenue in the 1980s. The company then decided to shift to large-scale open-pit and bulk mining methods to sustain the profitability of its gold operations in the area.

Many of the local communities, however, opposed the use of such mining methods, because of their widely recognised adverse effects on environment and the possible massive physical displacement of the people, many of whom are small-scale miners or farmers and are made up of indigenous people. The people's opposition took the form of a sustained campaign starting in 1989. This campaign, which caught national and international attention, witnessed the organisation and mobilisation of numerous POs and NGOs. Earlier studies[4] have indicated that, to a large extent, the concerted efforts of these POs and NGOs have been successful in pushing government to adopt stricter measures designed to protect the environment. Thus, even without provisions for decentralised governance Itogon has, in the past, been presented as a case study of how people's actions can directly influence government policies. In 1990, for instance, the municipal government responded to the people's opposition by unanimously adopting a municipal ordinance providing for the abatement of open-pit mining which was declared to be particularly injurious to the health and safety of the community and damaging to the peace, comfort, harmony, prosperity and general welfare of the people of Itogon. In 1992, Benguet Corporation announced the closure of its Benguet gold operations, except for its open-pit operations. Because of its unique historical and contemporary experience, Itogon proves to be an interesting case study of the implementation of the Local Government Code.

## The Municipal Government of Itogon

Since the macro level paper on the Philippines provides a general overview of the Local Government Code, this section presents the significant features of decentralisation provided by the Code as it applies to the municipality of Itogon.

The Local Government Code of 1991 devolves to the municipal government the provision of basic services including, but not limited to, the following:

1. agricultural extension and research services (formerly provided by the Department of Agriculture);
2. community-based forestry projects (formerly handled by the Department of Natural Resources and Environment);
3. health and hospital services (formerly provided by the Department of Health);
4. public works and infrastructure projects, excluding projects funded wholly or partially through official development assistance (formerly managed by the Department of Public Works and Highways);
5. social welfare services, such as projects pertaining to the welfare of children, youth, the elderly and disabled persons, the family, and the community, as well as livelihood and pro-poor projects (formerly provided by the Departmet of Social Welfare and Development).

In addition, the regulatory functions of certain agencies are also devolved to the municipal government. These include the processing and approval of housing projects, the enforcement of environmental laws, the inspection of food products, the implementation of the National Building Code and the enforcement of quarantine regulations.

The devolution of the responsibility for the provision of basic services and facilities was to take place within six months from the Code's effectivity, that is, by 30 June 1992. It was further provided that the basic services referred to above would be funded from the share of the municipality in the proceeds of national taxes and other local revenues, with funding support from the national government. In this connection, regional offices of national agencies, or offices whose functions were devolved to the Local Government Units (LGUs), were to be phased out within one year from the effectivity of the Code, that is, by 31 December 1992.

In support of its development plans and priorities, and in the fulfilment of its responsibility to provide the foregoing basic services, the municipality is empowered by the Code to create more of its own sources of revenue, including new taxes and even floating municipal bonds if it so chooses. The municipality is further entitled to a 40 per cent share of the real property taxes collected within its boundaries, and a much higher share in the internal revenue collected by the national government. Likewise devolved to the municipal government is the power to expropriate private property for public use, as well as the power to reclassify agricultural lands for other uses which would yield greater economic gains.

From the foregoing, it is evident that the Code devolves significant powers and responsibilities to the municipality. The Code likewise provides for unprecedented de-bureaucratisation of governance, as it seeks to promote the establishment and operation of POs and NGOs to make them active partners in local governance. One way is by providing for PO/NGO representation in the legislative body, in this case, the municipal council. As the elected legislative body, the eight-member municipal council is mandated to enact ordinances, approve resolutions and appropriate funds. Specifically, the Code provides that the municipal council shall include one sectoral representative each from the women's and workers' sectors and one from any of the following sectors: urban poor, indigenous cultural communities, disabled persons or any other sector as may be determined by the council. These sectoral representatives are to be elected by their peers in their sector. De-bureaucratisation is further provided in the direct involvement of the POs, NGOs and the private sector in various local special bodies, which include the municipal development council, the prequalifications, bids and awards committee, the school board, the health board, and the peace and order council.

In addition, it is also important to point out that the Code recognises the power of the people to recall an elective official for loss of confidence. Moreover, local initiative or the right of the people to directly propose, enact, repeal or amend an ordinance is also mandated by the Code.

## The Municipal Development Council and the Local Planning Process

The Local Government Code of 1991 provides for the creation of the municipal government council to be responsible for initiating the formulation of a comprehensive multi-sectoral development plan for approval by the municipal council. The development council would assist the municipal council 'in setting the direction of economic and social development and coordinating develop-ment efforts' within the municipality. In fulfilment of this goal, the Code defines the functions of the municipal development council as follows:

(*a*) Formulate long-term, medium-term and annual socio-eco-nomic development plans and policies.
(*b*) Formulate the medium-term and annual public investment programmes.
(*c*) Appraise and prioritise socio-economic development pro-grammes and projects.
(*d*) Formulate local investment incentives to promote the inflow and direction of private investment capital.
(*e*) Coordinate, monitor and evaluate the implementation of development programmes and projects.
(*f*) And perform such other functions as may be provided by law or competent authority.

The municipal development council is headed by the mayor, with the following as members: all barangay captains, the chair-man of the municipal council's committee on appropriations, the congressman or his representative, and representatives of NGOs operating in the municipality who should constitute not less than one-fourth of the members of the fully organised council. With regard to the designation of NGO representatives to the municipal development council, the law provides that NGOs shall choose from among themselves their representatives to the development council within a period of 60 days from its organisation. In this connection, the municipal council is mandated to accredit NGOs in accordance with the prescribed criteria. As of mid-January 1993, it was reported that the Itogon municipal development council was functioning, although this was without any NGO/PO representatives. Despite this flaw in its composition, the development council was already carrying out its perceived task of reviewing project proposals from the various barangays, either for endorsement to higher agencies, such as the Department of Public Works and Highways, or for consideration in the programming of the 20 per cent development fund[5] for 1993.

Meanwhile, there is also the municipal planning and development office which is responsible for formulating integrated plans and policies for consideration of the municipal development council. The planning and development office is now in the process of formulating the long-term (1993–1998) plan, which it hoped to complete by 15 March 1993, and the annual (1993) plan of Itogon. The formulation of the two plans is in compliance with a directive from higher authorities.

The Itogon six-year development plan, in its present preliminary form, has the overall vision of improving the social, economic and political conditions of the municipality, through the effective implementation of balanced development with emphasis on infrastructure, agriculture, industry, social services and human resource development. The plan hopes to realise its goals of sustained economic growth, ecological preservation and improved public services. It further envisions that these goals will be realised by providing functional physical infrastructure in order to effectively deliver the needed socio–economic services, promoting an intensive campaign for the protection in the environment and improving the technical and management capabilities of local officials and community leaders. The aforementioned goals and objectives have already been reviewed and approved by the municipal council. The long-term plan also contains a listing of prioritised projects to be submitted for funding by the provincial government or the Department of Public Works and Highways. All these projects involve the construction, rehabilitation or improvement of community infrastructure, such as waiting sheds, foot, animal and vehicular bridges, stone masonry walls, pavements, barangay halls, waterworks, pathways, public toilets, and feeder and barangay roads.

On the other hand, the annual plan contains the various projects approved for implementation using the 20 per cent development fund of Itogon, which amounts to P 2,872,720 for 1993. 87 per cent of the 1993 development fund has already been allotted for specific projects, almost half of which was allotted for infrastructure maintenance and development. There were 34 community infrastructure projects, including 12-foot trails or pathways, nine waterworks projects, seven footbridges, two waiting sheds, two feeder roads or 'tire paths', one school ground pavement and the fencing and enclosure of a village health centre.

Among the projects which did not involve the construction, repair, maintenance or improvement of community infrastructure, the biggest allocations went to the establishment of a municipal breeding/demonstration farm and agri-training centre (P 450,000), the renovation, repair and painting of the municipal building (P 300,000) and attendance in meetings, conferences, seminars for municipal officials and employees (P 150,000). Other projects for which funds allotted are at amounts ranging from P 10,000 to P 90,000 are social services, nutrition development programme, integrated development program, livelihood/entrepreneurship skills training, establishment of silkworm breeding house, maintenance of municipal plant nurseries, sports and youth development programme, peace and order fund, engineering supervision and design, municipal profile preparation, purchase of equipment for development purposes, project documentation, monitoring and management, and farmers' training and seminars.

Comparing the above-mentioned development projects with those accomplished in 1992, it is notable that all projects accomplished in the past year were basically community infrastructure projects. The list of accomplished projects for 1992, which was obtained from the municipal planning and development office, did not include a single *non-infrastructure project*, of which there are a significant number planned for 1993. Still more notable is the lack of skills training programmes and livelihood projects in the annual plan for 1993, which are urgently needed now that Benguet Corporation has announced the closure of its underground mining operations.

The municipal planning and development office works under a set of guidelines for an effective planning process. For one, it is mandated by law that the local development council initiate the preparation of the plan. In this connection, the participation of the private sector, including NGOs and POs, should be encouraged. Officials are expected to participate in the planning process which, on the whole, should employ the 'bottom up' approach where plans originate from the village level.

Adherence to these guidelines, however, is not necessarily widespread. For example, it is the municipal planning and development office, rather than the municipal development council, that has initiated and spearheaded the formulation of the six-year and annual development plans thus far. Moreover, since there has been a delay in the official constitution of the municipal development council due, in turn, to the delay in the selection of private sector representatives, there has been no participation whatsoever of NGOs, POs and the private sector in the planning process.

It is also significant to note that some members of the municipal development council are not even aware of the ongoing planning process. This was highlighted when a municipal councillor, who is also a member of the development council, declared that, with regard to its planning function, the municipal development council at this point does not intend to formulate any long-term or medium-term development plan for the municipality. According to this informant, the municipality decided to 'adopt the annual term for development planning'. His conception of an annual socio–economic development plan for the municipality is simply programming the use of the municipality's development fund and deciding which projects proposed by the various villages be approved for implementation. Relatedly, his view of the annual plan is nothing but a list of development projects proposed for funding under the municipality's development fund. Presently, therefore, it appears that instead of taking the lead in the formulation of a comprehensive socio–economic development plan for the municipality, the municipal development council is reduced to a mere reviewer of proposed development projects.

## Initial Development of the Code in Itogon, Benguet

### *Devolution of Powers*

National law mandates that the devolution of the responsibility for the delivery of basic services and the transfer of personnel, assets and liabilities from national government agencies to local government units should have been completed not later than 30 June 1992, provided that those services which were not devolved by that date should have been devolved not later than 31 December 1992. In the event that devolution was not completed by 30 June 1992, the concerned national government agencies were expected to enter into a memorandum of agreement with local government units on the schedule and extent of devolution. Between 30 June and 31 December 1992, the municipal government entered into memoranda of agreement with the Departments of Agriculture, Social Welfare and Development, Budget and Health. These memoranda essentially provided for the immediate devolution of functions and services, and the transfer of all personnel, assets, equipment, facilities, liabilities, records and documents corresponding to the devolved functions and services from national agencies to the municipal government. It appears on paper, therefore, that devolution has indeed taken place.

However, information gathered from the municipality produced conflicting reports regarding the actual status of the devolution of services. The devolution of agricultural extension services of the Department of Agriculture is a case in point. One municipal councillor claimed that, as of January 1993, agricultural extension services had actually been devolved to the municipal level. Reportedly, all personnel of the Department of Agriculture assigned to the municipality have been transferred to the municipal government. Funds for personnel and operation costs for such agricultural extension, however, continued to be sourced from the Department of Agriculture. The municipal government, moreover, simply retained policies previously adopted by the Department. But the municipal agricultural officer presents a different perception on the status of devolution. According to him, agricultural extension services have not yet been devolved, since actual devolution has been postponed on at least two occasions—

from October 1992 to January 1993, then reportedly again from January to March 1993. The officer, however, does not have a clear conception of what devolution will mean in concrete terms. In early 1993, the staff of his office thought that devolution had already been carried out, but this was simply because there was a delay in the issuance of the salaries for that period. For them, devolution was simply a transfer of which office would disburse their salaries, i.e. the municipal government or the Department of Agriculture. The agricultural extension personnel, moreover, expressed concern that their salaries and other fringe benefits might be reduced once they are transferred from the Department of Agriculture to the municipal government. According to them, under the Department, their salaries were pegged to the level of a first class municipality, while Itogon's current classification is as a third class municipality, with the possibility of being re-classified to fourth or fifth class with the closure of the Benguet Corporation's gold operations in the area.[6] Their fears, however, may be unfounded, because the rules governing the transfer of personnel provide that there will be no diminution in pay or benefits of devolved personnel.

As of January 1993, the devolution of health services despite the existence of a memorandum of agreement between the Department of Health and the municipality of Itogon was reportedly still subject to further deliberation and reconsideration, particularly at the national level. A proposal for the Department of Health to retain the responsibility of providing health services was being seriously considered in Congress due to anticipated financial problems to be faced by various LGUs. While supervision of health personnel had already been devolved to the municipality, funds for their salaries for the first quarter of the year were released by the national government. Municipal officials recognised that the municipality may not be able to allocate the funds necessary for the salaries and other privileges of health personnel.

On the other hand, the devolution of the responsibility of overseeing the maintenance and construction of school buildings has caused some apprehension on the part of the municipal government. A compounding problem is the shutdown of Benguet Corporation's gold operations in Itogon. The cessation of mining operations caused apprehension on the part of the newly-created school board which would have to consider the funding necessary for the maintenance of the school buildings inside the mining communities. Benguet Corporation recently announced that it would continue subsidising the maintenance of the school buildings only until March 1993, and then turn these over to the Department of Education, Culture and Sports effective from 1993–1994. The affected parents, teachers and other school personnel have already requested the municipal government to address the situation. The local government realises that the maintenance and improvement of these school buildings will require additional financial appropriations.

The devolution of social welfare services and public works and infrastructure has not been discussed yet by the municipal council. Local officials expressed apprehension over the impending devolution of the social welfare services. They expect that the municipality will face major problems in addressing the social services and welfare needs of its residents.

## Inclusion of Sectoral Representatives in the Municipal Council

The country's Commission on Elections (COMELEC) promulgated on 27 October 1992 the rules and regulations, as well as schedule of activities, governing the first election of the three sectoral representatives to the legislative bodies of various local government units. One of the critical phases of the sectoral elections was the formal decision of each local legislature on the choice of the two other sectors, in addition to women as the mandatory first sector, which would be represented in the local legislative body. This decision should have been reached by the municipal council not later than 29 November 1992. COMELEC rules designated 1 December 1992 to 15 January 1993 as the accreditation period for sectoral organisations interested in fielding candidates for the positions of sectoral representatives.

Although fully aware of the above rules and regulations, the municipal council of Itogon has adopted a resolution providing that the municipality would, at this time, forego the election of sectoral representatives. According to the municipal secretary, anticipated financial constraints pose the major stumbling block in the appointment of sectoral representatives to the municipal council. As of January 1993, only the youth representative had been given an official seat in the council which had, of course, been mandated by law even before the enactment of the Local Government Code.

Elected local officials estimated that the inclusion of three sectoral representatives to the municipal council would require an additional budgetary outlay of P5 million to cover their salaries and other entitlements as council members. Presently, the local government cannot contemplate any possible sources for the financial requirements. Moreover, the municipality was expecting a sharp decline in revenue because of the announced closure of Benguet Corporation's underground mining operations. Furthermore, a certification from the municipal treasurer's office implied that the municipality was likely to suffer serious budgetary constraints. Local officials had also been informed that a bill was recently passed in the Philippine Congress proposing the deferment of the inclusion of sectoral representatives in the local legislatures to 1995. Local officials further noted that some municipal mayors felt that the selection of sectoral representatives is not necessary considering the present composition of the local legislative bodies. These officials were of the opinion that, in most municipalities, the various sectors are already well represented by the incumbent members of their respective councils. They cited, for instance, municipalities where elected councillors came from the ranks of farmers or labourers. They also expressed the view that the women's sector could very well be represented by men! They cited the example of the country's House of Representatives, where most of the bills, numbering more than 100, concerning the rights of women were sponsored or drafted by men. Generally, they held the view that the functions and responsibilities of the various sectoral representatives could be absorbed by the existing committees.

## Formation of the Local Special Bodies

As of January 1993, municipal officials claimed that the local special bodies had been constituted, although some were still without their NGO/PO representatives. Local officials claimed that, with the exception of the health board, all other special bodies had been formed and were already engaged in planning out their respective programmes of action. As of that date, the local peace and order council had been constituted, together with representatives from the women's and the veterans' sectors. It was learned that the peace and order council was conducting regular meetings and was engaged in an information dissemination campaign regarding its role and functions, although it still had to formulate its programme of activities for the year. There is nothing novel in this arrangement. However, even before the enactment of the LGC, existing rules already prescribed the inclusion of private sector representatives in the peace and order council. The local school board had likewise been constituted together with its private sector representative coming from the local Parents–Teachers Association in the locality.

The municipal government is still in the process of constituting the local health board. They cited a number of problems which have delayed the creation of this body, foremost among them being financial constraints. It was noted that, prior to the implementation of LGC, medicines and other medical needs had always been provided through funding sources external to the municipality. Traditionally, the municipality has appropriated only a minimal amount for health programmes and services. In addition, health programmes and activities have always been carried out in accordance with standards set by the Department of Health. It was observed that the municipal government seemed to be at a loss as to the provision of adequate health services to its constituents.

## Accreditation of NGOs and POs

According to the law, the accreditation of NGOs and POs for membership in the local special bodies should have been completed as early as September 1992. Most local government units, however, did not meet the prescribed deadline. In the case of Itogon, no certificates of accreditation had been issued as of the end of January 1993. By January 1993, 114 POs/NGOs had applied for accreditation in the municipality of Itogon. It should be pointed out that this is a huge number compared with most other municipalities in the country. Based on a tentative classification of the applicants, the majority were found to be POs, while only about eight were NGOs. The NGOs which applied for accreditation comprise three associated with the people's anti-open-pit mining campaign, the foundation established by Benguet Corporation to undertake development projects in the mining communities, three religious organisations, and one civic organisation. Among the POs, on the other hand, was the Itogon Inter-Barangay Alliance (IIBA)[7] and 10 of its member organisations plus two of its support organisations. Other PO applicants included farmers' associations, people's cooperatives, Parent–Teacher Associations, small-scale miners' associations, women's associations, civic organisations, etc.

Although not all of the applicants for accreditation had submitted a complete set of the required documents,[8] the municipal council had agreed in principle that all 114 NGO/PO applicants would be accredited. The council decided that all applicants who completed the requirements would be automatically accredited, while those which lacked some requirements would be accredited on the condition that they meet those requirements before they participate in the selection of representatives to the local special bodies. The municipal council had decided that deficiencies in the requirements would not hamper the accreditation of concerned NGOs and POs. The resolution providing the formal accreditation of the 144 applicants was expected to be passed by the municipal council by January 1993. For no apparent reason, however, it was not pushed through and was set aside for some future date. The municipal staff is still in the process of classifying the various applicants, as to whether these are POs and NGOs.

## People's Responses to and Perceptions about the Effectiveness of Decentralised Governance System

Local government officials of Itogon, as well as their counterparts in NGOs and POs, have ambivalent responses towards the Local Government Code. Local officials expressed that, despite all the problems attendant to the implementation of the Code in the municipality, decentralised governance is more effective and poses greater challenges to local government units. They cited that devolution of power provides the municipal council with the authority to directly address the problems of the municipality, bypassing the need for obtaining the go-ahead signal from higher authorities. They also citied as significant the power of the local government to create its own sources of revenue for the interests of the community. Furthermore, since the appointing authority of government personnel has been transferred to the local government, they feel that this will remove political pressure on the matter of appointments.

On the other hand, these same local officials make no attempt to hide their apprehension about or even non-acceptance of the devolution of the responsibility for the delivery of basic services. Is this apprehension simply due to their concern about insufficient budget or even inadequate training? Or is there perhaps a political consideration behind their apprehension? Can it be that they are even now foreseeing that, when the next local elections come, their constituents will hold them accountable for any inadequacy in the delivery of basic services or lack of tangible accomplishments?

Ambivalence also characterises the sentiments of local officials regarding the inclusion of sectoral representatives in the local legislature. On the one hand, they declare that NGOs can contribute much to development planning and legislation. On the other hand, their resistance to this innovation is evident in their resolution to seek deferment of the election of sectoral representatives to the municipal council. They have also verbalised, on numerous occasions, their willingness to work with NGOs. However, they feel that the NGOs and POs currently active in the municipality should first have a change of orientation. They suggest that NGOs should be re-oriented such that they see themselves as partners rather than as adversaries of government. They believe that NGOs can be of great assistance to the municipal government by conducting research in aid of legislation. If this is what they envision the role of NGOs and POs to be, then they are bound to be disappointed. NGOs and POs in the municipality have traditionally taken on a much more active and militant role. Local officials also expressed that there was need to review and look deeper into the incorporation of private sector representatives in the local special bodies.

A positive response is, of course, the application of no less than 114 POs and NGOs for accreditation. It is notable that the more militant NGOs, as well as the POs under the banner of the Inter-Itogon Barangay Alliance, unanimously agreed to apply for accreditation. Together, these groups constituted the major political force in the people's campaign against open-pit mining. The reason for their collective decision to seek accreditation was the belief that recognition by the municipality would allow their organisations to put forward their interests on a more formal plane. Three NGOs and 13 POs identified with this alliance applied for accreditation and are now looking forward to some representation in the local special bodies. These groups perceived the Code as a breakthrough in that it allows them to participate directly in local governance. They see the Code as an instrument for strengthening their position vis-à-vis the government and for gaining official recognition for their various activities and programs. Some POs and NGOs also believe that their accreditation will pave the way for better coordination with municipal officials. It is their view that the Code will provide them the opportunity to participate directly in local governance through their representatives in the local special bodies.

Previously, NGOs and POs acted as mere pressure groups vis-à-vis the municipal government. A case in point is when their sustained campaign against open-pit and bulk mining pushed the municipal council to pass a resolution in 1990 calling for the abatement of open-pit and other destructive mining methods in the municipality. The people considered this as a major achievement, which was gained only by the concerted efforts of the local population through a series of mass actions, and through the continuous sharing of ideas with individual municipal councillors. Even then, the municipal council consulted leaders of NGOs and POs, especially on matters concerning the environment. These NGOs and POs feel that the Code can provide them with an official identity, such that they no longer remain mere pressure groups but participate directly in local governance and become active partners in development.

These same NGOs, however, also have some misgivings about the Code. Now that the national line agencies have been relieved of the responsibility of providing basic social services, the burden for doing this has been shifted to the LGUs and the private sector. The NGOs point out that local government units may not have the financial and administrative capability to carry out such responsibility. At the same time, they hold the view that the provision of basic services should not be the responsibility of the private sector.

It was also learned that NGOs and POs in Itogon were generally informed about the Local Government Code even before the municipal officials. These NGOs and POs cite, for instance, the undue delays in the accreditation process. They claimed that accreditation could have been undertaken earlier but that the municipal council was not aware of the guidelines for accreditation. Presently, while most POs/NGOs have already completed and submitted the necessary documents to the municipal council, they are still awaiting issuance of their certificates of accreditation. Expectedly, NGOs and POs are not too happy about this.

Most of the members of POs learned about the Local Government Code through a series of consultations and training seminars sponsored by Baguio-based NGOs which are active in the mining communities. These consultations and training seminars took place mostly in the latter part of 1992. Participants of these consultations and seminars then conducted echo seminars in their respective localities. Officers of various POs who had earlier attended various seminars or training sessions on the LGC are now actively engaged in disseminating information regarding the Code at the village level.

## Conclusion

The following are some preliminary conclusions regarding the implementation and impact of the Local Government Code of 1991, as drawn from the experience of Itogon.

### Initial Implementation and Procedural Problems

During its initial year, procedural problems plagued the Code's implementation. These procedural problems caused undue delays in the accreditation of NGOs and POs in the municipality and, consequently, corresponding delays in the selection and inclusion of private sector representatives to the various bodies. For one thing, the municipal council was not clear on the guidelines for accreditation, nor on the procedure for convening the various accredited NGOs and POs for the purpose of choosing their representatives to the various local special bodies. Procedural problems, however, are easily surmountable and may thus be considered the least worrisome as far as the Code is concerned.

## Financial Stability of LGUs

At this early stage, it appears that the implementation of the Local Government Code, especially in its first three years, is likely to be wrought with problems concerning financial stability.

Regarding the devolution of the functions formerly reposed in the national line agencies, municipal officials expressed insecurity regarding the capability of the municipal government to provide basic services. They declared that they were suddenly made to shoulder the burden of various problems ranging from unemployment arising from the closure of Benguet Corporation's underground mining operations to insufficient social services. Local officials assert that financial considerations are at the core of their reservations to fully accept the devolution of powers provided by the Code. This appears to have been aggravated with the sudden closure of Benguet Corporation's underground operations in the municipality. For instance, the municipal government had already identified areas where infrastructure development, in the form of roads and bridges, are a priority. Some of these development projects, which were dependent on the anticipated revenue from the real property taxes to be paid by the Corporation, were derailed and the municipal council faced the major problem of having to identify alternative sources of funding to implement its projects.

This raises an important question. It appears that the LGC favours administrative units with larger potential tax bases. An unanticipated consequence of the Code may thus be the widening of the gap between rich and poor municipalities and provinces. Presently, the Itogon municipality has its share only from the Internal Revenue Allotment supplemented minimally by sources of local revenue. With the closure of Benguet Corporation's gold operations in Itogon, the municipal government will lose its anticipated 40 per cent share in the mining taxes to be collected by the national government from such operations. Local officials accept that financial resources will have to be generated from other sources.

Moreover, pertinent to the devolution of social welfare services, it was feared that retrenched workers would swell the growing ranks of the unemployed in the municipality. There are few alternative sources of livelihood in Itogon for these retrenched workers. In this regard, despite the financial constraints of local government units, the paramount consideration is to ensure continuity in the delivery of basic services. The national government has set aside a special augmentation fund which is to be used specifically to respond to the financial inadequacies of LGUs, particularly in providing the devolved services. However, guidelines on the management and allocation of this special fund, designed to bail out financially strapped LGUs, still have to be developed.

## Administrative Capability of LGUs

Aside from financial constraints, local officials have also pointed to the ill-preparedness of the LGU to take on the functions and responsibilities provided in the Code. Questions of administrative capability have thus been raised. From the problems that surfaced during the data-garnering phase of this research, it is evident that there is an urgent need to provide capability building seminars and workshops for local government personnel to help them carry out their expanded roles under the Code. For instance, they should be trained in the foundations of development planning to ensure that the development of each administrative unit is guided by a comprehensive socio–economic plan.

## GO–NGO Collaboration

On the whole, there is an evident sense of apprehension among local officials about the participation of the private sector in local governance. The same sense of apprehension, however, is also perceptible among development workers in NGOs and POs. Both sides express a degree of cynicism about how effective the Code can be in terms of bringing about fruitful GO–NGO collaboration. This is understandable, given that GO–NGO partnership in local governance is a new and rather revolutionary reform.

What has the Code achieved thus far in terms of bringing about actual cooperation and collaboration between the government and non-government sectors? Not much, if the case of Itogon is anything to go by. The municipal government has decided that it will defer the election of private sector representatives to the local legislature. Financial constraint was, of course, the convenient reason for this decision. However, interviews also revealed that at least some local officials feel that there was no need at all for sectoral representatives in the municipal council since its present composition was already representative of the various sectors of the local population, and because the inclusion of sectoral representatives would merely result in overlapping roles and functions. Worse, there was the view that NGOs and POs should first undergo a re-orientation in order to maximise their contributions to local legislation. There have also been undue delays in the accreditation process and, consequently, in the designation of private sector representatives to the various local special bodies. It thus appears that, at this point, the local government is not ready or, worse, unwilling to enter into partnership with NGOs and POs.

Some NGO workers have also pointed out that the hard decisions are not really made in the municipal councils or the development councils. They feel that their mandated representation in these bodies will not result in any significant changes in the decision-making process. Can it be said that the Code gives a semblance of greater participation of the private sector in local governance but not the substance of true participation?

### The Code in the Context of Political Patronage

Also notable is the concern among development NGOs that while the LGC provides for decentralisation of governmental functions and authority, there has been no significant change in the nature of politics and political culture in Itogon. They see no future for decentralisation in the context of patronage and elite-domination in local politics. The themes found in the Philippine local politics and the weaknesses of traditional government structure are also true for Itogon. It may be pointed out, for instance, that the incumbent mayor belongs to what may be considered a political dynasty which has held power in the municipality since 1971.

Has the Local Government Code resulted in any fundamental changes in the structure of local politics? While it is much too early to give firm answers to this question, early indications are not promising. To some extent, it can be said that local politicians may have lost an opportunity to provide some patronage through hiring, because the municipal government is expected to simply absorb the existing staff of national line agencies. However, it appears that the fundamental structure of local politics in Itogon, with its patronage, elite-domination and personality-oriented elections, has not changed at all.

## The Role of NGOs and POs

Direct participation in governance is neither the thrust nor the expertise of NGOs and POs. That they do not perform at their best in governance is reflected in the relatively poor showing of cause-oriented groups and individuals in past electoral services. Undoubtedly, NGOs and POs perform best in the arena of development work. Direct participation in the bureaucratic structures and procedures of governance may drain the energy of these NGOs and even distract them from their primary mission.

Will NGOs and POs be more successful in their development work with the Code? While NGOs and POs have on the whole decided to avail themselves of the opportunities presented by the Code, it is clear to them that the Code is only one avenue of promoting their interests. Indeed, they are not pinning all their hopes on the Code. For some NGOs it can even be said that their decision to seek accreditation is only to prevent pseudo NGOs or 'fly-by-night' POs to monopolise the power that is being shared in accordance with the Code. Their participation, at best, will simply enable them to safeguard whatever gains they have thus far achieved in their development work.

We have noted earlier that the salient features of the LGC— local autonomy, decentralisation, mandatory consultations, participation in governance and delivery of basic services, local taxation, recall and initiative—provide broad unprecedented opportunities for people's empowerment. At this point, however, it appears that people's empowerment is not likely to be realised through the Local Government Code.

Finally, all sectors need to work hard at the implementation of the Local Government Code. The national government should have the political will to work for the realisation of the goals of the Code. LGUs should build their capabilities to respond adequately to the needs of their constituents. NGOs and POs should take advantage of the opportunities provided by the Code to empower

local communities. In the final analysis, the successful implementation of the Code rests on the shoulders of everyone.

## Notes

1. A municipality or town is a geographical and administrative unit consisting of a group of villages called barangays. A municipality may either be urban or rural, and may be classified from first to sixth class depending on its annual income.
2. Sources for data on population growth include *Municipality of Itogon Town Plan (1986–1995)*, Benguet Provincial Health Office, *A Survey on Family Profile 1985*, and National Statistics Office, *1990 Census of Population and Housing*.
3. Athena Lydia Casambre *et al.*, 'Population Mobility and Development in the Mining Sector', *Population Mobility and Development in the Baguio Area*, Baguio City, ARTC-UP College Baguio, 1987, pp. 253–55.
4. Jessica K. Carino, 'People's Organisations, Non-Government Organisations and Open-Pit Mining in the Cordillera'. Paper presented at the Fourth International Philippines Studies Conference, Australian National University, 1–3 July 1992, passim.
5. The Code provides that each local government unit shall appropriate in its annual budget no less than 20 per cent of its annual internal revenue allotment for development projects.
6. Classification is on the basis of revenue earned, with a first class municipality earning the highest revenue and a fifth class municipality earning the lowest revenue.
7. The IIBA is a municipality-wide federation of POs which is committed to the protection of the land and environment from destruction. It was born out of the people's struggle against the implementation of open-pit and bulk mining in their communities.
8. Applicants for accreditation were required to submit their certificates of registration with duly recognised government agencies, latest financial statements, articles of incorporation, constitution and by-laws, statement of objectives and proof of their track record in community development work.

## Select Reading

Agra, Al. 1992. *Batas Alternatibo*, Tomo 2, Bilang 1 at 2. San Juan, Metro Manila: Scentro ng Alternatibong Lingap Panlegal.

Brillantes, Alex Jr. April 1992. 'Essay on the Local Government Code'. *CSC Issue, Paper No. 1*. Baguio City: College Baguio, Cordillera Studies Centre, University of Philippines.

Carino, Jessica K., (*a*) July 1992. 'Non-Government Organisations and Peoples Organisations and their Impact on Development Policies in Ifugao and Benguet'. Paper presented during the 4th International Philippine Studies Conference at the Australian National University.

—————. (*b*) 1992. 'The Local Government Code of 1991 and People's Organisations and Non-Government Organisations in Northern Luzon'. *CSC Working Paper No. 20*. Baguio City: Cordillera Studies Centre.

—————. (*c*) 1992. 'Forging Unity Towards Development'. *1st National NGO Congress Proceedings*. Quezon City: CODE-NGO.

—————. (*d*) 1992. *General Primer, RA 7160: The Local Government Code of 1991*.

Hollnsteiner, Mary R. (*a*) 1963. *The Dynamics of Power in a Philippine Municipality*. Quezon City: Community Development Research Council.

—————. (*b*) 1992. *Local Government Codes and the NGOs*, (LDAP-PBSP)

—————. (*c*) 1992. 'Head of Heels: Decentralising Government'. *Ibon Facts and Figures*, Vol. 15, No. 1. Manila: Ibon Databank.

Mendoza, Lorelei C. (ed.) (*a*) 1992. *Building Local Administrative Capability for Regional Autonomy in the Cordillera: Some Implementing Guidelines*. Baguio City: Cordillera Studies Centre and Friedrich Ebert Stiftung.

—————. (*b*) 1992. *Nationwide Mechanism for NGO/PO Selection and Representation in Local Special Bodies*. Baguio City: Cordillera Studies Centre and Friedrich Ebert Stiftung.

Research, Databank and Publications Department. (*a*) 1992. *Primer on the Local Government Code*. Manila: Council for People's Development.

—————. (*b*) 1992. *Rules and Regulations Implementing the Local Government Code of 1991: Republic Act No. 7160*

Tabunda, Manuel S. 1991. *Review and Analysis of the Local Government Code of 1991*. Philippines: Local Development Assistance Program—Associates for Rural Development, Inc.

# 13

# Devolution of Governance and Self-government in Sri Lanka

## C. SURIYAKUMARAN

The phrase 'local self-government' could have different meanings, according to the countries concerned. Local self-government and decentralisation of governance functions, as used in certain countries, ostensibly have their origins in US terminology and tradition. In certain other countries, local self-government has been too closely equated with just local government; and *decentralisation with enabling the latter* and not really local 'self-government'.

In the case of the second group of countries, local government has been quite acceptably associated with local bodies enjoying limited functions, handed down by the central government at its pleasure and enjoyed at its will; and, therefore, retractable or changeable by simple legislation or ministerial decision. This is quite in contrast to the exercise of functions at local levels by embedded right in the constitution of a country, which may then not be varied except by change of the constitution itself.

A third form of governance of local areas, of course, existed particularly exemplified in colonial experience, where local areas were administered by out-posted officials of central government with or without consultative bodies at the local levels.

It is, therefore, useful to make these distinctions clearly, that is, between administration of local areas by officials with absolute power, governance by local bodies with limited functions and circumscribed jurisdictions, and self-rule by really autonomous organs of government. Classically, these three would be described respectively as 'de-concentration', 'decentralisation' and 'devolution'.

The theme of the seminar at which this paper was presented is entirely reflective of these concerns, when it describes its purpose as examining the endeavours 'to create a system of politico–administrative decentralisation with a view to upgrading local self-governance'. The decentralisation of political power, administrative capacity and self-governance contained in this description, without doubt, is equal to devolution—a term which a distinguished Sri Lankan leader in as early as the 1940s, succinctly described as contained in 'the decentralisation of Administration, the decentralisation of Democracy, and the decentralisation of Development'.

A further clear theme that emerges is the importance of the grassroots level areas, equally with any of the other tiers of self-government. In this respect, perhaps it might be well to keep a few basic thoughts in mind. One is the dual nature of local areas bodies. Originating historically for the most part as centres of commerce, or concourse, or around natural or man-made ecosystems (typically the irrigation tanks, etc.), they were centres of self-sufficiency and self-reliance and in that sense truly autonomous. In a practical sense, in later times, there also emerged created local bodies or authorities as we know them, responsible for 'the amenities of civilised living', namely, essential services (water, lighting, roadways, conservancy, scavenging), utilities, culture, recreation, education, health, housing and other welfare provisions.

While the former have romantically been held up as 'little republics', neither they, nor the latter types, were politically self-governing units. They were more in the nature of decentralised local governments, the former under patriarchal systems, the latter, more likely than not, under an elective pattern. Yet, for present and future perspectives, their most outstanding characteristic had been something which has not always been adequately emphasised, perhaps even realised. This is that, right through history, and anywhere in the world, the only 'organic unit' in a body politic has been the 'local area'—not the state, not a region or sub-division or other area similar to these. Any view of devolution and local self-governance, therefore, must base itself on that premise of the village as the only organic unit of history in the body politic of countries or nations. Even as no state is large enough to replace the world, and to be by itself, no stable is small enough to speak for the people, or substitute for the individual's expression of 'identity' through the local area. The descriptions and evaluations on devolution in Sri Lanka contained in this paper are therefore made in the background of the foregoing realities.

## The Setting

Despite impressions to the contrary, in Sri Lanka devolution in its substance has had a history as long as that of centralised government. Dictated by 'logistics, administrative constraints and other aspects of governance and economy' and the existence in any case of local societies even prior to the emergence of the state (broadly dated from about 2,300 years ago), there were larger divisions of the country into three or four major regions, and within them 'finely tuned patterns' of sub-regional, district, divisional and sub-divisional areas below, up to the level of the well-established village areas themselves, known as the gansabhavas (the equivalent of the ancient panchayats of India).

With the colonial phase, beginning about the early 19th century, a gradual disappearance of this devolutionary pattern, and its integration into a unitary one, took place. It was, par excellence, a period of 'local government by de-concentration', in which some of the earlier indigenous heads of the sub-regional and other areas below were utilised, but purely in order to advance colonial government and management, and a unitary system. In this transportation from the ancient to the modern, democracy was either absent or minimal; in these later years, 'development' was only a handmaid of 'law and order' maintenance; and administration was the acme of government, of which the symbol was the classical 'kachcheri system', well known in South Asia, and its 'government agent' (the 'Collector' of India).

However, certain encouraging trends also emerged in this process. As a response to colonial needs, but also as a reflection of the liberal traditions in England, the first steps in decentralisation were taken as early as 1871, with the enactment of the Village Communities Ordinance which, with amendments and parallel legislation from time to time, eventually saw the entire country covered by elected village committees at the grassroots, and town, urban and municipal councils in the conurbations.

From the 1920s, however, the perceptions of and the demand for true devolution were loud and clear and coterminus with the demands for increased national autonomy and finally, independence. In the mid-1920s, the Kandyan community (of the central highlands of the country) which had only lost its independence a few years earlier, demanded a federal system of government, pressing this in the early 1930s with what was known as the Donoughmore Commission that had been sent by the colonial power to consider political reforms at the national level.

The report of the Donoughmore Commission resulted in a central legislature called the state council, with considerable autonomy in internal affairs but with little else at the lower levels, although interestingly it had expressed itself favourably on the idea of devolution through 'regional councils'.

From about that period in the 1920s right through into the 1940s, one of the outstanding political leaders of the country, S.W.R.D. Bandaranaike, expressed himself eloquently in favour both of federal government and of a truly devolutionary system of regional councils, which included the total abolition of the 'kach-cheri system'. Little came of it, perhaps more due to the vicissitudes of leadership at the level of central government.

A central feature of all these developments and thinking on governance and self-government was that, whilst they were based on 'local loyalties' and ethnicity in the healthy sense of the term, they were not based on ethnic conflicts. Their roots were in concepts of autonomy and government. However, from the 1950s and thereafter, devolution and self-governance began to get increasingly associated, and therefore confused, with the issues of 'permanent' majority rule at the centre and a deep sense of ethnicity both at the centre and the periphery. Thus, increasingly, the true issues of devolution and self-governance became less amenable to evaluation, judgement and decision, at both governmental and societal levels, on their own merits and for their own sake. The process came to rest in the 1980s with the establishment, in this atmosphere, of a system of provincial councils. Established by amendment of the Constitution, this system was therefore devolutionary, and in that sense a watershed in political evolution.

In the meanwhile, during the 1970s and after, the village committees at the grassroots level had been abolished and substituted by a non-elective unit called the 'gramodaya mandalaya'. In 1987, a body called the 'pradeshiya sabha' (divisional council) constituted on a fully elective principle was established, each covering a group of village areas. Most recently, however, from 1992, separate divisional secretaries, with a secretariat, have been appointed and instituted alongside, to be in charge of the divisional responsibilities of the central government and provincial councils.

The progress on devolution and self-governance rests at this point for the present. It is certainly not the end of the process; and an evaluation of the experience so far, as also any assessment of potentials for the future, has to be made with this knowledge.

## The Experience

In terms of looking at the country's 'recent experience', what is 'recent' may be considered broadly to span the last four decades. Coincidentally, this is also the period of both national independence and the growth of the 'ethnic dimension' in the national and political framework. From an older time, however, a pure strand of local government was carried over into this period, manifested in universal commitment within the country to the ideas and values of that local government through the fully elected local bodies or authorities as they were called. Extending from the municipal councils right down to the village committees, it was common to refer to them as cradles of democracy and training grounds for national politicians.

A by-product of the background of these four decades was also, unfortunately, that the clear, though brief, period of thinking in favour of federalism and devolution, as manifested from the 1920s to the 1940s, failed to be carried over and was even forgotten.

As pointed out earlier, the devolutionary system presently with the country was the product of two streams simultaneously, of the ethnically driven and later rationalised provincial councils structure, and a 'de-democratised' village area structure. At the same time, by the end of this phase, there was also a 'third stream', reflected in an earnest and honest desire by the government to give true form and substance to people's participation in government and development. This 'third stream' was what was noted at the close of the preceding section in the setting up of the elected divisional councils.

In the circumstances of the case, however, all these streams taken together formed a mixed bag. In the north-east council area of the country whose political situation, in fact, led to the provincial system, the continuing dissonances on the larger political issues prevented the system itself from functioning. In the other provinces of the country, the entire structure of devolution came as a provision from the centre and, therefore, as something which was not demanded at the periphery at the time.

The government itself had gone into the programme after the adoption of the relevant Constitutional Legislation in 1987, known as the 13th Amendment—without adequate prior provisions on the essential arrangements therefore, whether in physical infrastructure (given the existence of the kachcheris), administrative capacity, finance, functions or the sheer continuation by the government's Line Ministries with jurisdiction over devolved functions. The government agents and the kachcheris, therefore, also continued during that phase as instruments of an uneasy 'dyarchy'.

By the 13th Amendment, all local bodies—that is, the municipal and urban councils, village committees and gramodaya mandalayas—were entirely under the provincial councils. However, the translation of the government's eminently justified policy of instituting elected divisional councils (the pradeshiya sabhas) was accompanied by their being identified as the point of transference of central functions directly from the centre, and from the kachcheris, without their going through the provincial councils. But as mentioned earlier, soon thereafter, by 1991, the elected divisional councils themselves entered a penumbra with the establishment of entirely separate divisional secretariats headed by independent divisional secretaries, to carry out the aforesaid functions of the centre and the kachcheris. The divisional secretaries were also similarly empowered to carry out, on behalf of the provincial councils, functions that may be devolved to them. But they were administratively appointed by, and responsible to, the centre. Doubtless, it seems a matter that must perforce evolve further in terms of effective devolution and self-governance, given particularly the sensitive importance of the divisional level in both democratic and developmental senses.

At the village area level, there is thinking currently on the re-institution of the elective principle for the gramodaya mandalayas, a matter which could undoubtedly have healthy consequences in many ways.

The commitment of the government itself to democracy and development at all levels is not in doubt. So much so, that the President, in the course of a programme of innovative presidential mobile secretariats (coupled with a poverty alleviation programme called 'janasaviya' which conducted face-to-face, on the spot resolution of problems with the people), has emphasised how once the divisional (pradeshiya) level structures are fully in place, the mobile secretariats would cease to be needed, and cease to exist.

The provincial councils, with their experience and maturing, have become major mechanisms of government in the country. Their needs, however, are still prominent and several, and a brief look at them is essential at this point. The observations that follow are under the headings of law, administration, functions, finance, development and participation.

Under law, the primary shortcomings would appear to be:

(*a*) the overall policy prerogative provided by the 13th Amendment to the centre on all functions;

(*b*) the somewhat unclear formulations on 'competence' in respect of key functions such as planning, transport, or environment; and

(*c*) the need to revise the so-called 'Concurrent List' (List 3 in the Schedule to the 13th Amendment) for the sake of effective functioning and delivery of programmes.

With regard to administration, considering the very difficult beginnings, an impressive picture of both endowment and capacity may be said to exist even though, as always, there is a recognised need for much further strengthening.

As implied in the remarks under law, where functions are concerned there is need for clearer provisions. Further, even where the written provisions may be clear, there is need for the Line

Ministries of the centre to move away from in-built reluctance to hand over designated functions where they have not so far been done.

In finance, the situation is clearly inadequate, with essentially a 'decentralised' system of grant and related financing, with the so-called independent local sources of financing being negligible. The system has still to move to a phase of true 'fiscal devolution', serving the needs of administration, services and development.

Closely linked is the development function, which presently is somewhat confused. Apart from the poor clarity earlier referred to, it is also confounded by:

(a) a perpetuation of allocations to Members of Parliament for expenditure in their areas, as an additional determinant of the level and direction of local area development;

(b) the inadequate perceptions on the linkages in planning for development from the centre through the provinces down to the grassroots, and back; and

(c) an absence of capacity for the provincial councils to plan objectively for 'all resources'—for all levels within their areas, and with all investment resources as they may be able to stimulate, whether local or foreign.

'Participation' in devolution still remains a matter for fulfilment, perhaps due to the multiple nature and the variations in the structures of government described earlier.

Yet, shortcomings notwithstanding, achievements have been notable. Above all, the whole is part of a process and there is little doubt that this evolution will continue.

## Assessments and Outlooks

The main plank from which an assessment of the position on devolution and local self-government in Sri Lanka should be made, in the overall, is its now deep-rooted tradition of the elective principle and universal franchise. Coupled with the very high level of literacy, and indeed of 'political literacy', it would be inconceivable to imagine any future position of government in the country other than on the basis of democracy and some form of self-governance in the periphery.

In that sense, compared to some other countries' experiences, any concept of local government on the basis of special groups, NGOs or such like, purportedly reflecting people's needs, however genuine, would not be considered a substitute. The experience of the gramodaya mandalayas, constituted by representatives of registered citizen's groups, goes against this notion. The explanation, perhaps, is that when these units were instituted in place of the elected village committees, they were not considered to be replacing the village committee proper. The gramodaya mandalayas were a much smaller unit while the village committees represented a cluster of village areas, and the proposed pradeshiya sabhas or divisional councils, although larger than the old village committee areas, were looked upon as the new grassroots level. The 'reversal' in local government that occurred was in the abolition of the village committees themselves.

That apart, on the specific assessments of the situation, it might be useful to classify them under legal, structural, financial and political or social categories. Official, media, public, academic or provincial level reports, articles, studies and conclusions, as the case may be, naturally have their emphases. While there was near-unanimity in all these on the validity of devolution, the primacy of development and the importance of people's participation at grassroots level, the variations in their assessments arose in the relative emphases given to those legal, structural, financial and political forms in giving substance to these goals.

Perhaps one of the more interesting assessments is by the provincial councils themselves, where they have had an opportunity to make one. Two such occasions were the regional workshops organised by the provincial council concerned and the Centre for Regional Development Studies (CRDS), in the central and north-western provinces, in June and December 1992 respectively. If one may use the experience of the later meeting, certain recommendations were made on the basis of assessments of progress with devolution, which may be said to reflect the outlooks and needs in the subject areas mentioned. That meeting called, inter alia, for: a commission on devolution (on specific as well as the basic issues of the subject); an inter-provincial councils study group on fiscal devolution; a review of 'Lists, *1, 2 and 3* of the 13th Amendment';

a review of the use by the central government of its role on national policy-making vis-à-vis the provincial councils; a review of the 13th Amendment in relation to other possible 'alternative forms' or structures for devolution; studies on the role of the divisional secretary, and on the organisational, administrative, devolutionary and developmental roles and relations of the division; an examination of the position and status of the gramodaya mandalayas, in relation also to the old village committees; a recommendation for the reintroduction, at the level of central government, of an effective National Planning Commission; the promotion of a mechanism for inter-provincial council cooperation (including on trade and marketing); and an acceptance and evaluation of the role and potential of 'consensual' (as opposed to 'confrontational') centre–province relations, and of conventions as essential accompaniments of successful devolution.

In addition, that meeting adopted an interesting declaration called 'The Wayamba Declaration on Devolution, Democracy and Development', which is included as Appendix 1 at the end of this paper.

While the directions of these may be predicted fairly reasonably and, in positive terms, the particular unknown continues to be the north-east regional provincial devolution, and the political or ethnic dimensions of government and governmental relations. It is not possible here to go into the prospects of its resolution, although one may assert that a resolution should emerge, sooner rather than later.

However, it contains a fundamental factor for a national assessment of the outlook for devolution at large in the future. It would be fairly correct to assume, and to assert, that the nature of the resolution of this particular, politically based, issue of ethnic relations, and the structures ultimately decided for them, will finally influence the parallel nature of the devolutionary structures in the other areas of the system. The reference here is not to the 'ethnic components' of the conflict resolution; it is to the competence, functions, finance, development capability and grassroots authority that would flow to the other provincial councils, depending on the former arrangements.

In a specific case, not particularly discussed in the country so far, namely that of the so-called plantation districts of the predominantly tea growing up-country areas, populated in large part

by an ethnic minority, the developments on divisional level government may prove to be of more than ordinary interest. Similar to
the 'cantons' and the concepts behind them, these pradeshiya
(divisional) councils may evolve as an important, if not the only
ingredient in the ultimate devolution structures that must come to
these areas.

In the overall, for an outlook on devolution and self-governance,
given Sri Lanka's traditions, experience, maturity and commitment—both to certain forms of government and to development—
one must declare oneself to be clearly optimistic. Without them,
the trend could be 'reactionary'; but with them, current shortfalls
and conflicts notwithstanding, the trends must be 'progressive'.

## Concluding Observations

Perhaps the best way to make any concluding observations that
may also be tangible is to look at a forward perspective of the
picture on devolution and local self-government, as it may be, say,
by the year 2000. They are given below as sets of issues and
conclusions.

1. The first thing that strikes, if at all, is an increased commitment to democracy and to people's participation in the future. In
that sense, there is a sharp distinction to be made between the
situation and prospects in Sri Lanka, where no political advance is
measured except in these terms (even to the detriment of economic
advance), and several other countries, where universal franchise
and people's participation, particularly at the lower levels, have
still to come and where, for instance, a change in provisions, such
as for NGOs to participate at local levels, is genuinely considered
to be an advance on devolution and local self-government.

2. The competence accorded to the central government under
the 13th Amendment for deciding on rational policy on all subjects
and functions of provincial councils is bound to receive more
enlightened interpretation than at present, distinguishing more
sharply between an essential central function of 'harmonisation'
and the counterproductive function of 'control'.

3. Similarly, in respect of functions of provincial councils, a
more understanding and pragmatic interpretation of natural resources, distinguishing between 'ownership' of resources, and the

'use' of all (provincial) resources, would be expected to evolve for sheer reasons of mutual harmony and the development imperative.

4. Likewise, in the matter of exploring and utilising foreign aid, particularly investment participation, there is bound to evolve a healthy distinction between 'negotiation' and 'exploration' and between 'authorisation' and 'management'.

5. The planning function itself should develop, by force of circumstances, with much fuller provincial council initiatives.

6. The system of financial relations is obviously bound to change from the decentralised and self-defeating 'grant pattern' to devolutionary 'fiscal finance', based on concepts of shared income and substantial local revenue assignments.

7. While the latent dyarchy in the first phase of devolution is disappearing with the phasing out of the system of government agents, the new dyarchy at the divisional level referred to earlier is bound to be sorted out, under pressures both of provincial government and popular demands from below, on a basis of 'dyarchy' vs 'responsibility'.

8. The unit of devolution itself, which now is the provinces, determined during the colonial phase, is likely to undergo change, not only for the ethnically related north-eastern provincial area, but even elsewhere, perhaps more in terms of larger regions.

9. The 'cantonal' concept, physically equivalent to the present divisional or pradeshiya areas, but totally different from the latter as they are functioning now, is bound to become a strong influence in determining the nature and scope of devolution and self-government at the lower level across the country, and for various situations.

10. The lowest grassroots level, what we termed the only organic unit in the body politic in history, namely the village area, is bound to regain its identity through elected representation and a strong invocation of the ancient concepts of gansabhava (or panchayat) governance in all aspects, as well as being essential for serving the needs of modern development.

11. Finally, with growing experience, the value and role of 'consensual' government relations between the centre and the periphery, and of 'convention', in the system of governance itself, are bound to become visible and valued.

12. Development success and enlightened international support are, of course, pre-conditions. Given them, the prospects cannot

be considered, from whatever angle we may view them to be dim. What is obvious are the evident 'challenges' for which one may venture to assert, in the context such as we have, that the 'responses' themselves would be convincing. Some of these may occur earlier, some later, and in that sense the year 2000 may only be a convenient peg to hang our targets on. Nevertheless Sri Lanka, it seems, should be able to look forward to the 21st century with much greater hope and confidence than it did during this century.

## Select Reading

Bandaranaike, S.W.R.D. 1963. *Speeches and Writings*. Colombo: Department of Broadcasting and Information.

Coomaraswamy, Radhika. 1992 *Devolution, the Law and Judicial Construction*. CRDS Monograph Series 4.

CRDS/Central Provincial Council Workshop Report on *Devolution Development and Environment*. 1992. CRDS Mimeograph.

CRDS/North Western Provincial Council Workshop Report on *Devolution Development and Environment*. CRDS Mimeograph.

*Donoughmore Commission Report*, 1931.

Fernando, Neil. 1992. *Training for Decentralised Administration under Devolution*. CRDS Monograph Series 5.

Gunatilleke, Godfrey. 1992. *Development Planning under Devolution*. CRDS Monograph Series 3.

Gunawardane, Asoka. 1992. *Provincial Councils: Structures and Organization*, CRDS Monograph Series 14.

Gunawardane, V. and D. Wesumperuma (eds.). 1987. *Constitutional Structures And Devolution of Power* SLFI Seminar Report.

Leitan, G.R. Tressie. 1992. *The System of Provincial Councils: Centre-Province Relations*. CRDS Monograph Series 13.

————. 1986. *Problems and Issues Pertaining to the Structures of the Proposed Provincial Council System*. Marga Institute Seminar Report.

Namasivayam, S. 1950. *The Legislatures of Ceylon 1928–1948*. Faber and Faber.

Nanayakkara, V.K. 1992. *Environmental Management under Devolution*. CRDS Monograph Series 7.

Pradeshiya Sabhas Act, 1987.

Shastri, Amita. *The Provincial Council System in Sri Lanka: A Solution to the Ethnic Problem?* Conference Draft prepared for the Conference on Asian Studies, Washington, April 1992.

de Silva, K.M. 1993. *History of Ceylon*. University of Ceylon.

Suriyakumaran C. *Devolution in Sri Lanka: Origins and Concepts*. CRDS Monograph Series 1, April.

————. *Fiscal Devolution*. CRDS Monograph Series 2.

Suriyakumaran C. 1992. *Regional Planning Design in Sri Lanka and the Institutional and Procedural Arrangements*. Paper presented at the Workshop on Provincial Administration, Postgraduate Institute of Management, University of Sri Jayawardenapura. University of Ruhuna in association with CRDS.

—————. 1992. 'Decentralisation of Administration through Pradeshiya Sabhas', *Sunday Observer*, Sri Lanka, 23 August 1992.

Sri Lanka Sessional Paper, Administrative Reforms Committee Report, 10 Vols. 1987/1988.

The Thirteenth Amendment to the Constitution of Sri Lanka, 1987.

Village Communities Ordinance, No. 26 of 1871.

Weinman, J.R. 'Our Legislatures' *Ceylon Daily News*, Published 1918, Langham House, London 1947.

# Appendix 13.1

# The North Western Provincial Council in Association With the Centre for Regional Development Studies

**(at Kurunegala on 3 December 1992)**

### The Wayamba Declaration on Devolution, Democracy and Development

*This second major regional workshop* on devolution, development and environment, held under the auspices of the North Western Provincial Council, with support of CRDS;

*Meeting* at a vital stage of the devolution process in the country;

*Having* the conclusions, also of the first Regional Workshop held at the Central Provincial Council at Kandy available to it;

*Having Further* the achievements and lessons of the Wayamba Provincial Council experience before it, and the lessons generally of other Provincial Councils, including, during its brief existence, of the North-East Provincial Council;

*Conscious* of the still transitional nature of the devolution process in the country, touching the aspirations of Provincial Councils, concerns of Central Government, and needs of subsidiary organs and mechanisms;

*Convinced* of the clear scope for and potentials of effective devolution, as contribution to the larger good of the entire country;

*Aware* that the final tests of true governance and devolution are the extent and nature of the genuine decentralisation of administration, democracy and development, with benefit to the people at all levels;

*Hereby affirms*

1. *The concrete benefits* of the Wayamba experience in using devolution to public benefit, as evidenced for instance by the planning of its

resources for development, its pursuit of foreign investments of various types, export promotion, industrial consultancy service, intensive arts and crafts development, establishment of special offices and facilities for tourism and tourist plant development, and other achievements.

2. *The use of consensual relationships* that it has developed with the Central Government in pursing its initiatives;
3. *The tacit emergence of conventions*, as a future, major institutional device for harmonious Central Provincial relations;
4. *Its perceptions of the lower levels*, that is below the Province, as enhancing the attainment of its own objectives in development, decentralisation and administration;

*Notes Still*

1. *The further need for understanding* of devolution and its implementation at Central levels both political and bureaucratic;
2. *The need for clear definition* of scope, functions and responsibilities respectively under the Lists, I, II and III of the Thirteenth Amendment;
3. *Similar need for change* from the current, largely decentralised financial system to proper fiscal devolution;
4. *The continuing relevance* of the overall policy functions of the Centre, not merely as legally provided by the Thirteenth Amendment, but as means for creative leadership in initiating country-wide, systematic or other ideas, as for example the initiative for the Pradeshiya Sabhas, with the clear intention that such initiatives eventually form integral parts of the devolutionary system;

*Calls on*

All concerned, in particular the Provincial Councils,

1. *To seize* these evidences and opportunities towards a strong, stable future pattern for Government;
2. *To join in further enhancing* the structures and provisions thereto as above;
3. *To assist* one another and join together whenever necessary in the resolution of special problems, or the achievement of national goals, without discrimination and with equal concern for all areas of the Country; and
4. *To consider and to pursue* the goals of Devolution, Democracy and Development as being means to further the Peace and Prosperity of the entire Country, in larger Freedom and for the Welfare and Happiness of all its Citizens.

# 14

# Decentralisation and Local Self-governance in Sri Lanka: The Field Experience

## H.A.P. ABEYAWARDANA

Decentralisation of administration had been the main objective of administrative reforms in Sri Lanka since Independence in 1948. The four types of local authorities, viz., the district development council (DDCs), the municipal councils (MCs), urban councils (UCs) or town councils (TCs), and village councils (VCs) created by the national legislature were responsible for selected services and amenities in their respective areas.[1] These authorities functioned through councils elected by the voters and delivered services through paid officials responsible for the execution of council policies. They fell within the definition of delegated authorities whose continuance rested on the will of the legislature which created them.

In the quest for more political power and authority, the urge had been to work out political decentralisation to authorities at the sub-national level with power to formulate policies and implement them. Experiments in the form of district political authority (1972–1977) and the subsequent district ministry system (1978–1987) were only attempts made to integrate political leadership with the administration of the Government Agent, the bureaucratic head of the district, and other decentralised units of administration in the district. The establishment of the District Development Councils Act No. 35, 1980, could be considered as the first attempt to set up a district-level elected political organisation.[2] The district development councils (DDCs) were vested with power to attend to 15 development functions relating to 11 Line Ministries at the centre in addition to local government activities hitherto performed by the town councils and village councils.[3]

While the DDCs functioned in the 25 administrative districts, municipal councils and urban councils continued to function in urban areas. The government agent served as the secretary to the DDC. The functions of government not entrusted to the DDCs were delivered through the decentralised units of administration, some under the authority of the government agent of the district and others under their respective local heads. All these activities were coordinated by the District Minister, who had the services of the government agent as ex-officio secretary.

The establishment of provincial councils in 1988[4] and pradeshiya sabhas[5] during the same period, followed by the repeal of the Development Councils Act[6] and the changes in administration in the interim (1988–1992) resulted in the emergence of an administrative structure at the national, provincial, district local and grassroots level, which can be tabulated as in Table 14.1.

Local government is a subject devolved on the provincial councils. The constitutional safeguard is that the provincial councils cannot take away their powers. They can be bestowed with additional powers. Thus municipal councils (MCs), urban councils (UCs) and pradeshiya sabhas (PSs) have received constitutional recognition. Gramodaya mandalayas, which had also been given corporate status by law, had been included along with local authorities in this constitutional amendment.[7] Their objective is to attend to civic functions in the village area and link the grassroots with the administration.[8]

The authority given to pradeshiya sabhas to attend to development functions is a feature uncommon to MCs and UCs.[9] The performance of a pradeshiya sabha will be evaluated in the background of its powers, functions and duties as an organisation representing the interests of the local population through its council and services. The performance of the Divisional Secretariat, which looks after the various devolved functions of the local level governments, will also be evaluated in the present paper.

**Table 14.1: Administrative Structure at Different Levels**

| Level | Democratic Institution | Bureaucratic Institution |
|---|---|---|
| National | Executive President Parliament | Presidential Secretariat. Line Ministries answerable to Parliament. |
| Provincial | Provincial Council | 5 Sector Ministries. Answerable to the Provincial Council. |
| District | | Office of the District Secretary: functions relating to district coordinating committee; resource allocation, disaster management, elections, census etc. |
| Local | Pradeshiya Sabhas, Municipal Councils, Urban Councils/answerable to rate payers. Delivery of services of a local nature within the ambit of local government laws, other ordinances and by-laws. | Divisional Secretary. Translate national and provincial policy into action.<br>i. Revenue<br>ii. Services<br>iii. Planning<br>iv. Coordination of development functions. |
| Grassroots | Gramodaya Mandalaya | Grama Seva Niladhari (Village Services Officer). Serving the PS and the DS and the public. |

## Methodology

The literature available in the form of laws, policy statements of government manuals, circulars and official reports have been examined for this study. The Pradeshiya Sabha Act, examined in the light of the debate in Parliament at the presentation of the PS Bill, provides an insight into the political thinking underlined in the adoption of this innovative law designed to obtain people's participation in both administration and development, and the statutory provisions made therein.

Laws applicable to the powers and functions of gramodaya mandalayas and study reports relating to their performance were also considered; regulations governing the restructuring of the divisional secretariats were examined. Field visits to the selected pradeshiya sabha area and the divisional secretariat in the corresponding division, examination of the organisational structures, study of important documents and progress reports compared in the field survey were used to analyse the problems. The administration of a questionnaire to a cross-section of enlightened citizens helped in arriving at well-considered conclusions.

## Background

### Pradeshiya Sabhas (PSs) and Local Self-government

The pradeshiya sabha with its distinctive characteristics is defined in the Pradeshiya Sabha Act 15, 1987, which is an innovative piece of legislation containing new features not available in the laws applicable to other local authorities, viz. municipal councils and urban councils functioning in urban areas. This law was designed to achieve a variety of objectives. Securing people's participation in development and local government was the primary objective. This system, it was felt, would relieve the government of many burdens and provide it with the opportunity to concentrate on matters of a more national nature. By the devices available to formulate policies and programmes and to implement them in their divisions, people themselves are to contribute to their wellbeing. The coordinated system of administration was intended to 'usher in a new era in development' where the beneficiaries themselves would be the planners. Further, it would involve youths in local self-government and later help them 'graduate into national politics'.[10] The preamble to the law sets out the intention in these words: 'to provide greater opportunities for the people to participate effectively in the decision-making process relating to administration and development activities at a local level'. The PS Act, which is the primary law, is reinforced by other laws and by-laws framed by the Minister and councils to discharge their powers, functions and duties. The traditional local government functions assigned to the

PS include responsibilities on thoroughfares, public health and a variety of public utility services.[11].

Development functions of a PS include subjects such as village works, experiments in agriculture and experimental farms, preparation of programmes for educational facilities, employment programmes, rural women's development activities, integrated development of selected villages, community development projects and commercial development projects to serve other local authorities and the public.[12]

Like other types of local authorities, the PS is empowered to generate its own revenue by way of rates, taxes, licence duties and, as recognised partners in administration to receive grants and aid from provincial councils and from the government on a nationally accepted formula. Several new avenues to raise income and to mobilise physical resources have been provided to generate the funds required for PS services.[13] There are certain features that the PS shares with other local authorities. For instance, the PS elects a council by popular vote conducted by the Commissioner of Elections for a period of four years; the body corporate status permits a PS to act within the ambit of the law; a PS is subject to the control of the provincial ministry and the Auditor General and is answerable to courts of law for its actions if challenged by a rate payer.[14]

## The Role of Gramodaya Mandalayas (GMs) as Grassroots Level Organisation in Governance

Gramodaya mandalayas gained recognition in the local government system in Sri Lanka shortly after the establishment of the DDCs in 1981.[15] It linked the village population with the services of the DDCs to set the planning process rolling at the grama sevaka division and to submit proposals to the next higher division viz. the assistant government agent's area and later to the DDC at the district level. Similarly, GMs would get involved in the implementation of plans at the village level when financial allocations were sanctioned.

The area of authority of a GM was the grama sevaka niladhari (GSN) division; the heads of voluntary organisations of a non-political nature in the area were the voters for the purpose. In their functions the officials in the division would be involved as non-voting members. The divisional level coordinating committee of GMs elected one of their members to the chairman, who was served by the assistant government agent of the division as the ex-officio secretary. Divisional level public servants too had to assist in the activities of the divisional coordinating committee.

This arrangement, which existed from 1981 to 1987, underwent substantial changes with the abolition of the DDCs and the establishment of pradeshiya sabhas from 1988. Through its committee system and by other consultative devices, PS law was given the facility to involve GMs as additional eyes and ears of the PS.[16] The coordinating committee established at the level of the PS and headed by its chairman has developed a consultative mechanism to ensure popular participation in PS services.[17] The GMs have been empowered by law to undertake a wide range of public service responsibilities, including construction activities, for which adequate facilities have been provided by the government.[18] In spite of the weaknesses inherent in the system, GMs have proved their capacity to serve as village based organisations linking individuals with local self-government institutions. After the abolition of the elective system of councillors on the basis of wards, first under the DDC system and later under the PS and other local authorities, the vacuum created was filled by relying on GMs to identify the felt needs of the people living in this lowest unit of administration. The grama sevaka niladhari (village services officer) is appointed as the secretary to the GM. The village based public servants are expected to help the GMs by making their services available as unofficial members. Thus GMs developed institutional arrangements to fit in with the local self-government system and also to help the government by offering their services on a voluntary basis.[19]

## Committee System in PS Administration

The committee system, spelt out in Section 12(2) of the PS Act, provides the legal base for the formation of the following four committees, with provision to co-opt the gramodaya mandalaya chairmen and other citizens: (a) finance and policy making; (b) housing and community development; (c) technical services; and (d) environment and amenities.

If a PS so desires, it can, under this law, form any number of other committees. These committees can be delegated with powers and duties of a PS other than the power to levy a rate or raise a loan.[20]

## Divisional Secretariat—Institutional Development

The evolution of the present office of the divisional secretariat (DS) as a bureaucratic institution can be traced back to the pre-independence period, when it was called the divisional revenue officers division (DRO), later re-named as the assistant government agents division (AGA).[21] After the provincial councils were established, it had to perform functions for the PCs and for the government and was called the divisional secretariat and office of the additional government agent. This office maintains its links with the gram sabha (GS) division at the village level through the office of the grama sevaka niladhari.

Considering the capacity of a PS as a local self-government body specially designed with power and responsibilities to undertake development and local government functions, arrangements were made during the period 1990–1992 to link the divisional secretary with the PS in order to transfer the delivery of devolved functions through the DS.[22] In this arrangement the DS was expected to serve as the official head of the PS administration, serving as its secretary to deliver the services relating to devolved functions through its secretariat. The purpose was to secure accountability through local authorities. Regarding non-devolved functions, accountability was to the appropriate Line Ministries and agencies, also to be achieved through the DS.[23]

A change in the government policy in 1992 led to restructuring the DS, upgrading the office to the level of an 'A' class department to undertake devolved and non-devolved functions of government. For this purpose, an Act of Parliament was passed in September 1992 bestowing legal authority on the DS.[24] As from 1993, the PSs and other LAs in the division are expected to perform their functions as elected local self-government institutions with administrative and financial support from the re-structured DS.

A total of 308 LAs function in Sri Lanka. Of these, 237 LAs comprising 194 pradeshiya sabhas, 10 municipal councils and 33 urban councils function under councils elected in May 1991. The remaining LAs, which include 63 pradeshiya sabhas, six urban councils and two municipal councils in the north-east provinces, have so far failed to elect their councils due to prevailing unrest in that territory.

A total of 205 DSs have been established in provinces other than those in the north and east. It is expected that 63 DSs will be established in these two provinces later.

## Focus on the Study Area

The selected study area is the PS Maharagama and the DS Maharagama. PS Maharagama is one among the six pradeshiya sabhas in Colombo district of the province council of the western province. It is 13 sq. kms in extent, with a population of 1,30,984 (in 1991). The area comprises 24 grama sevaka niladhari (village services officer) divisions. As a local authority, it is characterised by rapid urban growth because of its proximity to Colombo, the metropolitan city, which is only three miles away from the city limits. Housing a large number of public and private institutions and industries and also the University of Sri Jayewardenepura, this area is rapidly transforming its character into a fast-developing urban area requiring priority attention in terms of physical development.

The divisional secretariat as the principal administrative authority covers a larger area that extends to 41 GSN divisions. Of these, 17 fall within the local authority in the adjoining area. The total population for the DS division is 1,54,330 (1991).

## Institutional Arrangements

### Pradeshiya Sabha (Maharagama)

PS Maharagama was constituted with effect from 1 January 1988. Administered by a special commissioner from the time of its constitution to June 1991, the first elected council assumed office from 1 July 1991. The council comprising 22 members was elected at the general elections held in May 1991 in which 41,468 out of a total of 60,623 voters cast their votes. Recognised political parties which contested and secured membership in the council were as follows: Mahajana Eksath Peramuna (13 seats), United National Party (8 seats), and Nava Sama Samaja Party (1 seat). By winning the majority of the votes, Mahajana Eksath Peramuna secured control over the local authority.[25]

The council, which functions as the policy-making body, derives its power from the PS Act and other laws. Monthly meetings conducted in keeping with the by-laws, form the main forum for the discussion of council activities. Committees, as set out in Section 12 of the PS Act, facilitate council business. Minutes of council meetings held in 1992 reveal that the decisions of the committees carry substantial weight.[26]

The council is served by a hierarchy of paid officials headed by the secretary who is the chief administrative officer. They maintain political impartiality in their services. While the general administration, with the help of divisions organised under the administrative officer and accountant are responsible for council administration, revenue and payments, other divisions such as health services, physical planning, water works, utility services and public welfare services are responsible for the delivery of services in accordance with the financial and manpower resources available to the council under the budget. The council has a total of 180 officers and employees.

## Status, Powers and Duties

The PS Act has bestowed a wide range of powers on the council and its officials in charge of duties relating to thoroughfares, public health and utility services for the comfort, convenience and welfare of the citizens. These laws have been drawn up to deal with any situation that may arise; the content and power given in the Act is such that the Councils are empowered to enforce the provisions of the Act either directly or through courts. By formulating and enforcing certain rules and regulations relating to laying of public thoroughfares and construction of residential and commercial buildings, the councils compel the tax payers to comply with the provisions of law relating to physical planning and zoning requirements.

Similarly in public health, services are organised as required by law to improve the sanitation of the area. On matters such as garbage collection, the council has arranged for the scavengers to sweep the streets in the city centre before dawn to avoid inconvenience to the users. However, collected garbage lying on public streets is posing a problem as the present disposal arrangement is unsatisfactory. Plans are afoot to educate the rate payers regarding the delivery of garbage to pre-determined collection points after its contents have been sorted out. The idea is to encourage the preparation of compost manure pits by rate payers wherever feasible. Technical advice for public health services is provided by the medical officer; while health inspectors and public health nurses employed in the area undertake field inspections. The council is vigilant in such matters as latrine accommodation in public and private premises, insanitary buildings, overhanging trees, etc. It plans to identify new sites for garbage disposal, purchase additional vehicles and employ additional labour, all of which will help improve the standard of public health services.

Electricity as a utility service is supplied by the Lanka Electricity Company and the proposed water supply network presently under construction will be the responsibility of the Water Supply and Drainage Board. Provision of street lamps will continue to be a responsibility of the PS as will the provision of street taps. The expenditure for all this will be borne by the PS through its own funds.[27]

## Finances

The budget approved for the year 1993 indicates the council's financial position. The council has budgeted to receive a total of Rs. 21,790,700 and incur an expenditure of Rs. 21,773,800—leaving a surplus of Rs. 16,900. The budget is arranged under six programmes covering general administration, health services, physical planning including roads and land acquisition, water supply, other public utilities and welfare expenditure.

Assessment rates levied on the basis of 6 per cent of the annual value of properties yielding Rs. 3,900,000 are the main source of the council's income. Other sources of income are trade licenses, vehicles and animals tax, markets and shops, entertainment tax, etc. Funds for capital expenditure, mainly to cover physical development, are received from the decentralised budget controlled by Members of Parliament and from the criteria-based grants given by the provincial councils. Based on the previous years experience, the council has budgeted Rs. 5.14 million as capital grants from these sources.

An analysis of the total expenditure according to projects presents the following picture:

**Table 14.2: Total Council Expenditure According to Projects**

| Project | Amount in Lakhs (Rs.) | Percentage of the Total Budget |
|---------|-----------------------|--------------------------------|
| General administration | 59 | 27 |
| Health services | 38 | 17 |
| Physical planning | 88 | 40 |
| Water service | 02 | 01 |
| Other public utilities | 23 | 11 |
| Welfare expenditure | 08 | 04 |

Note: One lakh = 100 thousand.
Source: Budget of PS Maharagama, 1993.

## Citizen's Participation

Gramodaya mandalayas within the division have not yet been co-opted into the committees in the PS area. However, their ability to represent the interests at the grassroots level in PS administration has been recognised. Meetings of GM chairmen of GMs in the PS area are held every month, with the chairman of the PS presiding. This has helped the forging of a closer relationship with the GMs.

Minutes of these meetings, which are held on the fourth Wednesday of every month, reveal that main topics of discussion relate to road construction and repairs, street lighting, scavenging services, pre-schools, mobile clinics and the awarding of contracts to GMs. They are attended, on an average, by chairmen of over half the 24 GMs in the division.

At this point, a brief look at one of the more successful and well organised GMs in the division might be in order. The Vaththegedera Gramodaya Mandalaya, covering GSN division 523C and comprising a population of over 6,500 people in nearly 900 houses, succeeded in resolving outstanding problems by mutual understanding and consent, and by pooling resources. Widening roads, maintenance of existing roads, opening new roads, naming streets and even fixing assessment numbers to individual households, have all been done on GM initiative. Construction of houses for the poor, helping several villagers to secure bank loans for self-employment projects, supplying well water, toilet facilities and water-scaled latrines for the poor were among the other services provided by the Vaththe-gedera GM. The Pradeshiya Sabha was persuaded to install street lamps along all roads developed by the GM, and where funds from the PS were spent, the beneficiaries contributed lavishly by providing communal labour.[28]

A large number of NGOs operating in the area have free access to the PS administration, councillors and chairmen to discuss their individual problems. The PS reserves every Wednesday as an office day, giving individuals and organised groups the opportunity to discuss matters affecting them with the PS administration.

In an interview, the chairman of the Rate Payers' Association of Maharagama expressed satisfaction with the way in which the council is resolving problems in the area. His opinion was that the PS would perform better if the authorities in the area considered it as the legitimate institution of the people to coordinate development activities.[29]

There are a total of 32 youth societies and two women's societies in Maharagama, all of which have been earmarked to receive assistance by the PS through grants and facilities. Feedback elicited through informal discussions at selected public places within the PS area arranged by the chairman in the company of senior PS officials have helped him guage the performance of these societies. In matters connected with public health, sanitation, scavenging and markets, such discussions have helped in identifying related problems.

Another issue which surfaced during research is the poor participation of women in decision-making at the grassroots level. It was observed that in Maharagama, only one of the two women's societies is active. Lack of confidence in politically motivated village organisations, household chores and the related responsibilities, ignorance and lack of awareness have been mentioned as reasons for the poor participation by women. The relatively better economic status enjoyed by households in the study area, appears to be an additional cause.

All 32 youth societies in the area were found to be very active, having taken a pledge to foster 'unity, friendship, cooperation and development'. The location of the National Youth Council Headquarters within the PS area is an added advantage that these youths enjoy. Self-employment projects and vocational training activities have received priority in programmes implemented for them.[30]

### Divisional Secretariat Maharagama

The mission of the divisional secretary is to bring administration to the people and deliver services relating to devolved and non-devolved subjects in the division. In the process, the DS has to comply with the mandate given to him to translate government and provincial council policy into action to bring about growth and development. To do this, the needs identified and prioritised by the people of the area have to be taken into account. In this context, close liaison has to be maintained with the democratically elected body in the division of the DS Maharagama in the performance of his functions.

Vested with authority given to him by 23 line ministries of the government and the functions of an agent of the government at the divisional levels, the DS is expected to play his role as the head of an 'A' class department and also as a leader of a multidisciplinary team of officers. His allegiance is to the national and sub-national level legislators. Financially, he is accountable to the Secretary, Ministry of Public Administration, Provincial Councils and Home Affairs and to the Chief Secretary of the Provincial Council. The total provision for 1993 in the budget of the DS is Rs. 4.8 million.

Our field study revealed the following points related to the functioning of this office:

1. The DS does not pay sufficient attention to the views of local authorities in the discharge of his functions. His administrative discretion is used to interpret the aspirations of the national and provincial level politicians.

2. Adequate consultation with the GMs through the PS does not take place, nor is the consultative mechanism available for the purpose properly utilised. The divisional-committee of GMs is not fostered either.[31]

3. Identification of projects for capital development from government grants in the division often does not match with the felt needs of the areas; due consideration is not paid to the authority which will be responsible for maintenance of public amenities after their completion.[32]

4. The DS is vested with supervisory control over the PS by being appointed Assistant Commissioner of local government for the division from January 1993.[33]

5. People are not represented properly in the various committees formed by the DS to monitor administrative functions assigned to his office.[34]

6. Decentralisation to the division of government functions relating to routine activities like payment of taxes, licenses, duties on motor vehicles, pensions etc., are commendable features in the new system.

7. Frequent transfers of the DS has caused considerable inconvenience to the public and a sense of insecurity among the public servants in the team.[35]

## Local Planning Process: Project Planning and Implementation

The ninth schedule of the 13th Amendment to the Constitution recognises the importance of development planning, stipulating planning and implementation of provincial economic plans to be one of the responsibilities of the provincial councils.[36] The process of devolution of powers and functions from the centre to the provinces is yet to be fully evolved. However, the experience during the past few years shows that the level of decentralisation has gradually shifted further down to the divisional level, with strong emphasis on divisional secretariats. The divisional level is thus the most appropriate focus for a discussion of the experience of local level planning and programme implementation.

A stronger political and administrative structure has been evolving at the local level. The local council elections held in May 1991 consolidated political power at the local level by electing members to pradeshiya sabhas, including other urban–local authorities, in seven out of the nine provinces. These PS provinces have subsequently been strengthened for the purposes of planning and administration as a national policy. The divisional level has assumed a new meaning and significance in the light of decentralised planning and programme coordination. It has, in effect, become the meeting point where national development efforts, provincial development strategies and people's needs as represented by village groups and elected members are brought together, appraised, reviewed and approved. Moreover, it is at this level that projects are monitored and implemented, and their subsequent impact evaluated.

The newly strengthened divisional secretariats are expected to achieve the following objectives:

(*a*) ensure that the delivery of services is undertaken at a level closer to the people, enabling them to adequately represent their needs and aspirations;

(*b*) ensure that the needs of public are attended to at a level closest to where they live;

(*c*) maintain accountability to the people;

(*d*) and provide at the local level means for the implementation of national policy on all matters.

### Institutional Framework

To facilitate the further devolution of economic development responsibilities of provincial councils, two types of local level institutions have been identified i.e. the pradeshiya sabha with statutory powers and the divisional secretariat (former AGA office upgraded to 'A' class department) with administrative powers.

It is noted that there are two distinct arms—democratic–political and bureaucratic—of the planning process. The inter-institutional relationships even at the divisional level are somewhat grey. The gramodaya mandalaya at the grassroots level maintains links with the division through the office of the GSN for the identification and implementation of projects.

The divisional planning council and the divisional co-ordinating committee are the two main planning institutions available at the local level, chaired respectively by the chairman of the pradeshiya sabha and the divisional secretary. The composition of the planning council is spelt out in the Manual for Provincial and Divisional Planning.[37] According to this, the structure of the council is to be broad-based, allowing the pradeshiya sabha to play a key role in the economic development of the area. It is understood that the divisional co-ordinating committee will comprise bureaucrats, technocrats and political representatives of the area to ensure the effective monitoring and co-ordination of the implementation of the development plan.

## Local Planning Experience

The divisional planning effort of the government has been primarily based on a pragmatic approach. The planning function at the divisional level is confined to the mere compilation of activities for the purpose of requesting funds from the decentralised budget and from other sources except in cases where Integrated Rural Development Projects are being implemented. No systematic effort had been made for programme coordination in the study area over the past several years. However, the PS members interviewed by us felt that there was an urgent need to establish a coordinating device. They suggested a common body/platform as a suitable device to allow genuine interaction over development decisions in the area. Such a body, they emphasised, should be free of any interferences or influences—political or otherwise.

The planning experience of both provincial and divisional level institutions with regard to decentralisation is rather unique. It has been one of trial and error, success and failure. The issues that emerged at the field level were taken into consideration by the planners and administrators and corrective measures proposed. Such corrective measures formed the basis of the guidelines and procedures to be followed thereafter for the purpose of local planning and programme implementation.

Financial planning of the capital development programme has received more attention during this period, with funding sources being the main consideration. Four sources of funding have been identified for capital development: (*a*) capital grants allocated through the provincial councils; (*b*) capital grants allocated through the Line Ministries; (c) funds from the decentralised budget (allo-cated to Members of Parliament at the rate of Rs. 2.5 million); and (d) funds generated by the pradeshiya sabhas themselves.

With regard to decentralised capital budget (DCB) funds, several guideline circulars have been issued with the objective of ensuring effective utilisation as well as balanced development in the district as a whole. The efforts made in this direction are evident in the guidelines issued by the Ministry of Public Administration, Provincial Councils and Home Affairs. These guidelines suggested the concept of a 'basket of capital projects' from which projects can be picked on a priority basis for implementation out of decentralised budget funds.[38]

All project and activities emanating from the gramodaya man-dalayas, pradeshiya sabhas, Members of Parliament and members of provincial councils were considered for funding on a priority basis and for inclusion in the 'basket'. The district coordinating committee, chaired by the Chief Minister (Provinces) and the Senior Cabinet Minister of the area is held responsible for moni-toring the programme.

The 'basket of projects' concept was proposed to remedy a number of weaknesses encountered in the planning and imple-mentation of the DCB, such as overlapping and duplication, waste, conflicts between and among Members of Parliament, provincial councils and pradeshiya sabhas, and inability to accept the total development plan. The implementation of this proposal in the study area, as also elsewhere, failed for the simple reason that Members of Parliament are more keen to invest their allocations according to their own priorities. The allocation of funds under the DCB and provincial council is given in Table 14.3.[14] It is noted that Maharagama division has received more funds from DCB due to a high degree of political patronage.

Another significant aspect of DCB lies in the planning process itself. It is expected that MPs, before making their proposals, consult the AGA and the local authorities in identifying the needs and priorities in the area. In reality, this did not happen in the study area. The people's response to the selection of projects for DCB funding was unfavourable.

Another important landmark in the local planning process is the guidelines issued by Secretary, Ministry of Policy Planning and Implementation on the preparation of the divisional development

Table 14.3: Availability of Funds 1989–1992 (Rs. million)

| Source | 1989 | 1990 | 1991 | 1992 |
|---|---|---|---|---|
| DCB | 4.23 | 6.29 | 5.73 | 4.74 |
| Provincial Grants | 0.50 | 3.03 | 4.09 | 4.09 |
| Total | 4.73 | 9.32 | 9.82 | 8.83 |

Source: DS Maharagama.

programme.[39] This can be considered as a concerted planning effort aimed at achieving consistency between the macro objectives and the local level planning strategies.[40] Accordingly, the preparation of a divisional development plan requires the classification of all capital development activities under six major sectors, i.e. economic infrastructure, social infrastructure, human settlement-related activities, income and employment generation and divisional administration.[41] This approach would presumably solve some of the issues relating to programme administration. Further, it will enable the diversion of adequate resources to backward areas, thereby providing immediate benefits to the disadvantaged and needy groups, as envisaged in the national policy.

However, it can be argued that the new approach might restrict the opportunity for people's participation in development decision-making. Under the new set-up, the divisional secretariats will be responsible for planning, monitoring and coordinating the divisional development programme using funds received from five main sources: allocation from the Treasury through the public investment programme, allocation from the DCB, allocation from provincial council grants, project-specific allocations from Line Ministries, and allocation for special projects such as from the Janasaviya Trust Fund, Integrated Rural Development Projects, UNICEF and other similar bodies.

A recent government circular requires divisional secretaries to monitor the programme through field visits, divisional coordinating committees and progress reports obtained from responsible officers/agencies. The role of elected bodies, i.e. the pradeshiya sabha, the provincial councils, the Parliament and the gramodaya mandalaya in this planning process is yet to be determined.

## Issues and Limitations of the Local Planning Process

The relatively low emphasis placed on the realisation of economic development objectives, as envisaged in the 13th Amendment, is considered to be a major limitation of the decentralised planning process. It is necessary to identify the role of the private sector in each economic area and the potential of its contribution in achieving the overall development goals of the country. In this way, the private sector can effectively participate and contribute in finding sustainable solutions to the critical problems of the masses, particularly unemployment and the high cost of living.

The study has revealed that the local level planning process is evolving at a fast pace. While planning documents are being compiled competently, the execution of the plans is not quite as competent. Effective plan implementation can only be possible through better coordination between the political representatives and the technocrats/bureaucrats. The mechanics of divisional planning need to be evolved within Sri Lanka's unique politico–bureaucratic system through a process of trial and error. While doing this, it is important that certain fundamental issues relating to local planning be resolved, particularly that of ensuring the sustainability of the PS area as a viable planning unit.[42]

## Physical Planning

The PS area has been brought under the Urban Development Authority (UDA) Law (Ch. 602), thus facilitating the application of the UDA to promote the physical development of the area.[43] The local authority is faced with several challenges pertaining to physical planning responsibilities. The planning committee headed by the chairman grants planning clearance to individual rate payers regarding building activities. In the process it has to handle a heavy volume of work connected with granting building approval, blocking out plans and issuing certificates of conformity.[44]

## Zoning Scheme: City Centre Development

The UDA has taken into account the urgent need to plan a zoning scheme for the entire area and to concentrate on activities relating to the city centre development on a priority basis. The physical, economic and social aspects of development have been considered, taking into account vital indicators. In a recent survey, the physical characteristics of the Maharagama area have been identified.[45] The PS has a total land area of 13.343 hectares of which 75 per cent is developed, 20 per cent is yet to be developed and the remaining 5 per cent comprise water resources. A dramatic increase in population from 92,981 in 1981 to 130,984 in 1991 indicates a 4 per cent population growth rate. The projected population for 2001 is estimated at 167,663. The value of land records a high escalation between 1980 and 1990.

In the town centre, the price of land has gone up from Rs. 20,000 in 1980 to Rs. 160,000 in 1990.[46] The increase in other areas is about 50 per cent over 1980 prices. Civic amenities such as safe water and extension of electricity supply need to be improved. The present growth is attributed to the push factor from the city of Colombo to its immediate environs and the escalation of land prices within the city centre.

The physical development of the area, therefore, receives high priority as revealed in the capital development grants invested for selected infrastructure projects. The strategy adopted for city centre development is to undertake on an urgent basis seven selected projects relating to road development, landscaping, construction of additional commercial complexes and new playgrounds. Funding sources have been identified and both public and private sectors have been involved.

A four-year development plan currently at the draft stage will be monitored by the PS with technical support from the UDA. All government and public agencies are expected to collaborate and participate in achieving the targeted development.[47]

### People's Responsiveness

A questionnaire was administered to a selected sample of enlightened citizens, knowledgeable persons in the PS and DS administration to obtain their perceptions and suggestions regarding devolution and decentralised administration, development and local participation. The majority felt that the PS should be the focal point for devolution while the bureaucratic institution should provide programme support. They also held that the PS should be the individual level development authority not only for the physical but also for the economic and social development of the people.

Where local participation is concerned, the survey highlighted the importance of restructuring the GM to suit the needs and aspirations of the villagers. It was suggested that the election of the GM chairman be by popular vote. This would help genuine leadership to emerge in the village, free of partisan affiliations.

## Conclusions

The decentralisation of administration and securing the participation of the people through democratic institutions at levels lower than the national is the emerging political culture in Sri Lanka. The selection of the division as the accepted unit of decentralised governance has now been stabilised and integrated into the provincial council system with the approval of the government.

The pradeshiya sabha as the appropriate local self-government institution, democratically elected by the rate payers of the area and designed to undertake and promote economic and social development, is not being invoked yet to discharge development functions earmarked for it by law. While rendering the traditional local government functions, the PS concentrates on the physical development of the area—a legitimate local government function. Its present state reveals a disparity between the ideal and the reality.

The DS as the bureaucratic institution at the divisional level has failed to invoke the mechanism available to it to consult the local populace through the PS and LAs in the division and to bring forth GMs at the grassroots and may, therefore, not be able to maintain accountability to the people they serve. This tendency depicts some trends in centralisation, which are contradictory to the principles of decentralisation.

The present system of resource allocation and identification of projects for funding from provincial and national sources need adjustment in order to conform to the philosophy of decentralised governance and administration with a commitment to encourage local level planning.

A model where the key partners, viz. the elected representatives, bureaucrats and the people, have a healthy interaction should emerge and announced as a matter of national policy. It was felt that the Pradeshiya Sabha should be given the power, recognition and financial resources to spearhead local level development strategies to achieve regional and national development. In this exercise, the bureaucratic institutions should ideally provide the necessary administrative and technical support.

## Notes

1. The ordinances relating to local authorities are: (*i*) municipal councils (MC) Ordinance (Ch. 576), (*ii*) Urban Councils (UC) Ordinance (Ch. 577), (*iii*) Town Councils (TC) Ordinance (Ch. 578), and (*iv*) Village Councils (VC) Ordinance.
2. Development Councils (DC) Act 35, 1980 (Ch. 5).
3. DC (Ch. 5): First Schedule.
4. 13th Amendment to the Constitution of the Democratic Socialist Republic of Sri Lanka, 14 November 1987, Provincial Councils (PC) Act 42, 1987.
5. Pradeshiya Sabha (PS) Act 15, 1987, of 16 April 1987.
6. DC (repeal) Act, 1988.
7. Ninth Schedule to the 13th Amendment to the Constitution Section 4: 1 Local Government.
8. DC Amendment Act 21, 1987.
9. PS Act Section 19 compared with provisions in MC and UC Ordinances.
10. Debate on the PS Act in Parliament on 23 January 1987. *Hansard of Parliament of the Democratic Socialist Republic of Sri Lanka*, pp. 346–28.
11. PS Act, Sections 21–107.
12. PS Act, Section 19.
13. PS Act, Sections 129, 153 and 154.
14. Abeyawardana, H.A.P. 1992. 'Constitutional and Legal Aspects of Local Government in Sri Lanka' in H.A.P. Abeyawardana (ed.) *Legal Environment for Local Government in Sri Lanka*. Colombo. Postgraduate Institute of Management, pp. 116–26.
15. DC Amendment Act 45, 1981.
16. PS Act, Section 12.
17. Circular PC/LG/3/87 of 15 July 1991 by the Secretary to the Ministry of Public Administration, Provincial Councils and Home Affairs (S/PA/PC/HA) on the Establishment of Gramodaya Consultative Committees.
18. DC Act 21, 1987.
19. Regulations made under Section 17A of DC Act 41, 1981.

20. PS Act, Section 12.
21. Fernando, Neil and K.P.G.M. Perera (eds.) 1980. *Regional Development in Sri Lanka*. Colombo. Sri Lanka Institute of Development Administration. (Ch. 8).
22. 'Taking the Administration to the People': a statement issued by the Ministry of PA/PC/HA.
23. Circular issued by the Ministry of PA/PC/HA.
24. Divisional Secretaries (Transfer of Powers) Act 58, September 1992.
25. Results of General Elections in Maharagama PS: summary prepared by Commission for Elections, June 1991.
26. Minutes of council meetings of PS and standing committees of PS held in 1992.
27. Official documents, interviews and observations in the field.
28. Administration report of the GM for 1992 and observations in the field.
29. Interview with the chairman, the Rate Payers Association of Maharagama held on 18 February 1993.
30. A programme to foster youth activities is being implemented jointly by the PS and DS Maharagama and National Youth Services Council headquarters.
31. The 10 consultative committees functioning in the DS Maharagama do not adequately provide opportunities for the PS and GMs to represent the citizens.
32. Circular RDD/DPS/25/P/1 of 18th January 1993 issued by the Regional Development Division of the Ministry of Policy Planning on the divisional development programme.
33. The DS served as the secretary to PS till 30 June 1992.
34. Vide reference 31.
35. Three transfers were made by government in quick succession within 15 days in February 1993.
36. Ninth Schedule of the 13th Amendment to the Constitution, List 1, Item 2: Planning—Implementation of Provincial Economic Plans.
37. *Manual for Provincial and Divisional Planning*. 1981. Marga Publications.
38. Circular FB/DCB/1990 of 20 November 1990 issued by the Secretary, Ministry of PC/PA/HA.
39. Circular RDD/24/C2 of 10 April 1992 issued by the Secretary, Ministry of Policy Planning and Implementation on criteria applicable in the implementation on the decentralised capital budget programme.
40. *Public Investment 1992–1996*. 1992. Colombo. Department of National Planning, Ministry Policy Planning and Implementation.
41. Vide reference 32.
42. This entire section, entitled Local Planning Process: Project Planning and Implementation, is based on a study specially undertaken for this research paper by Mallika Karunaratne, Deputy Director, National Planning of the Sri Lanka Planning Service.
43. Dickson, N.D. 'Urban Planning in Sri Lanka' in *Legal Environment for Local Government in Sri Lanka*.
44. Planning Manual for UDA Declared Areas, 1991.
45. City Centre Development Proposals for Maharagama UDA, 1992.
46. *Ibid.*
47. The zoning scheme for Maharagama PS area is still at preliminary stage.

# 15

# An Overview and Conclusions

N. SIVANNA
ABDUL AZIZ

The foregoing chapters have discussed at length the structural and functional aspects of decentralised governance as practised in South-Asian countries such as Bangladesh, China, India, Nepal, Philippines and Sri Lanka. The experiences of these countries have brought out many important aspects and issues related to the working of local self-government institutions and possibly contributed to an understanding of the third world perspective on the subject. The present chapter, which is mainly based on the seminar discussion, discusses the significant aspects of these institutions and relates them to the larger issues of decentralised governance such as the electoral process, autonomy, people's participation in decision-making, the role of people's organisations and NGOs, planning and implementation and so on.

One of the striking features of decentralised governance in Asia is that all the six countries, notwithstanding their differences in governmental set-up and machineries, have made provisions in their constitutions to establish local government institutions. This underscores the importance accorded to the grassroots level governmental institutions in the overall political and governmental systems and reflects the concern for decentralised governance shown by the higher level governments. However, there appears to be a considerable degree of variation across countries in the structures of, and the devolution of resources, powers and functions to, the self-governing institutions. In fact, in some countries the political and financial autonomy afforded to these institutions is so minuscule that it has proved to be a great constraint in their effective functioning.

Owing to the limited autonomy enjoyed by the decentralised governments, these institutions by and large have been reduced to the position of instruments or agents of state governments instead of functioning as decentralised units or levels of governments. Also, since the powers delegated to them have not been commensurate with the responsibilities given, it has also created some doubt as to whether such a political development at the grassroots level would really infuse democratic values at all, and if yes, would it infuse these values among all sections of the society. The experiences of the countries under reference has shown that steps taken by the higher level governments in respect of grassroots level institutions sometimes appear to be progressive and sometimes regressive! In India, of course, efforts have recently been made to restructure the panchayati raj institutions and to give them a statutory status by amending the constitution. But it is yet to be seen as to how far this precept is translated into practice.

The reluctance of many governments to give these institutions the required degree of autonomy raises some doubts and questions: Is there any real dichotomy between decentralised governance and national unity and integrity? Or, is it just an alibi for not devolving powers to people? Alternatively, is the concept of decentralisation the product of the political games pursued by the central and the state governments? Answers to these questions can be given only after a proper assessment of the political system that obtains in the country in question. However, there is a view that the state is, after all, an artificial creation of the people for governance and only when it reaches maturity and is secure can it show real concern towards the development process. When that happens, devolution of power to sub-regional governments would become a reality. Another view is that real devolution of power to grassroots level institutions can take place only when the country is ruled by a national party that has organisational links throughout the country. And also, it would be easier for such a political party to maintain national unity and integrity. If there are sectarian political parties in the system there will always be a fear of disintegration and this might deter the spread of decentralisation. A definite view on this point can only be formed after a detailed study of the politico–

administrative set up of the country in question. Hence, this may well be an important area for future research efforts.

Political and financial autonomy apart, a few more pre-requisites are considered important for the successful functioning of local self-government institutions. A detailed reference to them is made in the following pages.

## Electoral Process

For the successful functioning and continuance of local level institutions, the nature of the electoral system and its process is an important pre-condition, for it gives people an opportunity to exercise franchise freely and without fear on issues about which they are informed and assured. More importantly, political parties cannot peacefully contest elections without a prescribed electoral system. Set in this direction, the experiences of countries like Bangladesh and China are very encouraging. With the establishment of a democratic form of government in these countries, violence in elections seems to have reduced drastically and, what is more, political parties appear to have played a significant role in ensuring free and fair elections. A point worth noting is that in countries like China, elections were conducted not on party basis but on the basis of the individual's qualifications—a factor which contributed greatly to the peaceful conduct of elections. The candidate's character, performance and achievements in public life were crucial in determining his success or failure in the election. This is quite a gain for political processes at the grassroots level.

## People's Access to Power

There has, however, been a disturbing trend in some countries as far as contesting elections is concerned. By and large elections were contested by the rural elites, with the rural poor participating as mere voters! As a result, rural elites dominate the affairs of local self-government institutions. One way of breaking the stronghold of rural elites would be to provide for reservation of seats to the weaker sections, as is done in some states in India. Notwith-standing this provision, the panchayati raj institutions in India have still been dominated by the stronger sections, much to the disappointment of the weaker sections. The latter have hardly made any dent in the rural power structure. It is hoped that the 73rd Constitutional Amendment, which provides for reservation of seats to weaker sections such as scheduled castes and tribes, women and backward classes, will reduce the dominance of the elites, and the weaker sections will be able to wrest power from the traditional dominant groups.

It is to be noted that the problems of the weaker sections, though of a social nature, are fundamentally political and so they can be solved by strengthening the political base of the weaker sections. It is therefore necessary that the system of reservation be applied not only to the seats being contested but also to the offices of chairpersons of the PR institutions, as is now being done in Karnataka. The aim of such a provision is to give more oppor-tunities to the weaker sections to participate in the electoral process and in decision-making so that more of the benefits of develop-ment would accrue to them and not be wrested by the elites and the dominant groups.

## Financial Adequacy

The established local self-government institutions generally suffer from inadequate financial resources which limits their sphere of activities. The financial crunch faced by them is mainly due to inadequate powers to raise taxes and the meagre grants given by the government. In a country like the Philippines, the central government allocates 40 per cent of its revenues to the local governments. Even then the local governments find this amount inadequate to meet their requirements. Contrary to this situation, in Sri Lanka there exists a tripartite system of sharing resources through finance commissions. The joint action committee, consisting of people's representatives and officials, take decisions relating to the sharing of financial resources with the local governments. It is very encouraging to note that in Sri Lanka a regular flow of funds is always ensured to local governments and, what is important, resource allocation is made in response to the felt needs of the sub-regions. This contrasts with the situation that prevails in India where formal systems of sharing of resources between the state governments and local governments are yet to be evolved. Even in a progressive state like Karnataka in India, where a state finance commission had gone into the question of financial devolution and made appropriate recommendations as far back as 1989, the report lay gathering dust. A new state finance commission has now been appointed to look into this question once again.

Shortage of finance is one of the main drawbacks of the local government system. There can be no two opinions on the need to strengthen the financial resources of the grassroots level institutions. This is essentially because the potential of local governments to perform the functions entrusted to the them depends, among others, on the adequacy of financial resources. Also, there is a need to maintain a balance between the expanding functions and the role entrusted to the local bodies and their financial resources. If local governments are to effectively administer services and provide goods and services to people, they must have a sound source of income which is independent of state and central governments. Otherwise, their capacity to plan and monitor development activities will be very much limited and their tendency to depend largely on grants given by the state governments would, to say the least, erode their operational autonomy.

## Planning Process

The decentralised planning process is in a way an indispensable part of the decentralised governance process and in the absence of it, decentralised governance may lose a major part of its rationale. In the countries under reference, though the local governments have the responsibilities of planning for the development of local regions, they have had to work under certain constraints. These constraints, such as lack of data and information, want of expertise at different spatial levels and delay in allocating and releasing funds by the higher level institutions, adversely affect the planning efforts of the local governments. More significantly, while it is important that people identify projects and priorities, they are constrained by the fact that the officials hardly encourage them to do so; nor is there a mechanism available for the people to give their inputs.

The constraints referred to in the preceding paragraph arise largely on account of the technical nature of planning. Both the language used and the content of planning specified are highly technical. The high sounding jargon coupled with unfamiliar technical words used in the planning process make the people and their organisations depend rather too heavily on technical personnel for a proper understanding of the process. Hence, it appears that the very nature of the planning process works as a hurdle to the democratisation of the decision-making process.

The planning process as observed and practised at the local level appears to be deliberately mystifying structures and processes. It is therefore imperative to provide training to people and their organisations so that they can fully participate in the decision-making process. It is very encouraging to note that in Nepal there are, at present, seven autonomous training institutes that impart planning skills to trainees. To make training a successful venture, it is also necessary that the language used in the teaching material is simple enough to be understood by the common man. In this context, it is more important to emphasise the utility of the planning process rather than its technicalities. Also, the methodology employed in the training process should be dialogical in nature. This kind of methodology would certainly provide a two-way flow of communication and information, and act as a continuous source of feedback both for the trainees and the trainers.

Besides imparting training in regard to the planning process, it is equally necessary to provide training on the various aspects of local self-governance. The training should be given to both the official and the non-official members of the local governments. This is absolutely essential because such training would not only improve the functioning of local governments but would also widen the scope for people's participation in the governance process. It would also promote political commitment among the leaders, thereby making them more responsive to people's needs. However, one serious drawback that has been observed in most of the developing countries is that the facilities available in terms of resources, skills of personnel, and the training methods and techniques employed are very poor. The governments should, therefore, give utmost priority to training by providing the necessary infrastructure in terms of both physical and human resources.

## People's and NGO Participation

Of the many important aspects of local self-governance, the participation of people in the governance process is considered to be very significant and crucial for the development and sustainability of grassroots level institutions. However, there is no appreciable achievement in this regard because of the absence of mobilisation of rural people, especially the rural poor. Experiences show that the system has remained 'external' to the local people, which in turn reflects the prevalence of entrenched vested interests. The rural poor are the people who have an extremely limited participatory role and are practically absent in the crucial stages of governance; they are generally used as targets rather than as participants in the rural development process. Therefore, some kind of training for them, with a thrust on creating at least awareness among them, is also necessary.

It is in this context that the role of voluntary organisations is crucial. The role of voluntary organisations like NGOs and User Groups is generally perceived in the context of the failure of formal governmental structures to deliver basic needs and services to the people. Today, NGOs are looked upon as the 'fourth estate'. However, there are varied experiences as far as the role of these organisations is concerned. For instance, in Bangladesh the role of NGOs has been disappointing; they have hardly played any part in people's mobilisation and in production-oriented activities. In India, the NGOs are by and large apolitical in nature and always keep themselves away from the party political process. However, in a country like the Philippines, people's organisations and NGOs have been playing a key and supportive role in local governance. Hence, they are rightly treated as partners in the system. Also their presence is seen as facilitating a healthy competition among the various agencies involved in local governance. In spite of all these developments, voluntary organisations, variedly referred to as users' groups, dalit groups, grameen banks, farmer's organisations, women's organisations, youth clubs and religious associations, have come to stay. Indeed, they have a crucial role in identifying and articulating the needs and aspirations of the people, launching awareness creation programmes, mobilising the rural masses and involving themselves in developmental activities in rural areas; their presence would certainly strengthen the hands of the local governments. They should therefore be encouraged and supported.

A related larger issue is the role perception of local governments. For promoting community and economic development, is it desirable to look upon the local government institutions as instruments of releasing people's energies? Or should we follow an approach where everything is given from above and the local governments are there only to implement programmes? These questions raise the issue of 'autonomy' which the local self-government institutions should legitimately have with them. There is a strong feeling that the national and the state governments take pride in establishing local government institutions but at the same time, they are not ready to share powers and resources with these institutions. There will always be some kind of reluctance to share power. It is not uncommon for arguments to be advanced against giving full autonomy to grassroots level institutions. In many cases, policies, programmes and priorities are worked out by the higher level governments keeping in view the macro development imperatives. Obviously, such practices cannot be expected to give autonomy to local governments. Besides, there is no guarantee that decisions taken at the top would be in conformity with the needs and aspirations of local people.

Seen in this perspective, it is imperative to strengthen these institutions with enough powers, functions and resources, especially financial resources. These institutions should not only function as implementing bodies but also be involved in designing development programmes for local areas. For performing this task, they should be properly empowered to augment their financial resources. While helping and encouraging these bodies to raise their own resources (by giving them more taxing powers and providing property valuation services through a central valuation committee), it is also necessary to provide a meaningful devolution of power and financial resources. The devolution of funds should be based not on the sympathy and generosity of the politicians but on a proper assessment of the needs of local governments and the availability of funds with governments at the higher level.

## Role of Political Parties

In the promotion of well-perceived and well-structured decentralised governance, political parties have a significant contribution to make. They could, for instance, nurture local leadership to take over the functions of local self-governments, provide necessary guidance and resources to local level political workers. It is these political parties which can bring about a change in the local institutions by reorganising or restructuring them. Also, any change in the local governmental systems is political in the sense that it is, in the final analysis, a product of legislative decision or sanction which is the handiwork of the political parties participating in the legislature.

However, whether or not the political parties can or will promote the development of local institutions depends on the nature of the political parties themselves: how democratic they are, to what extent internal structures and mechanisms allow for democratic participation, and how they understand and propagate the rationale of decentralisation. But past experience has shown that the internal structures of political parties and their functioning are highly autocratic. It is also doubtful that political parties are representative in nature. The representation of women and other weaker sections of society in political parties was (and even now is) merely cosmetic. Moreover, there is a dichotomy in the thinking of political parties as far as national and state level politics is concerned. Their interests and priorities hardly coincide. At the root of all this lies the rise of hegemonic leadership styles in almost all parties and consequently insufficient understanding of the nature and process of local self-governance. In view of all these factors, political parties have not shown much interest in the decentralisation of power and governance. It is in this context that a need has been felt for people to mobilise themselves into organisations and exert pressures such that the central and the state governments take serious note of the needs and aspirations of the people at the grassroots level.

## Community Development

Notwithstanding these problems and issues relating to self-government institutions, the time has come now for reorienting ourselves in response to the changed socio–economic and political conditions. Local governments should emphasise social development, community development and economic development as their principal objectives. More than ever before, there is a need now to eliminate rural poverty and promote the sustainable development of the local economies. To attain these goals, only a group approach seems to be ideal because it will help promote community development. Also, under this approach, it will be easier to mobilise resources, monitor progress and empower weaker sections.

In order to promote community and economic development, there is a need to have small, governable states. In such states, it is easier to carry out planning from below. More than this, it is very important to work out a basic local government which will provide opportunities to the people to participate in decision-making and be economically viable at the same time. Given such a basic structure, it will be necessary to upgrade the skills and knowledge of the members of these units. More importantly, the local governments would need to develop a spirit of self-help and take initiatives to identify and utilise local resources such that local energies for development are released. In order to streamline the planning process, it would be necessary to establish planning cells in the local governments to carry out local level planning. Encouraging the private sector to invest in rural development projects and thereby to participate in local development activities would also be desirable.

In order that local governments can effectively promote the overall development of rural areas, there should be:

(*a*) A viable set of local institutions which can efficiently implement social development programmes.
(*b*) An apparatus to reconcile the priorities of decentralised planning with those of national and state planning.
(*c*) A bigger role for local governments in implementing self and wage employment generating programmes which have the potential to promote community and social development.

(*d*) The ability in local governments to take initiatives which would ensure greater equity in development.

Governments at the higher levels should take necessary steps to create an atmosphere conducive to the establishment of full-fledged local government systems with a genuine devolution of powers and resources. In this context, governments should make serious and conscientious attempts to reorganise and revitalise grassroots institutions. This is necessary because in the changing context of 'new economic policies' and 'structural adjustment programmes' which are placing new agendas before the countries for the ultimate cause of development, even the local governments are expected to take upon themselves new responsibilities to bring about substantial changes in the countryside.

# NOTES ON CONTRIBUTORS

H.A.P. Abeyawardana has written extensively on decentralised planning and related issues and is associated with the Post-graduate Institute of Management, Sri Jayawardevepura University, Colombo, Sri Lanka.

Abdul Aziz is Professor of Economics at the Institute of Social and Economic Change, Bangalore, where he holds the Chair in Micro-level Planning. Prior to joining the Institute in 1975, Dr. Aziz worked at the Shri Ram Centre for Industrial Relations and Human Resources, New Delhi, and taught economics at Mysore University. Besides directing numerous research projects, he has published several research papers and books, among them being *Decentralised Planning: The Karnataka Experiment.*

Soorya Lal Amatya is Professor of Geography at Tribhuvan University, Nepal. Prior to this.he has been Dean of the Institute of Humanities and Social Sciences, and Executive Director of Centre for Economic Development and Administration (CEDA), Tribhuvan University. He has authored a number of books and has contributed research papers on decentralisation, structural plans for towns, agricultural problems, rural development and other topics. He is currently serving as a member of the University Grants Commission and Tribhuvan University Service Commission.

David D. Arnold is currently the Ford Foundation's Representative for India, Nepal and Sri Lanka. Mr. Arnold holds a Master's degree in public administration from Michigan State University. Before joining the Ford Foundation, he worked as a staff director for the National Governor's Association and later as Executive Director of the Coalition of Northeastern Governors in Washington, DC. His work at the Foundation has included undertaking liaison activity for the Foundation's governance work in Africa, Asia and Latin America as well as directly participating in projects focusing on the shift to democracy in Eastern Europe and the former Soviet Union.

Devendra Babu holds a Master's degree in economics and is currently working at the Institute for Social and Economic Change, Bangalore, as a field officer on the Ford Foundation-sponsored project entitled 'Decentralised Governance and Planning in South India'. He has published many articles of interest on rural development. He is the co-author of a book entitled *Scheduled Castes and Scheduled Tribes: Socio Economic Programmes*. Earlier he taught economics in a degree college and worked as a research assistant.

Alex B. Brillantes has made significant contributions to the field of decentralised governance by way of research and is currently working in the Institute for Strategic and Development Studies, University of Philippines, Quezon City, Philippines.

Jessica K. Carino teaches history at the University of the Philippines College Baguio. Her research interests include grassroots participation in local governance, particularly in the Cordillera region of the northern Philippines. Presently she is Dean of the University of the Philippines College Baguio.

Cao Guoying is Deputy Director of the Research Institute of Management Cadres, College of Rural Economy, Ministry of Agriculture, People's Republic of China. He is also the Permanent Director of the Research Society of China's Political Power Construction at the Basic Level.

Sant B. Gurung completed his Masters in rural sociology from Agra University, following which he obtained his MPA in economic social development from the University of Pittsburgh, USA. Mr. Gurung served as Executive Director of Centre for Economic Development and Administration (CEDA), Tribhuvan University, 1986–1990, and was Vice-President, Board of Management of the Association of Development Research and Training Institute of Asia and the Pacific (ADIPA), Kuala Lumpur, Malaysia, 1987–1991. He has published several papers and project reports on the areas of rural development, urban planning and regional planning. His publications include *Planning with People: Decentralization in Nepal* (1988) and *Human Resource Development in South Asia: The Much Taken for Granted Domain* (1992).

Zhang Houan teaches political science in the Central China Normal University (CCNU) Hubei, People's Republic of China. Prior to this, he has been Director, Centre for Rural Grassroots Organs of State Power; Standing Director, China Research Society of Construction of Grassroots Organs of State Power; and Standing Director, Bubei Society of Political Science.

Mohammad Mohabbat Khan is Professor of Public Administration, University of Dhaka, Bangladesh. Professor Khan has undertaken research and taught at universities in Bangladesh, Jordan, Nigeria and the USA. He has authored several books including *Bureaucratic Self-Preservation and Politics of Administrative Reforms* and has contributed to many edited volumes. Professor Khan's major areas of research interest are administrative reform and change, democracy, governance, public sector management and urban management.

Zarina Rahman Khan is Associate Professor in the Department of Public Administration, University of Dhaka, Bangladesh. Her areas of research interest include decentralised governance. She has carried out many field-based studies on local government and published her research results in academic periodicals.

Rajni Kothari, an eminent political scientist, is a former member of the Planning Commission. He founded the Centre for the Study of Developing Societies and is founder-editor of *Alternatives*, an international journal. Earlier he has been Chairman, Indian Council of Social Sciences Research (1977–1988) and President, People's Union of Civil Liberties (1974–1978). He is the author, among other books, of *Politics in India; Footsteps into the Future; State against Democracy: In Search of Humane Governance*; and *Politics and the People* (two volumes). He has also edited *Caste in Indian Politics*, and *State and Nation Building: A Third World Perspective*.

George Mathew obtained his Ph.D. in sociology from Jawaharlal University and is Director of the Institute of Social Sciences, New Delhi. His articles on issues of the state and society have appeared in national dailies, scholarly journals and books. His major works include *Communal Road to a Secular Kerala; Panchayati Raj from Legislation to Movement*; and the following edited works: *Shift in Indian Politics; Dignity for All: Essays in Socialism and Democracy; Panchayati Raj in Karnataka Today;* and *Panchayati Raj in Jammu and Kashmir*. He is the general editor of the reference book, *Status of Panchayati Raj in the States of India 1994.*

Charles Nelson is an economist and is presently working in the Institute for Social and Economic Change as a field officer on the Ford Foundation-sponsored project, 'Decentralised Governance and Planning in South India'. He has worked on several projects including 'Mandal Panchayat System in Karnataka' in the past and is the co-author of a book entitled *Impact of Irrigation.*

N. Sivanna obtained a Ph.D. in development studies from the University of Mysore. He is Deputy Director of the training project 'Decentralisation' at the Institute for Social and Economic Change, Bangalore. He has authored two books—*Panchayati Raj Reforms and Rural Development* and *The Land Army and Rural Development*—and is a regular contributor to various professional journals.

C. Suriyakumaran is an economist, environmentalist and administrator. He is presently the Chairman of the Centre for Regional Development Studies, Colombo. In the past he has been UN Deputy Executive Secretary for Asia and the Far East; UNEP Regional Director for Asia and the Pacific; and Global Director for Education, Training & Technical Assistance. He was directly involved in the creation of various international programmes and institutions, among them, the Asian Development Bank, the South Asia Co-operative Environment Programme (SACEP), the Asian Clearing Union, and the Asian Coconut Community. He has authored several books including *The Wealth of Poor Nations; The Methodology of Environment and Development Management; Origins and Concepts of Devolution in Sri Lanka*; and *Fiscal Devolution*. He has lectured widely in India and abroad and was knighted by the King of Thailand for outstanding services to Asia during his UN career.

Wang Zhenyao is currently Vice-Director of the Department of Basic-Level Governance, Ministry of Civil Affairs, People's Republic of China. He is also Chairman of the Commission for Rural Work, China Research Society for Basic-Level Governance. Mr. Wang has published widely on the areas of rural elections, local government and political reform.

# INDEX

**Abdul Aziz** is Professor of Economics at the Institute for Social and Economic Change, Bangalore, where he holds the Chair in Micro-level Planning. Prior to joining the Institute in 1975, Dr. Aziz worked at the Shri Ram Centre for Industrial Relations and Human Resources, New Delhi, and taught economics at Mysore University. Besides directing numerous research projects, he has published several research papers and books, among them being *Decentralised Planning: The Karnataka Experiment;* and *Decentralisation: Mandal Panchayat System in Karnataka.*

**David D. Arnold** is currently the Ford Foundation's Representative for India, Nepal, and Sri Lanka. Mr Arnold holds a Master's degree in Public Administration from Michigan State University. Before joining the Ford Foundation, he worked as a staff director for the National Governors' Association and later as Executive Director of the Coalition of Northeastern Governors in Washington, DC. His work at the Foundation has included undertaking liaison activity for the Foundation's governance work in Africa, Asia and Latin America as well as directly participating in projects focusing on the shift to democracy in Eastern Europe and the former Soviet Union.